W9-BFK-257

Praise for the "Kids Love" Guidebook Travel Series
On-Air Personality Comments (Television Interviews)

"The great thing about these books is that your whole family actually lives these adventures" – (**WKRC-TV**, Cincinnati)

"Very helpful to lots of families when the kids say, I'm bored...and I don't want to go to same places again!" – (**WISH-TV**, Indianapolis)

"Dividing the state into many sections, the book has something for everyone...everywhere." – (**WLVT-TV**, Pennsylvania)

"These authors know first-hand that it's important to find hands-on activities that engage your children..." (**WBNS-TV**, Columbus)

"You spent more than 1000 hours doing this research for us, that's really great – we just have to pick up the book and it's done..."
(**WTVR-TV**, Richmond)

"A family that's a great source for travel ideas..."
(**WBRA-TV**, Roanoke)

"What a great idea...this book needed to be done a long time ago!"
(**WKYT-TV**, Lexington)

"A fabulous idea...places to travel that your kids will enjoy"
(**WOOD-TV**, Grand Rapids)

"The Zavatskys call it a dream come true, running their own business while keeping the family together. Their goal, encourage other parents to create special family travel memories." - (**WLVT-TV,** Pennsylvania)

"It's a wonderful book, and as someone who has been to a lot of these places...you hit it right on the money!" – (**WKRC-TV**, Cincinnati)

Praise for the "Kids Love" Guidebook Travel Series
Customer Comments (actual letters on file)

"I wanted to tell you how helpful all your books have been to my family of 6. I rarely find books that cater to families with kids. I have your Indiana, Ohio, Kentucky, Michigan, and Pennsylvania books. I don't want to miss any of the new books that come out. Keep up the great ideas. The books are fantastic. I have shown them to tons of my friends. They love them, too." – H.M.

"I bought the Ohio and Indiana books yesterday and what a blessing these are for us!!! We love taking our grandsons on Grammie & Papaw trips thru the year and these books are making it soooo much easier to plan. The info is complete and full of ideas. Even the layout of the book is easy to follow...I just wanted to thank you for all your work in developing these books for us..." – G.K

"I have purchased your book. My grandchildren and I have gone to many of the places listed in your book. They mark them off as we visit them. We are looking forward to seeing many more. It is their favorite thing to look at book when they come over and find new places to explore. Thank you for publishing this book!" - B.A.

"At a retail price of under $15.00, any of the books would be well worth buying even for a one-time only vacation trip. Until now, when the opportunity arose for a day or weekend trip with the kids I was often at a loss to pick a destination that I could be sure was convenient, educational, child-friendly, and above all, fun. Now I have a new problem: How in the world will we ever be able to see and do all the great ideas listed in this book? I'd better get started planning our next trip right away. At least I won't have to worry about where we're going or what to do when we get there!" – VA Homeschool Newsletter

"My family and I used this book this summer to explore Ohio! We lived here nearly our entire life and yet over half the book we never knew existed. These people really know what kids love! Highly recommended for all parents, grandparents, etc.." – Barnes and Noble website reviewer

KIDS ♥ LOVE MARYLAND

A Family Travel Guide to
Exploring "Kid-Tested" Places
in Maryland...Year Round!

George & Michele Zavatsky

Dedicated to the Families of Maryland

© Copyright 2007, Kids Love Publications

For the latest major updates corresponding to the pages in this book visit our website:

www.KidsLoveTravel.com

All rights reserved. No part of this book may be reproduced or transmitted in any form or by any means, electronic or mechanical, including photocopying, recording or by any information storage and retrieval system without the written permission from the authors, except for the inclusion of brief quotations in a review.

Although the authors have exhaustively researched all sources to ensure accuracy and completeness of the information contained in this book, we assume no responsibility for errors, inaccuracies, omissions or any other inconsistency herein. Any slights against any entries or organizations are unintentional.

REMEMBER: Museum exhibits change frequently. Check the site's website before you visit to note any changes. Also, HOURS and ADMISSIONS are subject to change at the owner's discretion. If you are tight on time or money, check the attraction's website or call before you visit.

INTERNET PRECAUTION: All websites mentioned in KIDS LOVE Maryland have been checked for appropriate content. However, due to the fast-changing nature of the Internet, we strongly urge parents to preview any recommended sites and to always supervise their children when on-line.

ISBN-13: 978-0-9774434-2-0
ISBN-10: 0-9774434-2-6

KIDS ♥ MARYLAND™   Kids Love Publications, LLC

TABLE OF CONTENTS

General Information...Preface
(Here you'll find "How to Use This Book", maps, tour ideas, city listings, etc.)

Chapter 1 – CAPITAL AREA...1

Chapter 2 – CAPITAL-DC AREA...23

Chapter 3 – CENTRAL AREA...39

Chapter 4 – EASTERN SHORE AREA...91

Chapter 5 – SOUTHERN AREA..123

Chapter 6 – WESTERN AREA...141

Chapter 7 – SEASONAL & SPECIAL EVENTS............................171

Master Index..227

Activity Index...237
(Amusements, Animals & Farms, Museums, Outdoors, State History, Tours, etc.)

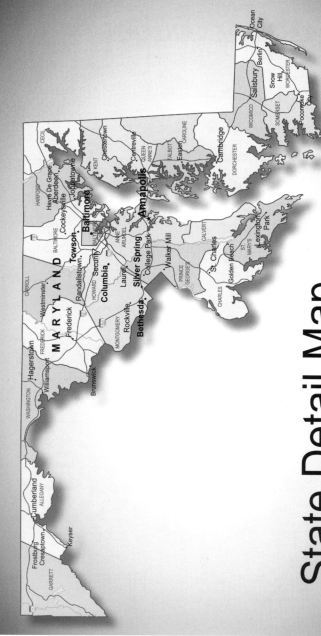

State Detail Map

(With Major Routes and Cities Marked)

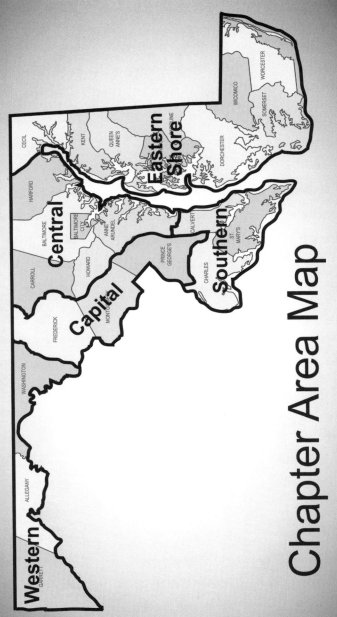

Chapter Area Map

(Chapters arranged alphabetically by chapter name)

CITY INDEX (Listed by City & Area)

Aberdeen, Central

Accident, Western

Accokeek, Capital

Annapolis, Central

Baltimore, Central

Baltimore, Inner Harbor, Central

Beantown, Southern

Beltsville, Capital

Berlin, Eastern Shore

Bethesda, Capital

Big Pool, Western

Boonsboro, Western

Bowie, Capital

Brookville, Central

Brunswick, Capital

Buckeystown, Capital

Burkittsville, Western

Cambridge, Eastern Shore

Camp Springs, Capital

Catonsville, Central

Charlotte Hall, Southern

Chesapeake Beach, Southern

Chesapeake City, Eastern Shore

Chestertown, Eastern Shore

Chevy Chase, Capital

Churchville, Central

Clear Spring, Western

Clinton, Capital

Colesville, Capital

College Park, Capital

Colton's Point, Southern

Columbia, Central

Conowingo, Eastern Shore

Cordova, Eastern Shore

Crisfield, Eastern Shore

Crownsville, Central

Cumberland, Western

Darlington, Central

Deal Island, Eastern Shore

Dickerson, Capital

Easton, Eastern Shore

Edgewater, Central

Elkton, Eastern Shore

Ellicott City, Central

Flintstone, Western

Fort George G. Meade, Central

Fort Washington, Capital

Frederick, Capital

Federalsburg, Eastern Shore

Frostburg, Western

Gaithersburg, Capital

Germantown, Capital

Glen Echo, Capital

Glenn Dale, Capital

Grantsville, Western

Grasonville, Eastern Shore

Greenbelt, Capital

Hagerstown, Western

Hampden, Central

Hancock, Western

Hanover, Central

Havre de Grace, Central

Hollywood, Southern

Hunt Valley, Central

Hurlock, Eastern Shore

Jerrettsville, Central

Jessup, Central

Kingsville, Central

Landover, Capital

Largo, Capital

Laurel, Capital

Leonardtown, Southern

Lexington Park, Southern

Linthicum, Central

Lonaconing, Western

CITY INDEX (Listed by City & Area)

Lusby, Southern

Lutherville, Central

Marbury, Southern

McHenry, Western

Mechanicsville, Southern

Middle River, Central

Millersville, Central

Monkton, Central

Mountain Lake Park, Western

Mount Airy, Central

New Market, Capital

Newburg, Southern

North Beach, Southern

North East, Central

Oakland, Western

Ocean City, Eastern Shore

Ocean City, West, Eastern Shore

Owings Mills, Central

Oxon Hill, Capital

Parkville, Central

Piney Point, Southern

Pocomoke, Eastern Shore

Port Deposit, Eastern Shore

Port Republic, Southern

Port Tabacco, Southern

Potomac, Capital

Powder, Capital

Princess Anne, Eastern Shore

Prince Frederick, Southern

Queen Anne, Eastern Shore

Queenstown, Eastern Shore

Ridgely, Eastern Shore

Rising Sun, Eastern Shore

Riverdale, Capital

Rock Hall, Eastern Shore

Rockville, Capital

Salisbury, Eastern Shore

Savage, Central

Scotland, Southern

Shadyside, Central

Sharpsburg, Western

Smith Island, Eastern Shore

Snow Hill, Eastern Shore

Solomons, Southern

Solomons Island, Southern

St. Leonard, Southern

St. Mary's City, Southern

St. Michaels, Eastern Shore

Stevensville, Eastern Shore

Suitland, Capital

Swanton, Western

Sykesville, Eastern Shore

Thurmont, Capital

Tilghman Isld, Eastern Shore

Timonium, Central

Towson, Central

Twiggtown, Western

Union Mills, Central

Upper Fairmount, Eastern Shore

Upper Marlboro, Capital

Vienna, Eastern Shore

Waldorf, Southern

Walkersville, Capital

Washington, DC – Capital – DC

Westminster, Central

West Friendship, Central

Whiteford, Central

Woodbine, Central

Wye Mills, Eastern Shore

> **Note: Listings in italics appear only in the Seasonal Chapter**

Acknowledgements

We are most thankful to be blessed with our parents, Barbara (Darrall) and Adrian Callahan & George and Catherine Zavatsky who help us every way they can – researching, proofing and baby-sitting. More importantly, they are great sounding boards and offer unconditional support. So many places around Maryland remind us of family vacations years ago…

We also want to express our thanks to the many Convention & Visitor Bureaus' staff *(especially Johanna Colburn, thanks for all your followup!)* for providing the attention to detail that helps to complete a project. We felt very welcome during our travels in Maryland and would be proud to call it home!

Our own kids, Jenny and Daniel, were delightful and fun children during our trips across the state. What a joy it is to be their parents…we couldn't do it without them as our "kid-testers"!

We both sincerely thank each other – our partnership has created an even greater business/personal "marriage" with lots of exciting moments, laughs, and new adventures in life woven throughout. Above all, we praise the Lord for His so many blessings through the last few years.

We think Maryland is a wonderful, friendly area of the country with more activities than you could imagine. Our sincere wish is that this book will help everyone "fall in love" with all of Maryland.

In a Hundred Years...
It will not matter, The size of my bank account...
The kind of house that I lived in, the kind of car that I drove...
But what will matter is...
That the world may be different
Because I was important in the life of a child.

HOW TO USE THIS BOOK

If you are excited about discovering Maryland, this is the book for you and your family! We've spent over a thousand hours doing all the scouting, collecting and compiling (*and most often visiting!*) so that you could spend less time searching and more time having fun.

Here are a few hints to make your adventures run smoothly:

- ☐ Consider the **child's age** before deciding to take a visit.
- ☐ Know **directions** and parking. Call ahead (or visit the company's website) if you have questions *and* bring this book. Also, don't forget your camera! *(please honor rules regarding use).*
- ☐ **Estimate the duration** of the trip. Bring small surprises (favorite juice boxes) travel books, and toys.
- ☐ Call ahead for **reservations** or details, if necessary.
- ☐ Most listings are **closed major holidays** unless noted.
- ☐ Make a **family "treasure chest"**. Decorate a big box or use an old popcorn tin. Store memorabilia from a fun outing, journals, pictures, brochures and souvenirs. Once a year, look through the "treasure chest" and reminisce. "Kids Love Travel Memories!" is an excellent travel journal & scrapbook that your family can create. *(See the order form in back of this book).*
- ☐ Plan **picnics** along the way. Many state history sites and state parks are scattered throughout Maryland. Allow time for a rural /scenic route to take advantage of these free picnic facilities.
- ☐ Some activities, especially tours, require **groups** of 10 or more. To participate, you may either ask to be part of another tour group or get a group together yourself (neighbors, friends, organizations). If you arrange a group outing, most places offer discounts.
- ☐ For the latest **updates** corresponding to the pages in this book, visit our website: **www.KidsLoveTravel.com.**
- ☐ Each chapter represents an area of the state. Each listing is further identified by city, zip code, and place/event name. Our popular **Activity Index** in the back of the book **lists places by Activity Heading** (i.e. State History, Tours, Outdoors, Museums, etc.).

MISSION STATEMENT

At first glance, you may think that this is a book that just lists hundreds of places to travel. While it is true that we've invested thousands of hours of exhaustive research (*and drove over 3000 miles in Maryland*) to prepare this travel resource...just listing places to travel is <u>not</u> the mission statement of these projects.

As children, Michele and I were able to travel extensively throughout the United States. We consider these family times some of the greatest memories we cherish today. We, quite frankly, felt that most children had this opportunity to travel with their family as we did. However, as we became adults and started our own family, we found that this wasn't necessarily the case. We continually heard friends express several concerns when deciding how to spend "quality" and "quantity" family time. 1) What to do? 2) Where to do it? 3) How much will it cost? 4) How do I know that my kids will enjoy it?

Interestingly enough, as we compare our experiences with our families when we were kids, many of our fondest memories were not made at an expensive attraction, but rather when it was least expected.

It is our belief and mission statement that if you as a family will study and <u>use</u> the contained information <u>to create family memories</u>, these memories will grow a stronger, tighter family. Our ultimate mission statement is, that your children will develop a love and a passion for quality family experiences that they can pass to another generation of family travelers.

We thank you for purchasing this book, and we hope to see you on the road (*and hear your travel stories!*) God bless your journeys and happy exploring!

George, Michele, Jenny and Daniel

General State Agency & Recreational Information

Call *(or visit websites)* for the services of interest. Request to be added to their mailing lists.

- [ ] State Park Camping & Cabin Reservations: (888) 432-CAMP or **http://reservations.dnr.state.md.us.**
- [ ] Maryland Association of Campgrounds: (301) 271-7012 or **www.gocampingamerica.com/maryland.**
- [ ] Maryland Department of Natural Resources: (877) 620-8DNR or **www.dnr.state.md.us.**
- [ ] Maryland Bicycle Maps and Publications: (410) 545-5656 or **www.sha.state.md.us/SHAservices/mapsbrochures/maps/oppe/maps.asp**
- [ ] Maryland Scenic Byways: (877) 632-9929 or **www.sha.state.md.us/exploremd/oed/scenicbyways/scenicbyways.asp**
- [ ] U.S. Fish & Wildlife Service, Maryland Fishery Resources Office: (410) 263-2604 or **http://marylandfisheries.fws.gov**
- [ ] Chesapeake Bay Gateways Network: (866) BAY WAYS or **www.baygateways.net**
- [ ] Maryland Tourism: (877) 209-5883 or **www.mdwelcome.org**
- [ ] CAPITAL - Tourism Council of Frederick County: (800) 999-3613 or **www.fredericktourism.org**
- [ ] CENTRAL - Annapolis & Anne Arundel County CVB: (888) 302-2852 or **www.visitannapolis.org**
- [ ] CENTRAL - Baltimore Area CVB: (800) 343-3468 or **www.baltimore.org**
- [ ] CENTRAL - Havre de Grace Tourism: (800) 851-7756 or **www.havredegracemd.com**
- [ ] CENTRAL - Howard County Tourism/ Ellicott City: (800) 288-TRIP or **www.visithowardcounty.com**
- [ ] EASTERN SHORE - Ocean City Department: (800) OC-OCEAN or **www.ococean.com**
- [ ] EASTERN SHORE - Wicomico County CVB: **www.wicomicotourism.org**
- [ ] SOUTHERN - Calvery County Tourism: (800) 331-9771 or **www.ecalvert.com**
- [ ] SOUTHERN - St. Mary's County Tourism: **www.stmarysmd.com/tourism**
- [ ] WESTERN - Deep Creek Lake / Garrett County Chamber: **www.garrettchamber.com**
- [ ] WESTERN - Hagerstown CVB: (888) 257-2600 or **www.marylandmemories.com**

Check out these businesses / services in your area for tour ideas:

AIRPORTS

All children love to visit the airport! Why not take a tour and understand all the jobs it takes to run an airport? Tour the terminal, baggage claim, gates and security / currency exchange. Maybe you'll even get to board a plane.

ANIMAL SHELTERS

Great for the would-be pet owner. Not only will you see many cats and dogs available for adoption, but a guide will show you the clinic and explain the needs of a pet. Be prepared to have the children "fall in love" with one of the animals while they are there!

BANKS

Take a "behind the scenes" look at automated teller machines, bank vaults and drive-thru window chutes. You may want to take this tour and then open a savings account for your child.

CITY HALLS

Halls of Fame, City Council Chambers & Meeting Room, Mayor's Office and famous statues.

ELECTRIC COMPANY / POWER PLANTS

Modern science has created many ways to generate electricity today, but what really goes on with the "flip of a switch". Because coal can be dirty, wear old, comfortable clothes. Coal furnaces heat water, which produces steam, that propels turbines, that drives generators, that make electricity.

FIRE STATIONS

Many Open Houses in October, Fire Prevention Month. Take a look into the life of the firefighters servicing your area and try on their gear. See where they hang out, sleep and eat. Hop aboard a real-life fire engine truck and learn fire safety too.

HOSPITALS

Some Children's Hospitals offer pre-surgery and general tours.

NEWSPAPERS

You'll be amazed at all the new technology. See monster printers and robotics. See samples in the layout department and maybe try to put together your own page. After seeing a newspaper made, most companies give you a free copy (dated that day) as your souvenir. National Newspaper Week is in October.

PETCO

Various stores. Contact each store manager to see if they participate. The Fur, Feathers & Fins™ program allows children to learn about the characteristics and habitats of fish, reptiles, birds, and small animals. At your local Petco, lessons in science, math and geography come to life through this hands-on field trip. As students develop a respect for animals, they will also develop a greater sense of responsibility.

RESTAURANTS

PIZZA HUT & PAPA JOHN'S

Participating locations. Telephone the store manager. Best days are Monday, Tuesday and Wednesday mid-afternoon. Minimum of 10 people. Small charge per person. All children love pizza – especially when they can create their own! As the children tour the kitchen, they learn how to make a pizza, bake it, and then eat it. The admission charge generally includes lots of creatively made pizzas, beverage and coloring book.

KRISPY KREME DONUTS

Participating locations. Get an "inside look" and learn the techniques that make these donuts some of our favorites! Watch the dough being made in "giant" mixers, being formed into donuts and taking a "trip" through the fryer. Seeing them being iced and topped with colorful sprinkles is always a favorite with the kids. Contact your local store manager. They prefer Monday or Tuesday. Free.

SUPERMARKETS

Kids are fascinated to go behind the scenes of the same store where Mom and Dad shop. Usually you will see them grind meat, walk into large freezer rooms, watch cakes and bread bake and receive free samples along the way. Maybe you'll even get to pet a live lobster!

TV / RADIO STATIONS

Studios, newsrooms, Fox kids clubs. Why do weathermen never wear blue/green clothes on TV? What makes a "DJ's" voice sound so deep and smooth?

WATER TREATMENT PLANTS

A giant science experiment! You can watch seven stages of water treatment. The favorite is usually the wall of bright buttons flashing as workers monitor the different processes.

U.S. MAIN POST OFFICES

Did you know Ben Franklin was the first Postmaster General (over 200 years ago)? Most interesting is the high-speed automated mail processing equipment. Learn how to address envelopes so they will be sent quicker (there are secrets). To make your tour more interesting, have your children write a letter to themselves and address it with colorful markers. Mail it earlier that day and they will stay interested trying to locate their letter in all the high-speed machinery.

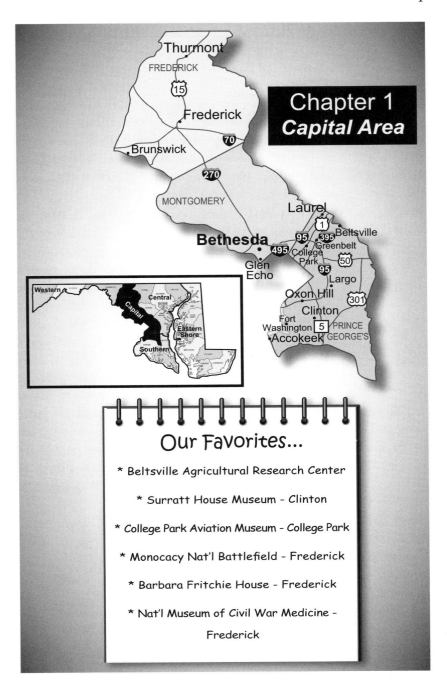

Thurmont

FREDERICK

15

Frederick

Brunswick

70

270

Chapter 1
Capital Area

MONTGOMERY

Laurel

1

Bethesda

95 · 395 · Beltsville

495 · College Park · Greenbelt

50

Glen Echo

95

Largo

Oxon Hill

301

Clinton

Fort Washington · 5 · PRINCE GEORGE'S

Accokeek

Western

Central

Capital

Eastern Shore

Southern

Our Favorites...

* Beltsville Agricultural Research Center

* Surratt House Museum - Clinton

* College Park Aviation Museum - College Park

* Monocacy Nat'l Battlefield - Frederick

* Barbara Fritchie House - Frederick

* Nat'l Museum of Civil War Medicine - Frederick

NATIONAL COLONIAL FARM IN PISCATAWAY PARK

Accokeek - 3400 Bryan Point Road (I-95 exit 3A to Rte. 210S to right on Bryan Point) 20607. Phone: (301) 283-2113. Web: www.accokeek.org Hours: Tuesday-Sunday 10:00am-4:00pm (mid-March thru mid-December). Weekends only (rest of year). Park open dawn to dusk. Admission: $0.50-$3.00 or $5.00 family. Miscellaneous: Weekend visitors may see sewing, cooking, spinning, dyeing, candlemaking, gardening, woodworking and colonial games. Best to plan a visit during a seasonal festival weekend as there is more going on to occupy kids' interests.

PISCATAWAY PARK, a national park, is on the shore of the Potomac River directly across from George Washington's home, "Mount Vernon".

Visitors enjoy the fishing pier; picnic areas; hiking trails; and open spaces. You can check out an excellent view of Mount Vernon from the fishing pier. At the NATIONAL COLONIAL FARM, costumed interpreters offer visitors a glimpse into the lives of middle-class colonial farmers, their animals, and their agriculture. The farm depicts life for an ordinary tobacco planting family in the 1770s. Check out the farm, barn, and smokehouse. A costumed character is usually stationed out in the kitchen, cooking something. Historic varieties of field crops such as Virginia Gourdseed corn and Red May wheat are cultivated

You can really see Mt. Vernon - way across the river

on a seasonal basis. The Museum Garden crops typify plants grown from different immigrants to the area (ex. Okra from Africa, planted in a circle vs. rows). The Livestock area contains live animals like the milking Devon Cattle or Hog Island Sheep. A modern

Learning about "farm life"

ecosystem farm near the property demonstrates sustainable, organic farming practices of service to the community co-op program.

BELTSVILLE AGRICULTURAL RESEARCH CENTER

Beltsville (Powder) - *Bldg. 302 BARC-W (Beltway 495/I-95 to exit 25A, Route 1 north. Turn right on Rte. 212 (Power Mill Rd). Go over bridge, cross thru light at Edmonston Rd into the BARC) 20705. Phone: (301) 504-8483. Web: www.ars.usda.gov/is/nvc/welcome.htm Hours: Monday-Friday 8:00am-4:30pm.*

Peer into the future of food and farm sciences using plant breeding, animal and human nutrition, products and new inventions based on agricultural science. Some of the best known accomplishments from work at Beltsville include the modern turkey, hog, and disease-resistant blueberries, strawberries and potatoes. Start at the Log Lodge to learn about exhibits and displays featuring photos of microscopic animals, scientists in labs, 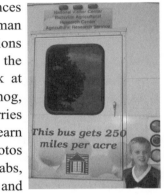 insects, and

other research topics. Most visitors view a short introductory video. You may be surprised that many products you use every day were developed here. Your morning orange juice, seedless grapes, thickening agents for gravies, and the fat substitute Oatrim.

Don't be a "couch potato!"

Other household products include wrinkle-resistant cotton shirts, fly traps, and super-absorbant corn starch molecules in disposable diapers and fuel filters. Check out the "bugs" that grow in humans and animals (ex. Tapeworms - ugh!) and the "couch potatoes."

BOWIE BAYSOX

Bowie - *Prince George's Stadium, Crain Hwy NE 20716. Phone: (301) 803-6000. Web: www.baysox.com*

Hot dogs, popcorn and peanuts for the entire family. The Baysox are a AA farm team for the Baltimore Orioles. Season runs April through

September and features endless special promotions and special appearances. Also, fireworks, a kids' play area and carousel.

BRUNSWICK RAILROAD MUSEUM / C&O CANAL VISITORS CENTER

Brunswick - 40 W. Potomac Street 21716. Phone: (301) 834-7100. Web: www.BRRM.net Hours: Friday 10:00am-2:00pm, Saturday 10:00am-4:00pm, Sunday 1:00-4:00pm. (April-December) Admission: $5.00 adult, $4.00 senior (60+), $2.50 youth (6-12) and $1.25 child (3-5). Regular admission is charged whenever a guest would like to view Museum Exhibits. Visitors may however, visit the National Park Service's C&O Canal Visitor center and browse the Museum Store without a fee. Miscellaneous: Nearby towns have Canal related aqueducts: Catoctin Aqueduct (catoctinaqueduct.org) is on Lander Road in Jefferson and Monocacy Aqueduct is at the mouth of Monocacy Road off Rte. 28 near the Frederick/Montgomery County Line.

The museum offers a giant interactive HO scale model railroad layout, which depicts the B&O Railroad's "Metropolitan Subdivision" from Washington DC's Union Station platforms to Brunswick's large rail yards. The big display takes up an entire floor and has many sight-

Have fun pretending to be a "local"...

and-sound push buttons that create smoke or move a carrousel. On the second floor, you will find the exhibits about Brunswick and the people and society located here in 1900. Brunswick went from a Canal town named Berlin to a booming railroad yard town named Brunswick. Railroad equipment is upstairs along with costumes, toys, baseball and medical history. Try on some Victorian era clothing for a picture or use a computer to transmit Morse Code to the conductor down the line. They recently opened a "Hands on History" Children's entertainment center for the kids (loads of trains to play with). This, and the C&O CANAL VISITOR

CENTER are located on the first floor. This visitor center, one of only 6 along the C&O Canal, shows a basic history of Brunswick, as well as showing the competition between the C&O canal and B&O railroad in the 1830s and beyond.

AUDUBON NATURALIST SOCIETY, WOODEND SANCTUARY

Chevy Chase - 8940 Jones Mill Road (I-495 exit Connecticut Ave, exit 33 toward Chevy Chase. Left on Manor Rd., right on Jones Bridge, and left on Jones Mill Road) 20815. Web: www.audubonnaturalist.org/cgi-bin/mesh/ sanctuaries/woodend_md   Phone: (301) 652-9188.

Enjoy the serenity of a wildflower meadow, hike meandering trails, explore the aquatic life of a pond at the 40-acre nature sanctuary, minutes from our nation's capital. Classes feature outdoor, hands-on experiences which build on children's natural curiosity.

SURRATT HOUSE MUSEUM

Clinton - 9118 Brandywine Road (Beltway exit 7A, Branch Ave. South (MD 5), right onto Woodyard Rd. (Rte.223W), left on Brandywine) 20735. Phone: (301) 868-1121. Web: www.surratt.org Hours: Thursday & Fridays 11:00am-3:00pm, Saturdays and Sundays Noon-4:00pm (mid-January thru mid-December). Closed Easter Sunday and 4th of July. Last tour of the day begins one-half hour before closing. Admission: $3.00 adult, $2.00 senior and groups, $1.00 child (5-18).

An1800s middle-class farm home, tavern and post office with special emphasis on the crucial years from 1840 to 1865. It explores the

impact of this period on our national history as well as on the family of John and Mary Surratt who became entangled in the web of conspiracy surrounding the assassination of President Abraham Lincoln. Today, much of the structure of the House & Tavern is original. Very engaging, entertaining costumed guides

Study the escape route on an electric map...

share little stories in every room. On a tour, you can see a reproduction of the original attic of the kitchen wing and look down a shaft where a rifle was hidden by Lloyd after Booth and Herold left the premises. The museum's permanent exhibit displays family artifacts, such as Surratt's wire-rim spectacles, pocket watch & a handkerchief with the family name embroidered on it. The kids really liked this tour and the guides, especially.

Probably not a coincidence that a rifle was hidden in the wall...

NATIONAL CAPITAL TROLLEY MUSEUM

Colesville - 1313 Bonifant Road 20905. Phone: (301) 384-6088. Web: www.dctrolley.org Hours: Thursday & Friday operations 10:00am-2:00pm, Saturday & Sunday Noon-5:00pm (mid-March to mid-May and October to mid-November). Thursday & Friday operations 11:00am-3:00pm and weekends (summer). Weekends only (rest of year). Holly Trolley Festival in December evenings.

The collections consist of 17 streetcars from Washington D.C. and other cities. Many of these are operated on a one-mile demonstration railway. Check out the O-scale model layout representing a Washington streetscape from the 1930s, a video or various street railway artifacts. Trolley rides.

COLLEGE PARK AVIATION MUSEUM & AIRPORT

College Park - 1985 Corporal Frank Scott Drive 20740. Phone: (301) 864-6029. Web: www.collegeparkaviationmuseum.com Hours: Daily 10:00am-5:00pm. Closed major holidays. Admission: $2.00-$4.00 per person. Miscellaneous: Notice the "ghost" screens of the first flights here, outside, near the parking lot.

The College Park Aviation Museum is located on the grounds of the world's oldest continuously operating airport. The Museum tells

Senior Captain Daniel says, "clear prop, ready for takeoff"

the story of flight from the Wright Brothers to today. An animatronic Wilbur Wright welcomes visitors to the exhibits. The museum gallery contains historic and reproduction aircraft associated with the history of the airfield, as well as hands-on activities and experimentation areas for children. Create your own Air Mail postcard using rubbings and stamps. Be an Air Mail pilot, work the controls, test the drag and lift, or air flow. While you're a test pilot, look the part and try on some bomber jackets and caps. Now, hop into the Imagination Plane and pretend you're the pilot of a 1939 Taylorcraft Airplane...a real plane. Next, write a short story about your "first flight." For the little guys, there is a mini-airport outside with small planes the kids can sit on and ride. The newer 1911 Model B Flight Simulator allows a visitor to fly over the airport with cockpit hand controls and state-of-the-art visuals (the 3 minute "ride" is $1.00 additional). The airport runway is just outside the glass windows of the museum - be sure to watch for a take-off or landing as today's pilots fly. The airport was founded in 1909 for the Wright Brothers' instruction of the first military aviators. One of the best aviation museums for kids.

WHITE'S FERRY

Dickerson - 24801 White's Ferry Road, US 107 (from I-270 & Route 28) 20842. Phone: (301) 349-5200.

There used to be 100 ferries operating on the Potomac, This is the last one and it's still pretty busy. Vehicles line up and fill up the barge ferry. The ferry follows a wire cable to the other side. It runs continuously, year round, from 5:00am-11:00pm. $4.00 one way or $6.00 round trip.

FORT WASHINGTON PARK

Fort Washington - 13551 Fort Washington Road (I-495 exit 3. Indian Head Hwy south 4 miles to Fort Washington Rd) 20744. Phone: (301) 763-4600. Web: www.nps.gov/fowa/ Hours: Daily 9:00am-4:30pm. Admission: $5.00 per vehicle. Miscellaneous: Civil War artillery demonstrations, first Sunday of the month from April to October.

Picturesque Fort Washington sits on high ground overlooking the Potomac River and offers a grand view of Washington and the Virginia shoreline. Today, only one silent gun stands behind the masonry wall- the last armament of the powerful fort that once guarded the water approach to our Nation's Capital. The old fort is one of the few U.S. seacoast fortifications still in its original form - although repairs for the crumbling structure occur often. Exhibits inside the Visitors Center include information and artifacts describing the history of Fort Washington as the Capital's Guardian. Audio-visual program explores the park's history and special exhibits from time to time depicting elements of the park's history.

The old FORT FOOTE is just down the road in Oxon Hill. (301-763-4600 or **www.nps.gov/fofo**) Open 10:00am to dark, the fort was designed in the 1860s to protect the river entrance to the surrounding sea ports. The National Park Service has cleared paths around the ruins of what is considered the best preserved Civil War fort in the region.

ROGER BROOKE TANEY HOUSE

Frederick - 121 S. Bentz Street   21701. Phone: (301) 228-2828. Web: www.hsfcinfo.org/taney_house/taney.htm Hours: Saturday 10:00-4:00pm, Sunday 1:00-4:00pm (April-mid-December).

Built in 1799, the site, including the house, detached kitchen, root cellar, smokehouse and slaves' quarters interprets the life of Taney and various aspects of life in early nineteenth century Frederick County. The docents are full of fun and interesting stories and the house creaks and groans as you climb the worn stairs to the top floor. Through guided tours, exhibits and special events, the lifestyle of Frederick's "middling class" is presented to visitors. It contains personal items of the Chief Justice Taney and the Key families (his wife was Francis Scott Key's sister). Taney is best remembered as the author of the majority opinion in Dred Scott v. Sandford (1857), overturning all restrictions on the spread of slavery into the territories, and declared that no African American, either slave or free, could ever be counted as a citizen under the Constitution of the United States. Francis Scott Key is the author of the Star Spangled Banner.

ROSE HILL MANOR PARK/ CHILDREN'S & FARM MUSEUM

Frederick - 1611 North Market Street, downtown (US 15, take the Motter Avenue exit; left on 14th Street, left on N. Market St.) 21701. Phone: (301) 694-1646. **Web: www.rosehillmuseum.com** *Hours: Monday-Saturday 10:00am-4:00pm, Sunday 1:00-4:00pm (April-October). Weekends only in November. Admission: $4.00-$5.00 per person (ages 3+).*

This living history museum specializes in early American life, historic tours and events designed for children and their adults. The tours focus on the early 1800s, the manor's owners, and their lifestyles. The Farm and Family Exhibit Building houses the following exhibit themes and displays: The Farm Family Kitchen; The Farmer's Carpentry Shop; The Farmer's Broom Shop; On the Farm Pork Butchering; a Rumly Steam Tractor; and a Wheat Thrashing Machine. The Bank Barn houses The Planting and Harvesting exhibit which includes a large collection of agricultural hand tools and machinery. The Carriage Museum exhibits a variety of restored carriages and sleighs. During the tour, children can card wool, weave on a table loom, play with replicas of old toys, dress up in period costumes, and experience old-fashioned daily chores. For the adult visitor, interpretation of architecture, furnishings, and site history is also included.

WAY OFF BROADWAY DINNER THEATER & CHILDREN'S THEATER

Frederick - 5 Willowdale Drive (Rte. 40 West at Willowtree Plaza) 21702. Phone: (301) 662-6600. **Web: www.wayoffbroadway.com** *Performances: Children's Theater: Performances every Saturday afternoon and the 2nd and*

4th Sunday of each month. Mainstage performances are on: Select Thursday Evenings throughout the month; Friday Evenings; Saturday Evenings; Matinees on the 1st, 3rd, and 5th Sunday of each month. Admission: $10.50 for everyone (Children's). Everyone gets a choice of an individual cheese pizza, a hot dog, or a peanut butter & jelly sandwich. All are served with chips. There's a choice of sodas or lemonade to drink. And for dessert there's ice cream. Mainstage serves a deluxe buffet $24.00-$38.00 per person. $13.00-$20.00 if no meal included.

Broadway musicals with live orchestra, comedies, mysteries, dramas, and Children's Theater lunch matinees (ex. Cinderella, Wizard of Oz). Every production includes a delicious buffet featuring bakery items.

FREDERICK KEYS BASEBALL

Frederick - 21 Stadium Drive 21703. Web: www.frederickkeys.com Phone: (301) 662-0013. Baseball action all summer long at Harry Grove Stadium. The season starts in April and ends in September. Tickets run $5.00-$11.00 for home games of the Carolina League Class A affiliate of the Orioles.

MONOCACY NATIONAL BATTLEFIELD

Frederick - 4801 Urbana Pike (I-70 exit 54. Proceed south on SR 355, just past the Monocacy River bridge) 21704. Phone: (301) 662-3515. **Web:** *www.nps.gov/mono/ Hours: Open Daily 8:00am-4:30pm (Labor Day-Memorial Day) and 8:30am-5:00pm (Memorial Day-Labor Day). Closed Thanksgiving, Christmas and New Years. Admission: FREE*

The center provides interpretive exhibits, an electric map orientation program (outlining the battle sequences) and an interactive computer program. The electric map is really engaging and the kids understand the strategy of the battle and why it was a win AND loss situation. On Saturday, July 9, 1864, along the banks of the Monocacy River, two armies clashed in a desperate battle for time. Confederates (led by General Jubal Early and his army of 15,000) were on the march towards overtaking Washington D.C. (the Federal Capital). At this battleground, they encountered Union Major General Lew Wallace, with only 5,800 troops, blocking the road to try to save advancement on the Nation's Capital. Greatly outnumbered, Wallace's Union forces lost the battle, but did cost the Confederates time allowing reinforcements to arrive in the Capital, saving Washington from capture. Brochures are available for the self-guided auto tour (this can be boring for kids, we recommend the short trail instead). Two trails are offered within the park: a one-half mile boardwalk loop trail near the visitor center and a six-mile trail on a historic farm within the battlefield.

BARBARA FRITCHIE HOUSE

Frederick - 154 W. Patrick Street, downtown 21705. Phone: (301) 698-8992. Hours: Saturday 10:00am-4:00pm, Sunday 1:00-4:00pm. Admission: $1.00-$2.00 per person. (students plus)

This woman was made famous by her comment to Stonewall Jackson "Shoot if you must, this old gray head, but spare your country's flag." Little is known of the truth of this incident or the facts of Barbara Fritchie's life, but a poem by Whittier about Fritchie made her a heroine to generations of school children in the US and abroad. From the street you enter, first, the Souvenir Shop. This was once the storeroom of Barbara's husband, John Casper Fritchie, who was a glove maker. Barbara Fritchie candy, cards, souvenirs and other items of interest are sold here. Perhaps the first object to catch your eye is Barbara Fritchie's desk, at which you are invited to register. While

registering, you sit in one of Barbara's dining-room chairs. The best part is next - your docent weaves the story (in first person) of Barbara on that eventful day in the 1860s - finishing with a vivid recital of the complete poem! Finally, you look out

Peering out the famous window...

of the window (which is directly in front of the bedroom), from which she always kept her flag waving; and, looking down, you see the very spot whereupon, more than 150 years ago, were enacted those stirring scenes which inspired Whittier's poem. The Confederates were approaching from your right -- coming on Patrick Street, moving westward -- when, "Halt! The dust-brown ranks stood fast!" -- right under the window out of which you are gazing.

HESSIAN BARRACKS

Frederick - 101 Clarke Place (I-15 along Maryland 355, known also as South Market Street) 21705. Phone: (301) 662-4159. Hours: Open for special events, by appointment, and on the second Saturday of every Month (May-December). Open the second Sunday in September. Noon-4:00pm.

The Hessian Barracks are located on the campus of the Maryland School for the Deaf. Built in 1777 to accommodate two battalions of soldiers, the Barracks soon became a repository for mercenaries fighting for England in the Revolutionary War. Afterwards, it was used as a staging point for Lewis and Clarke's expedition, a state armory in 1812, a Civil War general hospital, and the first Maryland School for the Deaf. Find out about the dreaded Hessian soldiers - who were they? As you are walking up to the building, you will notice a large cannon sitting there which was actually used to signal the end of the Revolutionary War. The interior of the Barracks transports the visitor back to the physical space of 1781. There are a vast array of objects for those who are interested in the history of deaf development in the Frederick area also. Everything from shelves of actual hearing aids from the early 1900s to civil war weapons. They show the actual place that students were taught and the set up of their classroom.

NATIONAL MUSEUM OF CIVIL WAR MEDICINE

Frederick - 48 E. Patrick Street, downtown (I-70 exit 56, Route 144 west - E. Patrick Street) 21705. Phone: (301) 695-1864. Web: www.civilwarmed.org Hours: Monday-Saturday 10:00am-5:00pm, Sunday 11:00am-5:00pm. Closes one hour earlier (mid-November thru mid-March). Closed New Years, Easter, Thanksgiving and Christmastime. Admission: $7.00 adult, $5.00 youth (10-16).

Immediately following the battles of Antietam and Gettysburg, Frederick was transformed into a hospital center. The town's "clustered spire" churches were used as makeshift infirmaries where as many as 8,000 soldiers were treated at one time. This museum is dedicated to telling the real story of medicine in the Civil War. Major advances changed medicine forever. Two floors of exhibit space cover topics such as: medical schools of the time; men enlisting with chronic diseases; the impact of infectious diseases, poor sanitation and diet on soldiers in camp (more died from illness than wounds); and transporting wounded and field stations. Do you know what the difference is between a Field hospital and a pavilion hospital? Most areas feature immersion exhibits that bring the visitor into a setting vividly illustrating different aspects of Civil War medicine. Walk thru a battlefield or hospital train, identify bones, or feed horses. While you're touring, look for the doctor's final exam, handmade paper chess board and fragrant pine. Each are significant. What an interesting place to study the medical side of a war! Every exhibit solicits conversation and questions - well done!

ADVENTURE PARK USA

Frederick (New Market) - 11113 W. Baldwin Road (I-70 East. Take Exit 62 – Rte. 75 (Libertytown/Hyattstown). Make a right off the exit ramp. Make first right. At intersection go straight) 21774. Phone: (301) 865-6800. Web: www.adventureparkusa.com Hours: Daily 10:00am-10:00pm. Remember outdoor park attractions may be closed due to cold or inclement weather. Admission: Parking and entrance is FREE. Choose the attractions you like best and purchase a Fun Pass and use it just like a debit card on all rides and attractions. Most cost $2.00-$5.00 per ride.

This Wild Western themed Family Entertainment Center features Go-Karts, Bumper Boats, Miniature Golf, Paint Ball arena, Laser Tag, Arcade, Kiddie-rides, and a café.

SENECA CREEK STATE PARK

Gaithersburg - 11950 Clopper Road (I-270 north towards Frederick, Maryland. Take Exit 10, Clopper Road (Route 117) 20878. Phone: (301) 924-2127. Web: www.dnr.state.md.us/publiclands/central/seneca.html

The park extends along 14 scenic miles of Seneca Creek, as it winds its way to the Potomac River. The Clopper Day-Use Area contains many scenic areas, including the 90-acre Clopper Lake, surrounded by forests and fields. Picnicking, boat rentals, trails and a tire playground are just some of its recreational opportunities. A restored 19th century cabin and a self-guided path interpret the history of the area. Traces of the Black Rock and Clopper Mills are still present today. Black Rock Mill has been stabilized and outdoor exhibits interpret its operation. The Seneca Sandstone Quarries historic site is near the Potomac River and contains a number of buildings, including the Seneca Stone Cutting Mill and the Seneca Schoolhouse, which is open to the public. The red sandstone was used in the construction of the C&O Canal and the original Smithsonian Institution "Castle." Nearby, the Schaeffer Farm Trail Area offers 12 miles of marked trails for hiking and mountain biking. Water activities include: boat rental, fishing, flatwater canoeing and kayaking.

CLARA BARTON NATIONAL HISTORIC SITE

Glen Echo - 3801 Oxford Road 20812. Phone: (301) 492-6245. Web: www.nps.gov/clba Miscellaneous: In Glen Echo Park, you can enjoy a carousel ride aboard a 1921 restored Dentzel Carousel or enjoy children's productions at Adventure Theatre.

Clara Barton was a Civil War nurse who went on to establish the American Red Cross. Clara lived here 1897 to 1912. Her late 19th-century home served as the first headquarters of the American Red Cross. Clara never put anything to waste. When construction began on a Red Cross supplies warehouse near our nation's capital, she thought of using the surplus lumber from relief work at Johnstown, Pennsylvania (see *Kids Love Pennsylvania*, Johnstown Flood). Having once served as a hotel for homeless victims of the epic flood, the large warehouse then served as the first permanent headquarters for the organization she started. Hear about her efforts at Antietam Battlefield, too. After the war, the President commissioned her to try to locate tens of thousands of soldiers still missing. It took an organized, systematic effort to locate many with her diligence.

NASA GODDARD SPACE FLIGHT CENTER

Greenbelt - Visitor Center, Soil Conservation Road, 8800 Greenbelt Road (I95/495 Capital Beltway- exit 23 to Greenbelt Rd., Rte. 193 east) 20771. Phone: (301) 286-8981. **Web: www.gsfc.nasa.gov/vc** *Hours: Tuesday-Saturday 10:00am-5:00pm (July, August); Tuesday-Friday 10:00am-3:00pm and Saturday, Sunday Noon-4:00pm (September-June). Admission: FREE*

The hub of all NASA tracking activities, Goddard is also responsible for the development of unmanned sounding rockets, and research in space and earth sciences including the Mission to Planet Earth. Through interactive exhibits, families explore the Flight Center with a focus on 1958 to the present. Collections include space flight artifacts and photographs. Check the website for the schedule of model rocket launchings. Science on a Sphere (SOS) is a large, mesmerizing 'earth ball' that uses computers and video projectors to display animated data on the outside of a suspended, 6-foot diameter, white sphere. Four strategically placed projectors work in unison to coat the sphere with data such as "3-D surface of the earth and Nighttime Lights," "moon and Mars" and "X-Ray Sun." To further enhance the experience, catch the movie, "Footprints." The movie consists of a visually rich presentation where the earth appears in a variety of guises, from depictions of the biosphere to planetary views of city lights at night to dramatic examinations about the science of hurricane formation. In the Science Center, students use the Hubble Telescope computer to "hit" Jupiter with a comet; attempt to put star clusters in order of age; use the Hubble Deep Field image to estimate the number of galaxies in the universe; match before and after images of colliding galaxies; and also learn about the different wavelengths of light by taking pictures of their hands in visible and infrared light. Numerous videos will be shown including, Shoemaker-Levy (a comet collision with Jupiter), Star Life Cycle Animations, Age of the Universe and the Hubble Deep Field. Outside, The Center features a full-size rocket garden with many types of rockets, mock-ups, and old flight hardware. This collection is 100% real NASA artifacts. Ask to see the tree that went to the moon.

WASHINGTON REDSKINS FOOTBALL

Landover - (FedEx Field, I-495/I-95 South to I-95 Exit 17A (Landover Rd. East), turn right on Lottsford Rd. Follow to Arena Drive) 20785. Phone: (301) 276-6800. Web: www.redskins.com

Home of the Washington Redskins NFL team playing August thru December (then playoffs). From the days of Slingin' Sammy Baugh through the Joe Gibbs era, Redskins fans have always been the most loyal and dedicated in all of sports. It takes teamwork to win a championship and Redskins fans are truly the twelfth man on the field.

SIX FLAGS AMERICA

Largo - 13710 Central Avenue (I-95 to Largo exit #15A Central Avenue. Head east 5 miles) 20775. Web: www.sixflags.com/america Phone: (301) 249-1500. Hours: Summer Break, daily 10:30am opening, closing near dark. Weekends only in May and September. Admission: Begins around $35.00 for little ones up to $50.00 for most riders. Discount tickets online.

Thrilling theme and water-park featuring more than 100 rides, shows and attractions, headlined by the constantly spinning Penguin's Blizzard River raft ride and eight exciting coasters. Younger families enjoy the Pirate themes at Bucanneer Beach and the classic amusement park rides at Looney Toons Movie Town (kiddie rides are plentiful and cute). Young families will also like that the music and noise is not loud here. There are plenty of shade trees - especially the entire area of rides near the entrance (right off Main Street). We also liked the fact that many rides were mild enough for many family members to enjoy. Gothan City and the Southwest Territory contained more "thrill" roller coasters although the Batman Thrill Show wasn't too scary for kids to watch as they cheered Batman on. For a classic wooden roller coaster, try the Wild One.

NATIONAL WILDLIFE VISITOR CENTER

Laurel - 10901 Scarlet Tanager Loop (off of Powder Mill Rd. between the Baltimore-Washington Parkway and Rt. 197 south of Laurel) 20708. Phone: (301) 497-5760. Web: www.pwrc.usgs.gov/ Hours: Daily 10:00am-4:30 or 5:30pm. Trails open at sunrise. Admission: Events are held at the National

Wildlife Visitor Center unless otherwise noted and are FREE. Tram Tours are $1.00-$3.00 per person.

The National Wildlife Visitor Center is the largest science and environmental education center in the Department of the Interior. It highlights the work of professional scientists who strive to improve the condition of wildlife and their habitats. Be a field researcher and travel through five life-scale habitat areas. Learn through hands-on interactive exhibits how wildlife research has led to important discoveries. See dramatic dioramas of gray wolves, whooping cranes, canvasback ducks and sea otters displaying true-to-life behavior - up close and in their own environment. If the weather is unkind, stay indoors and peer out their giant Pond Window.

The Visitor Center also offers hiking trails. The Loop Trail - (0.5 km/0.3 mi.) is a paved and fully accessible trail. It leaves the visitor center gallery door and offers views of both Lake Redington and Cash Lake. Goose Pond Trail - (0.3 km/0.2 mi.) parallels the wood's edge as it wanders first through a forested wetland area as it leads to Goose Pond. Laurel Trail - This woodland trail (0.6 km/0.4 mi.) was named for the many Mountain Laurels found along the trail. Visitors have the opportunity to see woodland songbirds and mammals (esp. deer). Cash Lake Trail - (2.3 km/1.4 mi.) travels along the edge of Cash Lake. This trail offers many opportunities to view the lake and its waterfowl, as well as a beaver lodge and evidence of their activity. There is also a seasonal fishing program at Cash Lake, with fishing by permit from the accessible pier and along parts of the shoreline. Patuxent is a research refuge where the air, land, and water are managed specifically for wildlife - keep this in mind when venturing outside to the hiking trails.

OXON HILL FARM AT OXON COVE PARK

Oxon Hill - 6411 Oxon Hill Road (I-95/495 Capital Beltway exit 3A) 20745. Phone: (301) 839-1176. Web: www.nps.gov/oxhi/ Hours: Daily 8:00am-4:30pm. Admission: FREE Miscellaneous: Venture beyond the hilltop and explore part of Oxon Cove Park's 512 acres by strolling along the lower fields or riding the bike path along Oxon Cove. The Woodlot Trail is a steep 1/2-mile trail, marked with yellow blazes on trees, from just below the farm house to the parking lot. Find out how this wooded ravine benefited early farmers.

Oxon Hill Farm operates as an actual working farm, representative of the early 20th century. You can see a farm house, barns, a stable, feed building, livestock buildings and a visitor activity barn. It exhibits basic farming principles and techniques as well as historical agricultural programs for urban people to develop an understanding of cropping and animal husbandry. The most unique story about this place is that of the early farmers of the wheat crops. From the 1890s until the 1950s, Oxon Hill Farm was operated by patients from St. Elizabeth Hospital. It provided therapy as well as food for the patients at the institution.

Each month offers a variety of programs, such as crafts, walks to observe plants and wildlife, wagon rides, and talks about farm life and the animals. Call ahead for reservations. Farming is a year-round business directed by the seasons. In spring, catch some planting corn or sheering sheep. June is dairy month with cows-a-milking. Fall brings the harvest season and cider pressing or sorghum syrup. Winter is a quiet time for walks, hayrides and tracking.

C & O CANAL NATIONAL HISTORICAL PARK

Potomac. - 11710 MacArthur Blvd. 20834. Web: www.nps.gov/choh Phone: (301) 299-3613. Hours: Open All Year 9:00am-4:30pm (extended summer hours). Admission: $5.00 per vehicle.

Take a mule-drawn barge ride on the historic canal. Footbridges are available to see Great Falls. Enjoy the Riley's Lockhouse, the only original C&O Canal lockhouse still open to the public. Displays and a short film interpret the site. Hiking and biking trails are along the historic towpath, a project which took 22 years to build and stimulated economic growth in little towns along the canal. This canal was considered an engineering marvel in its day. The marshy Dierssen Wildlife Management Area is also on site, with trails teeming with wildlife.

AIRMEN MEMORIAL MUSEUM

Suitland - 5211 Auth Road (just off Branch Avenue (Maryland Route 5) 20746. Web: www.afsahq.org/AMM/amm-htm/mwelcome.htm Phone: (301) 899-8386. Hours: Weekdays 8:00am-5:00pm and during special events.

The Airmen Memorial Museum stands as a tribute to enlisted airmen who have served in the United States Air Force, the U.S. Army Air Forces, the Army Air Corps and their predecessor organizations. The focus of the Museum's exhibits, programs, publications, oral history interviews and video documentary histories is the "enlisted experience" - the enlisted people. Stories of pioneers in air/space service are sprinkled with Aeronautical Division signal flags, a 1912 leather flying helmet, and a 1st Aero Squadron banner. World War I artifacts include; recruiting posters, an enlisted pilot's uniform, an American bomb and a Distinguished Flying Cross. Items from Sgt. Ray Gallagher and MSgt. John Kuharek, enlisted participants on both atomic missions, are displayed in this comprehensive exhibit detailing the enlisted sacrifices made to ensure the success of the atomic missions. Other World War II artifacts on exhibit include the Norden Bombsight, an A-2 flight jacket, Adolf Hitler's personal stationery (retrieved by an enlisted airmen in war-torn Berlin), and the China-Burma-India Theater sketches of enlisted artist Nathan H. Glick. Bring an enlisted or veteran Airman with you to honor him.

COTOCTIN WILDLIFE PRESERVE AND ZOO

Thurmont - (US 15 north of town) 21788. Phone: (301) 271-3180. Web: www.cwpzoo.com Hours: Open daily, 9:00am-6:00pm (April-October), last admission taken one hour prior to closing. Weekends only in November and March. Admission: $13.95 adult, $11.95 seniors (60+) / military, $8.95 child (2-12). Miscellaneous: Camel rides offered May to September.

From bears to boas, lions to lemurs, macaws to monkeys, panthers to pythons, you'll meet over 450 exotic animals on your Zoo adventure. Newest to the zoo (besides new babies born) is the Amazing Africa exhibit with lions, zebra, antelope and the deadliest snakes of Africa. Look for recent editions including cougars, dingos, tortoises, parrots and lizards. You'll be surprised how close you can get to these creatures at the Conservation Theater Contact Shows. Safely meet and touch a chinchilla, prickly hedgehog, smooth snake or bumpy lizard. Hand-feed animals in the petting area and maybe get to toss a Grizzly bear a special snack.

CUNNINGHAM FALLS STATE PARK/ CATOCTIN FURNACE/ GAMBRILL STATE PARK

Thurmont - 14039 Catoctin Hollow Road (The Manor Area, on U.S. Route 15 and the Houck Area, three miles west of Thurmont, off RT 77, on Catoctin Hollow Road) 21788. Web: www.dnr.state.md.us/publiclands/western/ cunninghamfalls.html Phone: (301) 271-7574. Hours: Daily 8:00am-sunset. Admission: Day use service charge is $3.00/vehicle year-round. Out-of-state residents add $1.00. Camping fees.

Cunningham Falls State Park, located in the Catoctin Mountains, is known for its history and scenic beauty, as well as its 78-foot cascading waterfall. The Falls are located one half mile from the lake in the Houck Area via the Falls Trail. Hiking, swimming, fishing, boating, playgrounds, nine camper cabins, and 171 campsites in two areas are available seasonally. The Houck area has a 43 acre lake and trail to the Falls. Manor area includes CATOCTIN FURNACE - in operation from 1776 to 1903, the iron furnace was an entire community. Founders, miners, clerks, charcoal makers, storekeepers, teamsters, and others were supervised by the iron master. A furnace stack, the iron master's Manor House ruins and a self-guided trail are available. GAMBRILL STATE PARK (off Rte 40) - All trails, except the Catoctin Trail, are loop trails, and return to the Trailhead Lot. All trails, except the White Oak Trail, are open for hiking, mountain biking, and horseback riding. Stunning overlooks of the surrounding areas. Camping.

MERKLE WILDLIFE SANCTUARY & VISITORS CENTER

Upper Marlboro - 11704 Fenno Road (Route 301 South to Croom Road/Route 382) 20772. Web: www.dnr.state.md.us/publiclands/southern/merkle.html Phone: (301) 888-1410. Hours: Merkle Wildlife Sanctuary is open daily from 7:00am to sunset. The Visitor Center is open 10:00am-4:00pm Saturday and Sunday only. Admission: $2.00-$3.00 per vehicle.

SANCTUARY: The geese arrive in mid-October and stay until late February or early March. About 100 geese stay the year round. During the peak of the season, more than 5,000 geese may be present. Corn, millet and other crops favored by geese are grown for them, adding to the marsh and aquatic plants that flourish in the ponds along the Patuxent River.

VISITORS CENTER: The exhibits focus primarily on the life history and management of the Canada goose. Other exhibits focus on the habitat of the area. A Discovery Room for children has live snakes, frogs, turtles and other wildlife species. The lower level includes a children's coloring table and a book nook. There is also a gift shop featuring nature items.

CRITICAL AREA DRIVING TOUR: The four-mile Chesapeake Bay Critical Area Driving Tour (CADT) is open for self-guided driving tours on Sundays from 10:00am-3:00pm throughout the year. The tour begins at Patuxent River Park. Take Croom Airport Road, off Croom Road (north of Merkle). The CADT travels across the Mattaponi Creek onto the Merkle Wildlife Sanctuary. The CADT is open for biking, hiking and horseback riding daily, January through September.

WATKINS REGIONAL PARK

Upper Marlboro - 301 Watkins Park Drive (just one mile south of Six Flags, left on Watkins Park Drive) 20774. Web: www.pgparks.com Phone: (301) 218-6700. Hours: Daytime park hours vary each season.

The park is 3 minutes from Six Flags and is a must see. It includes the Old Maryland Farm with farm animals petting zoo, Watkins Nature Center, miniature train that runs through the park, miniature golf, an antique carrousel, walking and biking trails and the like. Most activities only require $1.00-3.50 per person. It's a good complement for Six Flags and a wonderful cost-friendly option for families.

WALKERSVILLE SOUTHERN RAILROAD

Walkersville - 34 W. Pennsylvania Avenue (Rte. 15 north toward Gettysburg. Follow 15 for 6 miles north then turn right onto Biggs Ford Road) 21793. Phone: (301) 898-0899 or (877) 363-9777. Web: www.wsrr.org Admission: $9.00 adult, $8.00 senior, $5.00 child (age 3+). Miscellaneous: Visitors to *the museum will be treated to many educational displays and an operating model railroad (HO scale) known as the "Monocacy Valley Railroad."*

Take a trip back in time . . . on the Walkersville Southern, established in 1991 on the Frederick branch of the old Pennsylvania Railroad. Ride in vintage 1920s passenger cars or on an open flatcar as your rail excursion runs past a 100-year-old lime kiln, and then out into the picturesque Maryland farm country. On a clear day, you can view the Catoctin Mountains west of Frederick. Before returning to the Walkerville Station you will cross the beautiful Monocacy River on the recently reconstructed railroad bridge. The Railroad offers a wide variety of excursion rides on rustic trains, including mystery dinner trains, Jesse James Day, Circus Trains and Teddy Bear Picnics.

SUGGESTED LODGING AND DINING

HAMPTON INN & SUITES, **Frederick** - Complimentary fresh, hot breakfast. Comfy new beds & linens. **www.hamptoninnfrederick.com**

RADISSON HOTEL LARGO. **Largo** - 9100 Basil Court (I-495 exit 17A). The Largo Hotel features 184 perfectly designed guest rooms featuring all of the amenities to make your stay enjoyable. Guest rooms feature the exclusive Sleep Number® Bed, well lit work desk and Complimentary Wireless High-Speed Internet Access. Just 4 miles from Six Flags and 12 miles from DC. When it's time to relax, guests at the Largo Hotel can enjoy the indoor swimming pool and fully equipped, 24 hour fitness center. The Radisson Hotel Largo features a full service restaurant and lounge (breakfast buffet, Kids Menu - $4.95). For your convenience, they also offer a lobby shop with light snacks, beverages and microwavable meals available. Micro and Frig in each room. Value rates start around $149.00.

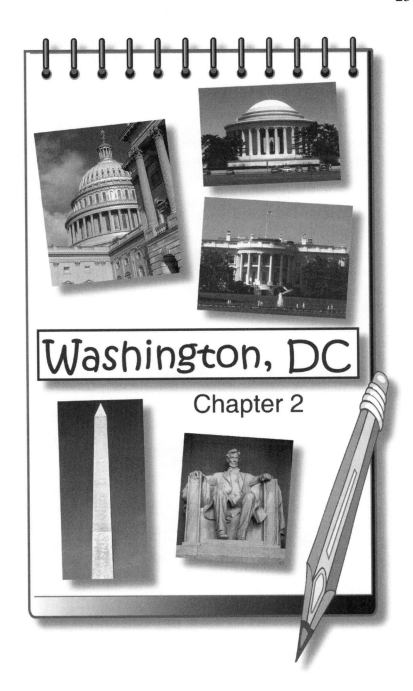

Washington, DC

Chapter 2

INTERNATIONAL SPY MUSEUM

Washington, DC - 800 F Street, NW (Metro: Gallery Place/ Chinatown), 20004. Web: www.spymuseum.org. Phone: (202) 393-7798, Hours: Daily 10:00am-8:00pm (April-October); 10:00am-6:00pm (November-March). Closed major winter holidays. Peak months the museum opens at 9:00am. Admission: $16.00 adult (12-64), $15.00 senior (65+), Active duty military, $13.00 child (ages 5-11). Children age 4 and under FREE. The Permanent Exhibition is most appropriate for ages 12+.

One of Washington, DC's newest attractions is a big hit with children and adults alike. Packed with high-tech, interactive displays and activities, visitors can take on a spy's cover, test their skills of observation and surveillance, while learning about the history and the future of espionage. Examine over 200 spy gadgets, weapons, bugs, cameras, vehicles, and technologies. Learn about the earliest codes--who created them and who broke them. A spy must live a life of lies. Adopt a cover identity and learn why an operative needs one. See the credentials an agent must have to get in - or out.

NATIONAL ZOO

Washington, DC - 3001 Connecticut Avenue, NW (I-395 north to exit 8B, Washington Blvd. To Arlington Bridge. Cross Bridge, veer left. Turn right on Constitution, left on 17th. Metro: Zoo), 20008. Phone: (202) 633-4800, Web: http://nationalzoo.si.edu. Hours: Daily 10:00am-4:30pm. Open until 6:00pm (April-October). Closed Christmas Day. Admission: FREE.

Most of you are thinking Giant Pandas at the National Zoo. See Tai Shan, the Zoo's newest panda, on the web cams. Information on viewing the cub during your visit can be read here. Like babies? Popular areas are: Dandula, the Zoo's young Asian elephant, Cheetah cubs, Tiger cubs or animals in the Kids' Farm. The new Prairie Dog Playland is designed for ages 2-6. It wouldn't be the National Zoo without a Bald Eagle Refuge. While many animals are always or usually in indoor exhibits, many others, including giant pandas, other bears, seals, and sea lions, and great cats, are usually outdoors. To make your walk around the Zoo more enjoyable, comfortable shoes are recommended. The Zoo is set on hilly terrain and some paths are steep. You can expect to see more animals early in the morning. Print off a scavenger hunt sheet before you visit (on the Info for Visitors web page).

ROCK CREEK PARK AND NATURE CENTER

Washington, DC - 5200 Glover Road, NW, 20008. Phone: (202) 426-6829. Web: www.nps.gov/rocr/naturecenter/. Hours: Wednesday - Sunday, 9:00am-5:00pm. Closed most national holidays. FREE.

This 2,000-acre park provides a perfect setting for an urban escape or a family outing. The park has a golf course, tennis courts, picnic tables, bike trails, jogging trails, and horseback riding.   The Rock Creek Nature Center is home to the only planetarium in the National Park system and a Discovery Room with a live beehive viewing area.

FRANKLIN D. ROOSEVELT MEMORIAL

Washington, DC - 900 Ohio Drive, SW (West Potomac Park at West Basin and Ohio Drive), 20024. Web: www.nps.gov/fdrm/. Phone: (202) 426-6841. Hours: Park ranger in attendance 8:00am-midnight. Wheelchair accessible. The Bookstore opens from 9:00am-6:00pm. All restroom facilities close at 11:30pm. Closed Christmas. Admission: FREE. Note: The memorial did not originally feature any renderings of the president in his wheelchair. FDR did not wish to be portrayed in his wheelchair, and designers honored this request. Many people with and without disabilities were angered by this omission, and a statue of FDR in his wheelchair was installed in 2001. The statue was placed at the entrance of the monument to remind visitors that FDR was confined to a wheelchair when he became one of the country's most revered leaders.

The rambling FDR Memorial (it spans 7.5 acres) consists of four "rooms" arranged chronologically to represent the 32nd President's unprecedented four terms in office. A fountain in the first room flows peacefully, representing the healing effect water had on the president during his term in the Navy and while at Warm Springs. The second room addresses the Great Depression and the hope FDR cultivated with his extensive social programs. The third room represents the

war years, 1940-1944 with choppy, unsettling stonework and water. In a stark contrast, the final room projects peace and optimism. A bas-relief resting above a pool of still water depicts FDR's funeral procession. Acknowledging FDR's own physical difficulties, his memorial was the first creation of its kind designed with easy access for people with disabilities.

JEFFERSON MEMORIAL

Washington, DC - *East Potomac Park, South end of 15th St., SW on the Tidal Basin, 20024.* **Web:** *www.nps.gov/thje/ Phone: (202) 426-6822. Hours: Park rangers available 8:00am-midnight. Admission: FREE.*

Easily recognizable to Jeffersonian architects, the colonnade and dome memorial reflect Jefferson's love of this architectural style. The graceful, beautiful marble design pays tribute to the third president and primary author of the Declaration of Independence. Inside, there is a large bronze statue and excerpts from his writings on the walls. Jefferson stands at the center of the temple, his gaze firmly fixed on the White House, as if to keep an eye on the institution he helped to create. Museum located in the lower lobby of the memorial.

LINCOLN MEMORIAL

*Washington, DC - 900 Ohio Drive, S.W. (west end of Mall, 23rd St. and Constitution Ave., NW), 20024. **Web: www.nps.gov/linc/**. Phone: (202) 426-6841. Hours: Visitors Center 8:00am-midnight. Park ranger in attendance 24 hours. Admission: FREE.*

The most famous of the monuments, this site was used for several of history's greatest moments (including MLK speech). The artist opted to portray Lincoln seated, much larger than life, a symbol of mental and physical strength. As the father of a deaf child, the artist positioned Lincoln's hands in the shape of the sign language letters "A" and "L." Lincoln faces the US Capitol. Murals sculpted by Jules Guerin adorn the temple's inner walls. Emancipation is on the

This famous memorial appears on the back of a penny...the huge, seated statue of Lincoln is amazing!

south wall and hangs above the inscription of the Gettysburg Address. Unification is on the north wall, above Lincoln's Second Inaugural Address. The view of the National Mall from this vantage point is spectacular.

NATIONAL MALL

Washington, DC - (stretches from 3rd St., NW and the Capitol grounds to 14th St., between Independence and Constitution Aves.), 20024.

Officially, the National Mall is green space that begins at 3rd Street and stretches to 14th Street. Visitors and locals, however, widely use the term to refer to the entire expanse of monuments and museums, from the grounds of the Capitol to the Lincoln Memorial. Pierre L'Enfant's original plans for the city called for this open space and parklands, which he envisioned as a grand boulevard to be used for remembrance, observance, and protest. Today, it serves this purpose, hosting concerts, rallies, festivals, as well as Frisbee matches, family outings, picnics and memorials: Vietnam Veterans Memorial (the Wall); U.S. Navy Memorial and Naval Heritage Center (701 Pennsylvania Ave., NW); Korean War Veterans Memorial (West Potomac Park, Independence Ave., beside the Lincoln Memorial; and National World War II Memorial (East end of the Reflecting Pool, between the Lincoln Memorial and the Washington Monument). Call a veteran from a Memorial to thank him/her for their service.

UNITED STATES HOLOCAUST MEMORIAL MUSEUM

Washington, DC - *100 Raoul Wallenberg Place, SW (Metro: Smithsonian, near the National Mall, just south of Independence Ave., SW, between 14th Street and Raoul Wallenberg), 20024.* **Web: www.ushmm.org**. *Phone: (202) 488-0400 or (800) 400-9373. Hours: Daily 10:00am-5:30pm, except Yom Kippur and Christmas. Extended hours in the summer. Admission: FREE. Timed tickets required for permanent exhibition; available same day or in advance at **www.tickets.com**. Usually sold out by Noon.*

Geared for visitors ages 11 and up, the permanent collection of the U.S. Holocaust Memorial Museum tells the moving story of the persecution of the Jewish people. A special children's exhibition, "Daniel's Story," presents the story of the Holocaust for younger visitors.

BUREAU OF ENGRAVING & PRINTING TOUR

Washington, DC - *Department of the Treasury, 14th and C Streets, SW, 20228. Phone: (202) 874-2330 (local) or (866) 874-2330* **Web: www.bep.treas.gov/locations/index.cfm/3**. *Hours: Public Tour: 9:00am-10:45am & 12:30pm-2:00pm (every 15 minutes). Extended Summer Hours (May-August): 5:00-7:00pm (every 15 minutes). Visitors Center: Weekdays 8:30am-3:30pm and summer early evenings. The Bureau is closed on weekends, federal holidays and the week between Christmas and New Years. Tours: Tickets are required for all tours from the first Monday in March through the last Friday in August, on a first-come, first-served basis. The ticket booth is* *located on Raoul Wallenberg Place (formerly 15th Street). They offer same day tickets only. The Ticket Booth opens at 8:00am - Monday through Friday, and closes when all tickets have been distributed. Lines form early and tickets go quickly; most days tickets are gone by 9:00am. Many are in line by 7:00am. No tickets required (September-February). Miscellaneous: Please be patient with them during this time of heightened security, and be advised that all tour policies are subject to change without public notification. If the Department of Homeland Security level is elevated to CODE ORANGE, the Bureau of Engraving and Printing is CLOSED to the public unless otherwise noted.*

You'll see millions of dollars being printed during a tour of the BEP. The tour features the various steps of currency production, beginning with large, blank sheets of paper, and ending with the paper money we use every day! The BEP designs, engraves and prints all U.S. paper currency. Did you know they also produce postage stamps and White House invitations? Established in 1862, the Bureau, at that time, used just six people to separate and seal notes by hand in the basement of the Treasury building. The Bureau moved to its present site in 1914. Though new printing, production and examining technologies have brought us into the 21st century, the Bureau's engravers continue to use the same traditional tools that have been used for over 125 years - the graver, the burnisher, and the hand-held glass. At any given time, you may see millions of dollars roll off the presses in a flash!

WASHINGTON MONUMENT

Washington, DC - 15th & Jefferson Drive (National Mall area, Tourmobile stop, Metro Smithsonian stop), 20228. Phone: (202) 426-6841 or (800) 967-2283 reservations. Web: www.nps.gov/wamo/. Hours: Washington Monument are from 9:00am-4:45pm, closed December 25th. Admission: Free tickets are distributed for that day's visit from the kiosk on the Washington Monument grounds on a first-come first-served basis. All visitors 2 years of age or older must have a ticket to enter the Monument. Hours for the ticket kiosk are 8:00am-4:30pm, but tickets run out early. Advanced tickets are available through the National Park Service Reservation System.

Reservations may be made between the hours of 10:00am-10:00pm. While tickets to the Washington Monument are free of charge, callers to this number will incur a $1.50 service charge and a 50¢ shipping

and handling fee. For ease of traveling with young kids, we'd recommend pre-purchased tickets. Miscellaneous: Bookstore, restrooms and concessions on site.

Take the fast elevator ride to the top of the Monument for a panoramic view of the city. Most rides make stops to allow viewing of the commemorative stones set along the inside walls of the elevator shaft. Many folks like to start here as Washington was our 1st President and the view gives you a good feel for the lay of the land in D.C. The 555-foot tall obelisk is marble and is the tallest free-standing obelisk in the world. Why are there two different colors of marble used? The immense structure represents Washington's enormous contribution to the founding of our republic.

What is an "obelisk"? A tapering 4-sided stone shaft with a pyramid on top!

NATIONAL AQUARIUM

Washington, DC *– 14th Street & Constitution Avenue, NW (Metro: Federal Triangle, only one block from the Washington Monument), 20230. **Web: www.nationalaquarium.com**. Phone: (202) 482-2826. Hours: Daily 9:00am-5:00pm. Admission: $5.00 adult, $4.00 senior & military, $2.00 child (2-10).*

Tucked inside the United States Department of Commerce building, the National Aquarium is a hidden treat for families that displays a variety of marine life. Features more than 270 species of native and exotic fish, reptiles, amphibians, and invertebrates. The aquarium features a touch tank, videos, and children's programs. Look for a surge around 2:00pm - feeding time for the sharks or piranhas.

WHITE HOUSE

Washington, DC - *1600 Pennsylvania Avenue, NW (Metro: Metro Center, McPherson Square), 20500. Web: www.whitehouse.gov. Phone: (202) 456-7041. Hours: Visitors Center: Daily 7:30am-4:00pm. Tours: The White House is currently open only to groups (of 10 or more) who have made arrangements through a congressional representative. Park Rangers lead Walks Around the Park at 9:30am, 11:30am (themed) and 1:30pm each day. Miscellaneous: The White House presents Life in the White House, an exclusive presentation of the rich history of the White House and West Wing by video online.*

White House Visitor Center: All visits are significantly enhanced if visitors stop by the White House Visitor Center located at the southeast corner of 15th and E Streets, before or after their walking or White House group tour. The Center features many aspects of the White House, including its architecture, furnishings, first families, social events, and relations with the press and world leaders, as well as a thirty-minute video.

America's most famous address... 1600 Pennsylvania Avenue

Allow between 20 minutes to one hour to explore the exhibits.

The guided OUTSIDE tour combined with the Visitor Center and online video presentations give you the best "feel" for the White House without actually going inside. I think they realize citizens still want to know about the President's house but can't always go through the "hoops" necessary to secure an inside visit these days. The White House Historical Association also sponsors a sales area. Please note that restrooms are available, but food service is not.

CAPITOL BUILDING, UNITED STATES

Washington, DC - (east end of the National Mall), 20540. Phone: (202) 737-2300 or (800) 723-3557. Hours: Monday-Saturday 9:00am-4:30pm. Admission: FREE. Tours: Guided tours of the building leave every 15 minutes from the Rotunda. Miscellaneous: A limited number of free passes to the House and Senate galleries are available by contacting your representative's office, by phone or stopping by their offices across the street from the Capitol building.

The Capitol is one of the most widely recognized buildings in the world. It is a symbol of the American people and their government, the meeting place of the nation's legislature, an art and history museum, and a tourist attraction visited by millions every year. The bright, white-domed building was designed to be the focal point for

DC, dividing the city into four sectors and organizing the street numbers. Begun in 1793, the Capitol has been built, burnt, rebuilt, extended, and restored. An 180-foot dome is adorned by the fresco Brumidi painting (took him 20 years to complete). The Rotunda, a circular ceremonial space, also serves as a gallery of paintings and sculpture depicting significant people and events in the nation's history. The Old Senate Chamber northeast of the Rotunda, which was used by the Senate until 1859, has been returned to its mid-19th century appearance. The third floor allows access to the galleries from which visitors to the Capitol may watch the proceedings of the House and the Senate when Congress is in session.. . learning firsthand how a bill becomes a law.

NATIONAL ARCHIVES

Washington, DC - 700 Pennsylvania Avenue, NW (Metro Archives station), 20408. The Rotunda entrance, which includes the Exhibit Hall, is on Constitution Avenue. Daily 10:00am-5:30pm. Admission: FREE.

The Rotunda of the National Archives Building in downtown Washington, DC, contains the permanent exhibit of the Constitution, Bill of Rights, and the Declaration of Independence. A new exhibit called the Public Vaults displays over 1,000 fascinating records (originals or reproductions) from the National Archives holdings. Often, the wait may be long, but most say worth it, to enter the Charters of Freedom.

LIBRARY OF CONGRESS

Washington, DC - 10 First Street, SW (Metro: Capitol South), 20540. Phone: (202) 707-8000. Web: www.loc.gov. Hours: Monday-Saturday 10:00am-5:30pm. Admission: FREE public tours. Tours: Docent-led scheduled public tours are offered Mondays through Saturdays in the Great Hall of the Thomas Jefferson Building of the Library of Congress. Tours are limited to 50 people. For more information on guided tours, ask at either of the information desks in the Visitors' Center of the Jefferson Building (west front entrance). You may enter this building on the ground level under the staircase at the front of the building, located directly across from the U.S. Capitol.

The world's largest library is home to much more than just books. At the Library of Congress, kids can see a perfect copy of the Gutenberg Bible, personal papers of 23 presidents, a collection of Houdini's magic tricks, the Wright Brothers' flight log books and more. Equipped with new information desks, a visitors' theater features a 12 minute award winning film about the Library and interactive information kiosks. The Visitors' Center enhances the experience of approximately one million visitors each year.

ALBERT EINSTEIN PLANETARIUM

Washington, DC – 7th Street & Independence Ave., SW (within the National Air & Space Museum), 20560. Phone: (202) 633-1000. Web: www.nasm.si.edu/visit/theaters/planetarium/. Hours: Daily 10:00am -5:30pm. Admission: $7.00-$8.50 per person (students and above).

Not only does this planetarium have a spectacular star field instrument, but it has been upgraded to include a first-of-its-kind, Sky Vision™ dual digital projection system and six -channel digital surround sound. For the first time, you'll feel the sensation of zooming through the cosmos with a blanket of color and sound. Infinity Express: A 20-Minute Tour of the Universe or Stars Tonight (free) program.

NATIONAL GALLERY OF ART

Washington, DC – 6th Street & Constitution Avenue, NW (Metro: Archives/Navy Memorial, on the National Mall between Third and Seventh Streets), 20560. Web: www.nga.gov. Phone: (202) 737-4215. Hours: Monday-Saturday 10:00am-5:00pm, Sunday 11:00am-6:00pm. Closed Christmas and New Years. Admission: FREE. Visitors with children can participate in drop-in workshops, take several postcard tours of the collection using a packet of cards with pictures of objects & questions for discussion, or rent a family-oriented audio tour.

This fine art museum contains a collection of European and American works in chronological order with recognizable names including da Vinci, Renoir, Monet and Whistler.

NEWSEUM

Washington, DC - (6th Street and Pennsylvania Avenue, N.W.), 20560. Web: www.newseum.org. Phone: (703) 284-3544 or (888) 639-7386. Hours: Tuesday-Sunday 10:00am-5:00pm. Closed winter holidays.

The world's only interactive museum of news. The exhibits take you behind the scenes to see and experience how and why news is made. Visitors here can act as editors and put together newspaper front pages. They can also step into a reality ride to the scene of a breaking news story and test their skills as investigative reporters or photographers. In the broadcast studio, visitors can watch "in person" a live TV newscast (most folks never get this chance). Try your hand at being a TV news anchor and then take home a tape of your "broadcast". A long news bar displays news from around the world. Below the wall are the front pages of daily newspapers from every state and many countries - all diversely covering the same stories. The dome theater presents great moments in news history or another theater offers a glimpse of vintage newsreels.

SMITHSONIAN INSTITUTION

Washington, DC 20560. Phone: (202) 357-2700 or (202) 633-1000 (voice). Web: www.smithsonian.org. Hours: All museums are open from 10:00am-5:30pm, daily. Admission: FREE.

A visit to Washington, DC is not complete without experiencing at least one of the 14 Smithsonian museums. The Castle is the original building, completed in 1855, which provides an overview of the entire offering to help your family determine which museums interest you the most (you probably can't do them all). The following are highlights of the myriad of exhibits and activities offered especially for children:

ON THE MALL: Outside the National Air and Space Museum, a scale model of the solar system entitled Voyage: A Journey through our Solar System helps children grasp the magnitude of the world around them. During the summer months, a ride on the world's oldest carousel, near the Arts and Industries Building, is a sure treat.

HIRSHHORN GALLERY: The Smithsonian's modern art museum's "Young at Art" program introduces young visitors to different artistic disciplines through hands-on activities. Participants can act in a play, create portraits in chocolate, make clay sculptures, and more. On Saturdays, drop in for an "Improv Art" program—including a tour of the gallery with a special activity sheet and an art project to take home. The museum also offers regularly-scheduled guided family tours.

NATIONAL AIR & SPACE MUSEUM: Provides a world-renowned collection of flying machines from the Wright Brothers' Kitty Hawk Flyer to the Apollo 11 Command Module. Kids can see a moon rock, Lindbergh's Spirit of St. Louis and a variety of special films. The museum's IMAX theatre provides large-format and 3-D glimpses of space and beyond.

Smithsonian Institution *(cont.)*

<u>NATIONAL MUSEUM OF AMERICAN HISTORY</u>: Also known as "America's Attic," this popular museum houses such treasures as the First Ladies' inaugural gowns, Dorothy's Ruby Red Slippers, and the flag that inspired "The Star-Spangled Banner." (see separate listings about the creation of this flag and poem in the *Kids Love Maryland* - Central Chapter - Baltimore). In the museum's Hands-on History Room, young visitors can explore American history with more than 30 special activities, such as operating a cotton gin and sending a message. In the Hands-on Science Room, kids can explore the scientific and social issues addressed in the museum. A new transportation exhibition (and the largest exhibition to open in the museum), America on the Move, explores the world of transportation, including real artifacts from historic Route 66.

<u>NATIONAL MUSEUM OF NATURAL HISTORY</u>: After visiting the Hatcher, seeing a digitally-restored Triceratops, dining in the special dinosaur café, and "ogling" the massive Hope Diamond, check out the famous Insect Zoo. Kids can learn all about these creatures and non-squeamish types are allowed to handle them for an up-close look. The newly-renovated Mammal Hall shows some of the museum's specimens in lifelike, realistic settings.

<u>NATIONAL MUSEUM OF THE AMERICAN INDIAN</u>: The Smithsonian has opened its final installation on the National Mall, the National Museum of the American Indian (4th Street & Independence). The four story brilliantly lighted atrium captures your senses to explore the simple chronicle of people's courageous survival to present day accomplishments. The site offers live performances by American Indians full of color and sound.

<u>NATIONAL POSTAL MUSEUM</u>: Located next to Union Station, the National Postal Museum offers its young visitors insights into the interesting world of mail service. Children can create a souvenir postcard, learn about the history of the Pony Express and the legend of Owney the Postal Dog, and participate in a direct mail marketing campaign. 2 Massachusetts Ave., NE. Metro: Union Station.

SACKLER GALLERY: Through the Sackler Gallery's ImaginAsia, kids visit a featured exhibition with a special guide written for children and create an art project to take home. Other special family programs include Asian dance and music lessons, storytelling, and more.

ADDITIONAL TOUR INFORMATION:

TOURMOBILE

*(Tours depart from National Mall and Monument stops - marked). (202) 554-5100 or **Web: www.tourmobile.com**. $10.00-$20.00 per person for the full package.*

Get ready for the sights and sounds of the Nation's Capital. Tourmobile's® narrated shuttle tours take you right where you want to go with unlimited free reboarding. You choose where to stop, stay as long as you want, then reboard and ride to another historic location. Friendly and courteous narrators will enlighten and entertain you with anecdotes and little-known facts. Tourmobile Sightseeing is the best way to see Washington, DC. Take a ride (on/off) along DC's National Mall area and/or Arlington Cemetery.

DC DUCKS

*(Tours depart Union Station). Phone: (202) 966-DUCK or **www.dcducks.com**. Tours: Daily every 30 minutes starting at 10:00am-4:00pm $29.00 adult, $14.00 child (4-12).*

DUCKS come from DUKW, a military acronym that designated the vehicle as amphibious military personnel carriers. D stands for the year built, 1942; U for its amphibious nature; K for its all-wheel drive; and W for its dual rear axles. This is the most unusual tour of our nation's capital you'll ever take. . . Land and water in the same vehicle. From Union Station you'll "waddle" down to the mall where you'll see the inspiring monuments and pass the Smithsonian Museums. Then, just after you reach the Potomac River, you'll splash down for a duck's view on the river. The Ducks return to land at Ronald Reagan Washington National Airport under the approach pattern. Hold your ears as incoming aircraft pass over just feet from where you're sitting . . . giving new meaning to "sitting duck"! The wise-quacking captains will entertain you with anecdotes, sneak in some interesting historical facts & tell corny jokes.

39

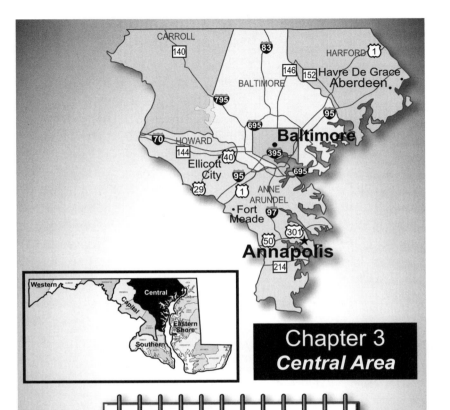

Our Favorites...

* HistoryQuest / Historic Annapolis
* Nat'l Museum of Dentistry - Baltimore
* Sports Legends, Babe Ruth BP - Baltimore
* B&O Railroad Museum - Baltimore
* Flag House & Ft. McHenry - Baltimore
* Inner Harbor - Baltimore
* USS Constellation - Baltimore
* Ellicott City B&O Railroad
* Nat'l Cryptologic Museum - Ft. Meade
* Havre de Grace Museums & Tours
* Ladew Topiary Gardens - Monkton

RIPKEN STADIUM / IRONBIRDS

Aberdeen - 873 Long Drive (I-95 NORTH take the MD-22 exit- exit number 85- towards ABERDEEN/CHURCHVILLE. Keep LEFT at the fork in the ramp. Turn LEFT onto MD-22) 21001. Web: www.ironbirdsbaseball.com Phone: (410) 297-9292. Home of baseball's best known family. Tours of the stadium, which includes the Ripken Museum exhibit, are offered during the Aberdeen Ironbirds off-season (October-May). The New York-Penn League affiliate for the Orioles plays seasonal home games, has a Kids Club, and hosts the Cal Ripken World Series and All-Star Games for the league. The name "IronBird" is a product of two distinct tie-ins that Cal wanted to incorporate into the team's image. "Iron" is a reference to Cal's streak of 2,632 consecutive games played, surpassing the record previously held by Lou Gehrig. Ripken is now known as baseball's all-time "Iron Man." The "Bird" part of the name refers to Cal playing his entire 21-year career in an Orioles uniform.

U.S ARMY ORDNANCE MUSEUM

Aberdeen - (I-95 exit onto Rte. 22 going towards Aberdeen. Exit Rte. 40 west to Rte. 715 south) 21005. Phone: (410) 278-3602. Web: www.ordmusfound.org Hours: Daily 9:00am-4:45pm. Closed National Holidays except for Armed Forces, Memorial, Independence and Veterans Days. Admission: The Day Pass will be issued only at the "Maryland Ave. Gate". This gate is on Rt. 715. The Rt. 22 gate will not issue any passes.

You can now visit the Ordnance Museum at Aberdeen Proving Ground as a civilian. Inside the museum, you'll find a collection of small arms, artillery, combat vehicles and ammunition. Outside is more impressive at the Proving Ground. Drive the "Mile of Tanks" at the 25 acre Tank & Artillery Park. A park full of real tank trucks is pretty eye-popping for little (and big) guys.

ANNAPOLIS SYMPHONY ORCHESTRA

Annapolis - Maryland Hall for the Creative Arts, 801 Chase Street 21401. Phone: (410) 263-0907. Web: www.annapolissymphony.org

The music you treasure, the orchestra that loves to play it. They present classics, Holiday Pops and kid-friendly Family Series concerts. Free Labor Day weekend concerts in the Parks.

HISTORYQUEST

Annapolis - *99 Main Street (historic Foundation site/Museum Store, corner of Main & Greene Sts.) 21401.* **Web: www.annapolis.org** *Phone: (410) 268-5576. Hours: Sunday-Thursday 10:00am-6:00pm; Friday-Saturday 10:00am-10:00pm. Open later on weekdays in the summer. Miscellaneous: Drive across the Spa Creek Bridge into Eastport on a mid-week evening and you'll see people lining the shore, on the bridge and anchored in the water to watch the Annapolis yacht Club's Wednesday Night Races. Locals and visitors time their trips to waterfront restaurants and the Naval Academy's sea wall (great spot for kids viewing) to watch more than 150 sailboats race, 20 at a time.*

Discover the Museum without Walls that is Annapolis – through the doorway that is HistoryQuest – where your Annapolis adventure begins! The complete orientation center (in a 1790s building) features movies, exhibits and artifacts on display...in a very simple, interesting format (free to look around museum). Kids need to do the scavenger hunt worksheet for a sweet prize once they complete it. Especially look for the Death's Head Printers Block reminiscent of the

Meet the folks who carved Maryland's future

Annapolis Tea Party. We liked their Window Rails. Look up at the present, look down at the past. Now that you're oriented, get your tour materials and then begin your walk past churches, a courthouse, the Old Treasury, The US Naval Academy (see separate listing), St. John's College campus, homes and taverns. Stop in for a visit to the BANNEKER-DOUGLASS MUSEUM (84 Franklin Street) in the first African American Episcopal Church of Annapolis which focuses on African-American life and history. The facility features an Annapolis Underground exhibit which explores the archaeology of African

American life in town and another exhibit, Deep Roots, Rising Waters, explores the history of African Americans in the state from the 1630s to the Civil Rights Movement. Wander some more and look for the house whose resident wrote "Anchors A Weigh" (Zimmerman House), or the birthplace of the only Roman Catholic signer of the Declaration of Independence (CHARLES CARROLL HOUSE). Other signers have homes here: WILLIAM PACA HOUSE (186 Prince George St) and CHASE LLOYD HOUSE (22 Maryland Avenue). Most are open to tour. Another home is named after the ship burned after a discovery of a hidden shipment of tea was found making Annapolis

its Revolutionary War "tea party" (PEGGY STEWART HOUSE). The Stewart House was also owned by the fourth (and youngest) signer of the Declaration, Thomas Stone. Pass by, and maybe explore inside, the State House - the oldest state capital in continuous legislative use.

Such a fun town to walk and explore!

Many linger at the heart of the city, the City Dock. City Dock has been the center of the town's maritime life for over 300 years. Today, work and pleasure boats share the use of "Ego Alley." There's a waterside park and a memorial commemorating the 1767 arrival in Annapolis of KUNTA KINTE, immortalized by his descendant, Alex Haley, in Roots. You'll love the endearing sculpture of Alex Haley reading to children. Story boards on Compromise street and a display at the Market House complete the memorial.

MARYLAND STATE HOUSE

Annapolis - 91 State Circle 21401. Phone: (410) 974-3400. Hours: Monday-Friday 8:30am-5:00pm, Saturday-Sunday 10:00am-4:00pm. Closed major holidays. www.mdarchives.state.md.us/msa/homepage/html/statehse.html

The Maryland State House is the oldest state capital in continuous legislative use, and the only state capital to have been a US capitol. Construction began in 1772; the legislature first met here in 1779.

Features include the largest wooden dome in country built without nails. To the right of the front door is the Old Senate Chamber where the Continental Congress met. This room has been restored to its original appearance and features a mannequin of George Washington dressed as he was when he resigned his commission. There are a number of portraits of early governors of Maryland by Charles Willson Peale, as well as Peale's celebrated portrait of Washington, Lafayette and Tilghman at Yorktown. The President's desk as well as some of the other desks and chairs in the room are original pieces

See a scale (15') working replica of the flagship, the Maryland Federalist

made for the State House in 1796-7 by Annapolis cabinetmaker John Shaw. The US Congress met here from November 1783 to August 1784 and ratified the Treaty of Paris in this building, formally ending the Revolutionary War.

SANDY POINT STATE PARK

Annapolis - 1100 E. College Pkwy 21401. Phone: (410) 974-2149. Web: www.dnr.state.md.us/publiclands/southern/sandypoint.html

Offering sandy beaches with swimming, playgrounds, hiking, crabbing, fishing and an excellent view of the Bay Bridge, the park also features boat ramps, a marina and boat rentals.

SCHOONER WOODWIND

Annapolis - 80 Compromise Street (Marriott Waterfront) 21401. Phone: (410) 263-7837. Web: www.schoonerwoodwind.com Admission: $29.00-$35.00 adult, $20.00 child. (mid-May to Labor Day)

"Woodwind" sails up to four times daily throughout the summer season from the Annapolis Marriott Waterfront Hotel. Raise the sails, steer the boat or sit back and relax on a two-hour sail. All cruises sail by the United States Naval Academy and then into the Chesapeake Bay. Sailing under the Chesapeake Bay Bridge is a fabulous experience as are the breathtaking sunsets over the historic Annapolis skyline. "Woodwind" is a replica of the classic, fast wooden schooners that were built as "yachts" in the early part of this century. Her handsome mahogany brightwork, gleaming chrome and roomy cockpit distinguish her from cargo carrying work vessels.

U.S. NAVAL ACADEMY

Annapolis - Armel-Leftwich Visitors Center, 52 King George St., Gate 1 (at the foot of King George Street) 21402. Web: www.navyonline.com Phone: (410) 263-6933. Hours: Daily 9:00am-4:00 or 5:00pm except holidays. Adults please bring photo ID to show at Gate 1 for entrance. Miscellaneous: Dry Dock Restaurant open for lunch. If taking the self-guided tour, be sure to get a campus map. It's not that hard to navigate the campus on your own. Navy Way Boot Camps are offered in the summer for youngsters to play pretend for a day.

The graduation hat toss is a recognizable Commissioning Week tradition and when you explore this 338-acre campus, known as "the Yard," you'll discover that the Naval Academy is defined by many traditions. Whether on self or guided tours, begin at the information

"...I have not yet begun to fight!"

center in the Armel-Leftwich Visitors center. The massive gift shop and the Freedom 7, America's first manned spacecraft flown by Naval Academy graduate Alan Shepard, are here, too. Begin by viewing the 12-minute film: "To Lead and To Serve", which chronicles the intensely structured and rigorous days and nights of the midshipmen. Stops on the tour include Bancroft Hall, known as "Mother B," the largest dormitory in the United States, and home to the entire brigade of midshipmen. If you are visiting during the school year, you may be able to see Noon Formation, when the entire brigade forms up to march to their midday meal. Another stop is the US Naval Academy Chapel, "The Cathedral of the Navy," located on the highest ground of the Yard, towering with its copper dome. The crypt and sarcophagus of Revolutionary War hero John Paul Jones lie beneath the chapel. His legend is forever linked to the immortal words, "I have not yet begun to fight!" The Naval Academy Museum (Preble Hall

John Paul Jones, "the Father of the American Navy" is buried here...

on Maryland Ave.) is packed with Academy memorabilia, beautiful model ships and exhibits on American naval history. What's that peculiar statue on the Yard? It's probably "Tecumseh." Midshipmen toss pennies in his quiver for good luck and refer to him as "the god of 2.0," the minimum passing grade. Before you leave, be sure to see the Herndon Monument, site of perhaps the most famous and enduring rite of passage in the USNA. To signal the end of their "plebe" status, first-year midshipmen work together to reach the top of the 21-foot monument, greased for the occasion by members of the upper classes. Legend has it that the student who successfully places his Dixie Cup hat on the pinnacle of the monument will be first admiral of his class. By the way, why is a goat the Navy's mascot?

ANNAPOLIS MARITIME MUSEUM

*Annapolis - Foot of Second Street & Back Creek on Bayshore Drive, 21403. Phone: (410) 268-1802. **Web: www.annapolismaritimemuseum.org** Hours: Saturday Noon-4:00pm, Sunday 1:00-4:00pm. Check their website for updated, expanded hours. Miscellaneous: Summertime maritime concerts are regularly scheduled. Thomas Point Lighthouse tours available mid-summer.*

Come to the Barge House to see the exhibit, the Thomas Point Lighthouse Experience, and the short documentary, Legacy of the Light, a virtual tour of the lighthouse. As the Museum is repaired from hurricane damage, it will again feature more than 300 years of historic and maritime artifacts, boats, maps and photographs in the larger structure, the McNasby Oyster Company building.

CHESAPEAKE CHILDREN'S MUSEUM

Annapolis - 25 Silopanna Road (pass the Naval Academy Stadium, right on Taylor, right onto Spa Road. Left on Silopanna) 21403. Phone: (410) 990-1993. Web: www.theccm.org Hours: Daily, except Wednesdays 10:00am-4:00pm. Admission: $3.00 per person (age 1+).

Live animals are the highlight of an exhibit on Aquatic and land-living creatures representing regional wildlife. Kids can then climb aboard a ten-foot boat and dock to act out their own watermen scenes (Props-life jackets, nets, plush crabs and fish- add to the realism of the exhibit). Toddlers adore the wooden train table, just at their height. Preschoolers make buildings and towns with the block set, often with help from their grown ups. In Body Works, kids can explore inside Stuffee, or climb up into a real dental chair (or, let mom do it and YOU be the dentist). There's an art workspace with creative, recycled materials or Center Stage full of costumes and a dramatic curtain. At Around the World, little visitors can visit a home in Colombia; Shop in the market place; Bring rainforest puppets to life; Say hello to Rosita the red-tailed boa constrictor or the new Owl on display.

DISCOVER ANNAPOLIS TROLLEY TOUR

Annapolis - (depart from Visitors Center, 26 West Street) 21403. Phone: (410) 626-6000. Web: www.discover-annapolis.com Admission: $15.00 adult, $7.00 youth (11-15), $3.00 (10 and under).

You will "Discover Annapolis" from a trolley–which is a little bus with big windows. The tour takes one hour. You'll travel down charming streets laid out over three centuries ago. Friendly guides point out all the major points of interest including the City Dock, the State House, handsome colonial mansions, beautiful Victorian homes, sailboats along the waterfront, and much more. You'll enjoy spectacular water views from three bridges. Drive along all sides of the Naval Academy as the guide describes the academic and athletic programs of Navy. There are about 1300 buildings in Annapolis at least a century old, representing 15 different architectural styles. This tour focuses on the largest and oldest of those 1300 buildings, with special attention on the Georgian style--harmonious and balanced--named after the Kings George who ruled Britain much of the 18th century. Annapolis has the highest concentration of Georgian buildings in America. The one-hour, air conditioned (or heated) trolley tour also promises some surprises.

PIRATE ADVENTURES ON THE CHESAPEAKE

Annapolis - 311 3rd Street 21403. Web: www.chesapeakepirates.com Phone: (410) 263-0002.

Come aboard for a Pirate Cruise as your children enjoy life as a pirate while you relax and enjoy the ride. We encourage you to arrive 30 minutes prior to sailing time to allow time to register and to transform your child into a pirate. Children will have the opportunity to have their faces painted with mustaches, mermaids, anchors, sharks, and more. Young buccaneers can also choose a pirate vest and sash from their treasure chest to wear for the voyage. The crew will gather the group for a rousing "AARGH" and then board Sea Gypsy for departure at sailing time. High energy staff fill the entire trip with activities. Watch out for their signature fire water cannons.

WATERMARK CRUISES & WALKING TOURS

Annapolis - Slip 20, Annapolis City Dock 21403. Phone: (410) 268-7600. Web: www.watermarkcruises.com   Admission: $10.00-$18.00 adult, $4:00-$10.00 child (11 & under). Tickets may be purchased at the time of cruise.

PIRATE CRUISES: Enjoy a romping good time with Captain Billy Baye as he and his sidekick, Grumpy Stumpy the Pirate Crab entertain audiences of all ages with music and imaginative tales of piracy. Mr. Long presents the character of Captain Baye in "first person" and in full 18th century garb. Musical instruments used during the performance correspond with instruments known during the colonial period. (60 minutes)

THOMAS POINT LIGHTHOUSE CRUISE: (90 minutes). Cruise out to the Chesapeake Bay to view the National Historic Landmark, Thomas Point Lighthouse. Built in 1875, it was the last to be manned on the Bay. You will learn more about the history of such points of interest as Providence, The Bay Bridge and Tolly Point as well as the historic lighthouses on the Chesapeake. Cruise departs at 4:30pm on weekends and holidays.

RIVER & BRIDGES CRUISES: (90 minutes) or (40 minutes): Just the right amount of time to take a leisurely, historical or natural cruise for younger sailors. Maybe the Spa Creek or Severn River, Chesapeake Bay bridges. The kids get to take turns being captain and receive a sticker!

WATER TAXI: Take a taxi to waterfront restaurants on Spa & Back Creeks. $2.00-$4.50 per person.

Capt. Daniel drives the boat...

COLONIAL STROLL (90 minute walking tour): Tour the heart of Annapolis and the U.S. Naval Academy as a colonial attired tour guide leads the way. Kids become history detectives, looking for unusual architecture, "speed bumps" and ghost marks. Your guide brings a basket of curiosities to visually connect the history told. Tour includes exteriors of the Maryland State House and famous historic mansions as well as the interior of the U.S. Naval Academy Chapel and Crypt. Tour leaves from the Visitors Center on 26 West Street (City Dock) at 10:30am. $13.00/Adults, $6.00/Children 3-11, Children ages 2 & under are free. PHOTO ID REQUIRED for adult admittance into Academy grounds. If you like to take walking tours of streets full of historic buildings - here's your match. Good tour for state history students and older.

MEDIEVAL TIMES DINNER & TOURNAMENT

Annapolis (Hanover) - *Arundel Mills, 7000 Arundel Mills Circle 21076. Phone: (443) 755-0011 or (888) WE-JOUST.* ***Web: www.medievaltimes.com*** *Shows: Wednesday - Sunday at 5:00pm or 7:00/7:30pm Admission: $37.00-$49.00 per person. Tax & gratuity not included. Includes dinner, beverages and live show. Children's and vegetarian menus available. Miscellaneous:*

Due to some choreographed fighting scenes in the tournament, small children may become frightened by the bashing sounds of sword against sword (it appears very real).

Set inside an 11th century-style castle, this show allows guests to become lords and ladies of the court. As you are assigned seating, you'll also be assigned a knight to cheer for and a "take home" crown to wear to show your support for that knight. You sit with others who join in cheering as serfs and wenches dressed in period costumes serve the feast of fresh vegetable soup, roasted chicken, spare rib, herb basted potato, a pastry and beverages. In order to honor medieval tradition, guests eat their meals without silverware (your kids will love having to eat with their hands!). As the lights dim, the story begins with the battle-weary King and his Knights returning to the Castle. The King calls for a grand tournament to determine the realm's new champion. As everyone is feasting, the Knights spar in games and jousts. AS the plot thickens - we all hope truth, honor and love will eventually triumph. The villain is revealed in the final minutes of the show bringing the crowd to their feet - cheering for the brave hero to defend the castle. The beautiful horses and quick displays of choreographed sword and jousting ability make this show so engaging!

BALTIMORE AREA SPORTS

Baltimore -

BALTIMORE RAVENS football. MT & T Bank Stadium. (410) 261-WAVE or **www.ravenszone.net**. The NFL Baltimore Ravens play home games here (not far from Inner Harbor) and the stadium gives tours on non-game days by appointment.

BALTIMORE ORIOLES baseball. Oriole Park At Camden Yards. (410) 685-9800 or **www.theorioles.com**. The famous park is home to the American League Orioles. Take A Stroll Through Oriole Park at Camden Yards On A Ballpark Tour! (by appointment, $5.00-$7.00) Come see Camden Yards from a whole new perspective! Enjoy the charm of the ballpark from club level suites, the press levels, and even the Orioles dugout!

BALTIMORE SYMPHONY ORCHESTRA

Baltimore - Joseph Myerhoff Symphony Hall, 1212 Cathedral Street 21201. Phone: (410) 783-8000. Web: www.baltimoresymphony.org

The Baltimore Symphony Orchestra has been playing strong since 1916. The Grammy Award-winning orchestra performs more than 150 concerts annually including outdoor summer concerts (which often conclude with fireworks) at Oregon Ridge Park.

GEPPI'S ENTERTAINMENT MUSEUM

Baltimore - Camden Station   21201. Web: www.geppismuseum.com Phone: (410) 427-9438.   Hours: Daily, 10:00am-6:00pm (April-October), Tuesday-Sunday, 10:00am-5:00pm (November-March). Admission: $10.00 adult, $9.00 senior, $7.00 student (3-18).

On TV and radio, in the papers and comic books - even toy stores - pop culture has performed magic for years. This new museum features colorful, chronologically arranged displays that explore 230 years of American life. From rare toys and antique advertising to comic books, movie posters and animation, the journey through history takes visitors from the late 1700s right up to today. Look for famous characters like Superman, Spiderman and Batman. Each chronological period highlighted in the museum is anchored by a centerpiece exhibit representing a historically significant character in pop culture. These artifacts have come from the world-famous private collection of museum founder and Diamond Comic President, Stephen Geppi.

MARYLAND HISTORICAL SOCIETY MUSEUMS

Baltimore - 201 W Monument 21201. Web: www.mdhs.org Phone: (410) 683-3750.   Hours: Vary by location. Society Museum: Wednesday-Sunday 10:00am-5:00pm. Civil War Museum: Daily 10:00am-5:00pm. Maritime Museum: Thursday-Monday 10:00am-5:00pm.   Admission: Varies by museum, call first for package rates.

Discover the people and events that shaped the state of Maryland. The bombardment of Fort McHenry, Francis Scott Key's original manuscript of the "Star Spangled Banner", hear the stories of civil rights activists, and the difficulties and successes of colonists. Don't miss Tench Tilghman's Revolutionary War uniform and Eubie Blake's eyeglasses.

BALTIMORE CIVIL WAR MUSEUM: 601 President St. (410) 385-5188. Daily 10:00am-5:00pm. The Baltimore Civil War Museum, housed in the 1849 train station - one of the oldest in the nation - examines the events of that day and highlights Maryland's divided loyalties and critical role as a border state during the war. Learn the story of the first deaths of the Civil War at the Pratt Street Riot. In addition, visitors will hear the story of the station's important role in the escape of enslaved African Americans via the Underground Railroad.

FELLS POINT MARITIME MUSEUM: 1721 Thames St. The museum tells the story of the notorious Privateer Clipper ships of the War of 1812 and the rich history of the town's ports. Privateers, shipbuilders, immigrants, merchants, and sailors sought their fortunes in this waterfront community, home to the world-famous Baltimore clipper schooners. These vessels, known then as pilot-boat schooners, were the fastest in the world and carried cargoes both legal and illegal. On a single voyage in 1814, one of the most famous captains, Thomas Boyle, captured 14 British vessels and 48 prisoners, and returned with cargo worth over $100,000.

NATIONAL MUSEUM OF DENTISTRY

Baltimore - 31 S Greene Street (MD 395 to downtown, exit ML King Blvd. Right on Baltimore, right on Greene) 21201. Phone: (410) 706-0600. Web: www.dentalmuseum.org Hours: Wednesday-Saturday 10:00am-4:00pm, Sunday 1:00-4:00pm. Admission: $2.50-$4.50 (age 7+). $7.00 for Admission and Audio Tour .

Discover the power of a healthy smile at this Smithsonian affiliate. The infamous Doc Holliday was a student at the Baltimore College

 of Dental Surgery, founded in 1840 as the first dental school in the world. An appropriate place, then, for the Dr. Samuel D. Harris National Museum of Dentistry, a fabulous interactive facility that showcases the evolution of dentistry. Interactives include:

Guess the Smile, Amazing Feats
- using teeth to write, to waterski,
to pull, to paint; Mouth Power -
meet Mouthy and take up a tooth
chair to pretend dentistry. Want
to know the history of the tooth
fairy? What about a whole room

devoted to Spit? Modern-day
forensics feature the section
Separate the facts from legends about
George Washington's teeth...
explaining how DNA in teeth can be used to identify missing persons
and solve criminal cases. Among the pieces in its collection are
George Washington's dentures (no, they weren't wooden; they were
ivory) and a set of dental instruments used by Queen Victoria. We
loved this museum!

SPORTS LEGENDS @ CAMDEN YARDS

*Baltimore - 301 W Camden Street (beside Oriole Park) 21201. Phone: (410)
727-1539. Web: www.baberuthmuseum.com Hours: Daily 10:00am-5:00pm.
Open later in the summer and Oriole or Raven game nights. Closed Monday
(November-March). Admission: $10.00 adult, $8.00 senior, $6.50 child (3-
12). Discount combo tickets with Babe Ruth BP.*

Sports Legends is located in historic Camden
Station passenger terminus at the gateway to

Oriole Park. Every fan
has favorite memories
from attending sporting
events. In these videos
and exhibits, fans
remember the great
plays, great games,
and great players of Maryland sports, plus
what makes going to a game such a special
part of the sports experience. Walk through
a simulated rail station terminal into the
theatre. The comical "Lucky Harry" intro
video is really cute. Then, Babe welcomes

"Photo ops" with
sports heros...

you to his gallery and famous "point" game. Interactives throughout include: Make a call to the Bullpen; sit on the bus to a game in the Negro Leagues; sit on the bench watching a Little League game; check your stance; listen to a post-game pep talk; try on actual official uniforms; radio call a game; go behind the scenes of a ball field pre-game; block the shot; catch like Berry; and get the "call" up for Johnny Unitas. The Colts, the Ravens, the Orioles and college teams are all here in spirit to learn about. Probably the most interactive sports museum we've ever seen!

WALTERS ART MUSEUM

Baltimore - 600 N Charles Street 21201. Web: www.thewalters.org Phone: (410) 547-9000. Hours: Wednesday-Sunday 11:00am-5:00pm. General admission FREE.

The Walters Art Museum offers a variety of extraordinary programs where you can make cool art, see live performances, play dress up, or tour the museum with a kid-friendly passport designed to foster discovery and engagement (scavenger hunt or audio tours). Listen to lively storytelling in the galleries during festivals, watch a family-friendly video in the cozy Family Art Center, create a piece of original artwork during drop-in hours, celebrate your birthday, and earn a scout patch. Every third Saturday of the month is Walk, Wonder and Create Family Tours. Their permanent collection includes Egyptian Mummies and medieval armor. The newly installed Renaissance and Baroque Galleries includes works by masters Raphael and Bernini. The Palace of Wonders features paintings, artifacts and furniture all arranged as they might have been in the home of a wealthy European collector during old time periods.

BALTIMORE PUBLIC WORKS MUSEUM

Baltimore - 751 Eastern Avenue, Pier 7, Inner Harbor 21202. Phone: (410) 396-5565. Web: www.baltimorepublicworksmuseum.org Hours: Tuesday-Sunday 10:00am-4:00pm. Admission: $2.50 - $3.00 per student and older.

Uncover how the city works. A place where you can climb down a manhole to explore Streetscape, a realistic re-creation of Baltimore underground set up outside as a maze. A sewer playground, this is

so fun to climb over, under and in the pipes. Indoors, with scavenger hunt in hand, run a water treatment plant or design manhole covers. With interesting videos, interactive computer challenges and exhibits, it's impossible to leave this place without learning something - in a fun and interesting way.

FLAG HOUSE & STAR SPANGLED BANNER MUSEUM

Baltimore - 844 E Pratt Street (Little Italy, 2 blocks east of Inner Harbor) 21202. Web: www.flaghouse.org Phone: (410) 837-1793. Hours: Tuesday - Saturday 10:00am-4:00pm. Admission: $5.00-$7.00 per person. Miscellaneous: Mary Pickersgill's flag still survives and now hangs at the Smithsonian Institution's National Museum of American History. A hands-on room is where the kids dress up and then color their own Star Spangled flag to take home.

A giant life-size flag awaits you at the entrance...

A museum dedicated to the story of Mary Young Pickersgill who made the enormous 30 x 42-foot Star-Spangled Banner that flew over Fort McHenry during the War of 1812 and inspired Francis Scott Key to write the poem that became our National Anthem. The new Star-Spangled Banner Museum, adjacent to the Flag House, houses an orientation theatre film and exhibits on the American Flag, Mary and the War of 1812. The unique feature of the museum is the Great Flag Window, a glass wall the same size, color and design of the original Star-Spangled Banner! Visitors to the Flag House are given a personalized tour of the 18th-century home of Mary

Young Pickersgill. You'll learn how Mary, a widowed flag maker and mother, made the flag. How do you hand sew a flag so large? The 90 pound flag made of wool bunting was recreated by local ladies and laid on display in the parlor to help you imagine the task these 1800 era women undertook. As you tour, you'll realize how contemporary  Mary and her family were for their time. Who would guess their large commissioned project would inspire patriotism even now! An American must-see visit!

FREDERICK DOUGLASS - ISAAC MYERS MARITIME PARK

Baltimore - *1417 Thames Street, Fells Point (near the intersection of Caroline St.) 21202.* **Web: www.livingclassrooms.org** *Phone: (410) 685-0295. Hours: Monday, Wednesday, Thursday and Friday 11:00am-5:00pm, Weekends Noon -6:00pm. Admission: $4.00-$5.00 (age 6+).*

This park features a re-creation of the first marine shipyard and marine railway operated by African Americans, as well as the Sugar House, the oldest remaining industrial building on the waterfront. Frederick Douglass lived in Baltimore for a time and worked in the maritime trades (before he became a famous abolitionist) and Isaac Myers founded the shipyard and the first black maritime unions. Baltimore was home to one of the largest populations of free blacks before the Civil War, many of whom worked here. After the Civil War, other ethnic workers asked not to work with Blacks and so many were fired - they needed work and new, black owned shipyards were established for a time. Wander through a once busy shipyard railway and a deep-water pier; monuments to Douglass and Myers; exhibits concerning African American maritime history; and the Sugar House view.

PORT DISCOVERY, THE CHILDREN'S MUSEUM

Baltimore - 33 Market Place (corner of Lombard Street and Market Place) 21202. Phone: (410) 727-8120. Web: www.portdiscovery.org Hours: Tuesday-Friday: 9:30am-4:30pm, Saturday: 10:00am-5:00pm, Sunday: Noon-5:00pm. Summertime open Mondays, too. Closed Thanksgiving Day, Christmas Day, and on Mondays during the months of October through May, except during select Maryland Public School holidays. Admission: $10.75 (age 2+). Miscellaneous: unlike most kids museums, this one is stroller accessible throughout.

Port Discovery, the Children's Museum in Baltimore, offers three floors of interactive, educational exhibits and programs for children ages 2-10 years old. Use your problem solving and critical thinking skills to climb, slide and glide your way through this three-story urban treehouse. Visit the farm area and look under interactive hanging signs to learn all about life on the farm, including how milk is made, or what a fowl is. Barter, sell or trade your new crops at the roadside market. Shop for farm-fresh fruits and vegetables and then use the giant crane to move hay bales from the market to the train for transport. Tinker here, in their R & D DreamLab, with real tools to build real stuff. Creative? Act, puppet or design skits or artwork. Step right up to a realistic gas station where you can pack the car, check the tires' air-pressure and fill the tank. Uncover secret hieroglyphics that provide clues to solving the mystery inside the tomb. Use giant sized MegaLogs to build anything or take some quiet time to read a story. Play hostess, waitress, cook or cashier in a realistic diner. Pick up clues using your detective-sharp research, literacy and problem solving skills to find out what happened to the missing members of the Baffled family. P.S. Don't forget to crawl through the sink, it could lead you to clues on the other side!

REGINALD F. LEWIS MUSEUM OF MARYLAND AFRICAN AMERICAN HISTORY & CULTURE

Baltimore - 830 East Pratt Street, just east of Inner Harbor 21202. Phone: (443) 263-1800. Web: www.AfricanAmericanCulture.org Hours: Tuesday-Sunday 10:00am-5:00pm. Admission: $6.00-$8.00 (age 6+).

See 400 years of progress in one day. The African American experience, from tobacco and ironworking to education and law, there is not an industry or profession that has not been touched by the accomplishments of African Americans. Often against incredible odds. Discover how ancient-African skills influenced laborers here. Try your hand at some of the most difficult occupations, including caulking and the art of oystering. Meet several families and follow their lives from slavery to freedom and equality. Listen to historical music. Get to know famous African Americans including Frederick Douglass and Harriet Tubman. Follow Benjamin Banneker, Eubie Blake, Joyce Scott and others as they guide you through understanding African American traditions of music, art, sculpture, storytelling and invention.

LACROSSE MUSEUM AND NATIONAL HALL OF FAME

*Baltimore - 113 W. University Pkwy. 21210. **Web:** www.uslacrosse.org/museum/ Phone: (410) 233-6882. Hours: Weekdays 10:00am-3:00pm (June-January). Tuesday-Saturday (February-May). Admission: $2.00-$3.00 per person (age 5 +).*

This modern museum spans the history of lacrosse from Native American origins to modern times. Relive the origins of America's oldest sport. View the all-time greats of lacrosse in the beautiful Hall of Fame Gallery and study their outstanding accomplishments through state-of-the-art computer interactives, striking sculptures, vintage equipment and uniforms, and ancient artifacts. Capture the thrill of playing lacrosse during the multimedia show "Lacrosse: The Spirit Lives" and our historical documentary "More than a Game: A History of Lacrosse."

BALTIMORE STREETCAR MUSEUM

*Baltimore - 1901 Falls Road 21211. **Web:** www.baltimorestreetcar.org Phone: (410) 547-0264. Hours: Sunday Noon-5:00pm. Open Saturdays (June-October). Admission: $6.00 adult, $3.00 senior and child (4-11). Family max + $24.00.*

Admission includes: Unlimited rides on original Baltimore streetcars and a guided carhouse tour. Visit Trolley Theatre and view the new 10 minute orientation video, Baltimore and Streetcars, about trolleys and how they built our cities, including, of course, Baltimore. The Trolley Theatre, is a 3/4 scale trolley model that you can sit in.

NATIONAL GREAT BLACKS IN WAX MUSEUM

Baltimore - 1601-03 E North Avenue (395 north onto South MLK Blvd. East onto E. Baltimore St. and quickly north onto SR-2. East onto US1) 21213. Phone: (410) 563-7809. Web: www.ngbiwm.com Hours: Tuesday-Saturday 9:00am-5:00pm, Sunday Noon-5:00pm. Open until 6:00pm (mid-January thru mid-October). Admission: $6.00-$9.00 (age 3+).

This unique museum, the first one of wax in Baltimore, Maryland is the first wax museum of African American history in the nation. The museum houses more than 100 life-size and lifelike wax figures presented in dramatic and historical scenes, and takes you through the pages of time with wax figures featuring special lighting, sound effects and animation. Harriet Tubman, Benjamin Banneker and Billie Holiday, as well as many other national figures, chronicle the history of African people from around the globe. The experience is highlighted by a dramatic walk through a replica slave ship complete with Middle Passage history. Visitors enter the cramped hold of a slave ship replica to witness a story of struggle, survival, and triumph. Another kid-focused area is the: And a Little Child Shall Lead Them: Black Youth in the Struggle delivers the message that children have been called upon to take up the mantle of freedom and justice throughout history and around the world.

MARYLAND ZOO IN BALTIMORE

Baltimore - Druid Hill Park 21217. Web: www.marylandzoo.org Phone: (410) 366-LION. Hours: Daily 10:00am-4:30pm. Extended summer weekend hours. Admission: $15.00 adult, $12.00 senior (65+), $10.00 child (2-11).

Journey from Africa to the Arctic on this wooded, 180-acre setting in Druid Hill Park. Otters, polar bears, bats and even skunk are here. Plus the regular lions, tigers and bears. A new tram system transports visitors from the main gate to the zoo's central plaza. Another highlight is the Polar Bear Watch, a new state-of-the-art exhibit about life on the edge of the Arctic, featuring an area where guests can watch Alaska and Magnet, the zoo's polar bears cavorting in and out of the water. Children will create lifelong memories as they hop across lily pads, perch in an oriole's nest, play on a giant barn silo slide, a tree slide or groom friendly goats at the hands-on Children's Zoo. Look for baby chimps or maybe a new elephant. In 2007, expect giraffe feeding stations and the return of the Zoo's flamingos.

BALTIMORE MUSEUM OF ART

Baltimore - Art Museum Drive at N Charles and 31st Sts. 21218. Phone: (410) 396-7100. Web: www.artbma.org Hours: Wednesday-Friday 11:00am-5:00pm , weekends until 6:00pm. General admisson FREE. (some admission charge for special exhibitions. See website for details).

Home to a wonderful collection of Matisse, Picasso and 19th century and contemporary art, plus a scenic sculpture garden. Three different self-guided kits invite kids to dress up, sketch, or sing their way through the galleries; available Thursdays, Saturdays, and Sundays 11:00am-3:00pm. A Grand Legacy Family Guide will help you explore five centuries of European art. Matisse for Kids Guide is a fun way to discover the Museum's renowned Cone Collection. During extended evening hours, enjoy family-friendly activities including music, performances, guided tours, hands-on workshops, and more.

MARYLAND AVIATION MUSEUM, GLENN L. MARTIN

Baltimore - 701 Wilson Point Road, Hanger 5 at Martin Airport 21220. Phone: (410) 682-6122. Web: www.marylandaviationmuseum.org Hours: Wednesday-Saturday 11:00am-3:00pm. Admission: FREE

The site is dedicated to the promotion, preservation, and documentation of aviation and space history in the state of Maryland. Outside planes with names like Thunderchief, Thunderflash, Phantom, Sabor and Voodoo entice the kids to look around some.

B & O RAILROAD MUSEUM

Baltimore - 901 West Pratt Street (I-395 exit to MLKing St. to Pratt St, west a couple of blocks) 21223. Phone: (410) 752-2490. Web: www.borail.org Hours: Monday-Friday 10:00am-4:00pm, Saturday 10:00am-5:00pm, Sunday 11:00am-4:00pm. Admission: $14.00 adult, $12.00 senior (60+), $8.00 child (2-12). Train rides are included in the price of admission.

Miscellaneous: A café is on the premises as well as a delightful, large gift shop.

The world's first telegraph line was erected between Baltimore and Washington, D.C., in 1844. Baltimore's Mount Clare Station, which

was built in 1830 as the first railroad station in the country, was the receiving point of Samuel Morse's famed "What hath God wrought" message. Today the station is the B&O Railroad Museum, a great place to learn about the history of the railroad that brought fame and fortune to Baltimore and which earned immortality on the Monopoly board! Ride the FIRST MILE of track in America, see them restoring old trains, learn the simple science of locomotion, get caught up in railroad flicks, and get a great view of the newly restored giant Roundhouse (the slumber house).

Baltimore & Ohio Railroad Pioneers

The 20-minute train ride (just the right length for antsy kids) has an interesting narrative accompanied by travel folk music. Younger kids marvel at the operating 60 foot HO gauge model railroad outside. The model railroad is a cute way for little engineers to push buttons to hear train whistles and horns or hear the conductor shout "all aboard." There are several trains you can board. Some are unusual - how was the spiked Clearance Car used? What a wonderful and incredibly historical train attraction!

See the First Stone of the First Railroad...the B&O...

AMERICAN VISIONARY ART MUSEUM

Baltimore - 800 Key Hwy, Inner Harbor 21230. Phone: (410) 244-1900. Web: www.avam.org Hours: Tuesday-Sunday 10:00am-6:00pm.

This museum only exhibits art produced by folks who have no formal training (farmers, housewives, doctors, auto mechanics...you get the picture). Between the six week themed temporary installations, you can gain access to the permanent collection on Level 1 for $2.00 a person (vs. much more for special exhibits). The Giant Whirligig & Sculpture Plaza is Baltimore's newest and already most beloved outdoor sculptural landmark. Fifty-five feet tall, this brilliant, multicolored wind-powered sculpture was created in the central plaza as a salute to Federal Hill and "Life, Liberty & The Pursuit of Happiness" by 76 year-old mechanic, farmer and visionary artist, Vollis Simpson. Free to visit anytime. The Sculpture Plaza functions as the ground level connector to Federal Hill and Baltimore's Inner Harbor.

BABE RUTH BIRTHPLACE

Baltimore - 216 Emory Street 21230. Web: www.baberuthmuseum.com Phone: (410) 727-1539. Hours: Daily 10:00am-5:00pm. Open later summers and nights of Oriole or Ravens games. Admission: $3.00-$6.00 (age 3+). Discount combo tickets with Sports Legends.

The Babe Ruth Birthplace is located just three blocks west of Camden Station (follow the 60 painted baseballs along the sidewalk). George Herman "Babe" Ruth was born February 6, 1895 on Emory Street, a Baltimore row house that is now just a long fly ball from Oriole Park at Camden Yards. The property was leased by Babe's grandfather, Pius Schamberger, who made

Compare the sluggers' bats of then and now...

his living as an upholsterer. The Baltimore Orioles signed Ruth to his first pro contract. Some of the priceless artifacts the Babe Ruth Museum holds in its collections are: a near-complete team set of 1914 International League Baltimore Orioles baseball cards (including the rookie card of a 19-year-old pitcher named George Ruth, Jr.) or a baseball bat given to Ruth by Shoeless Joe Jackson sometime between 1915 and 1916. This thick-handled, 38 3/4 ounces of baseball history is the only one known to exist — a game-used bat shared by Shoeless Joe and the Babe. A wonderful place to "get to know" a baseball hero!

BALTIMORE MUSEUM OF INDUSTRY

Baltimore - 1415 Key Hwy, Inner Harbor 21230. Phone: (410) 727-4808. Web: www.thebmi.org Hours: Tuesday-Saturday 10:00am-4:00pm, Sunday 11:00am-4:00pm. Admission: $10.00 adult, $6.00 senior, student/child.

Step back in time to the Industrial Revolution at the Baltimore Museum of Industry, with its vividly recreated workshops on machining, printing, garment-making and metalworking. Walk through an 1886 bank building or step into the 1910 Bunting Pharmacy where Noxzema

 was invented. Experience the local innovations that touched the world - from the world's first disposable bottle cap to America's first umbrella company. Students become garment workers and hand sewers and learn about life in a turn-of-the-century garment shop. As they work, they hear about labor activist "Mother Jones" and her crusade to rid the world of abominable working conditions for children. Learn Baltimore's role as one of the busiest and most important ports in America. See a replica of an early dock and dockmaster's shed. Walk through the original 1865 Platt Oyster Cannery structure, the only surviving cannery building. Look outside and see the coal-fired S.S. Baltimore, the only operating steam tugboat on the East Coast. To get the best value, it is better to visit on weekends or part of a group tour so the kids can actually dress up and participate in the re-enacting areas like the cannery and clothing factory.

FORT MCHENRY NATIONAL MONUMENT & HISTORIC SHRINE

Baltimore - End of E. Fort Avenue 21230. Web: www.nps.gov/fomc Phone: (410) 962-4290. Hours: Daily 8:00am-5:00pm. Admission: Entrance fee to the historic fort is $7.00 for adults 16 and over. Children 15 and under are admitted free of charge.

Fort McHenry National Monument and Historic Shrine is a star-shaped fort best known for its role in the War of 1812, when its successful defense against the British bombardment inspired Francis Scott Key to write the words that became our national anthem. "O say can you see, by the dawn's early light, ...Whose broad stripes and bright stars ...were so gallantly streaming!" This historical event happened over Fort McHenry during the Battle of Baltimore, September 13-14, 1814. Watch the orientation film and look at the day's calendar of interpretive programs (in season). The movie is wonderfully done

just like GIANT bottle rockets...

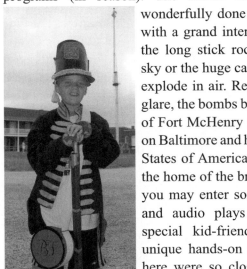

with a grand interactive patriotic finish! See the long stick rockets that glared red in the sky or the huge cannonball bombs designed to explode in air. Regardless of the "rockets red glare, the bombs bursting in air," the defenders of Fort McHenry stopped the British advance on Baltimore and helped to preserve the United States of America – "the land of the free and the home of the brave." Within the actual fort you may enter some rooms that have visuals and audio plays or an electric map. The special kid-friendly Defenders' Room has unique hands-on activities. Because soldiers here were so close to the harbor and town, they could purchase seafood, chocolate and spices. Touch and smell everything they ate and then try on some very authentic looking apparel and be a soldier for a moment. Following the Battle of Baltimore during the War of 1812, the fort never again came under attack. However, it remained an active military post off and on for the next 100 years. Highly recommended National site!

TOBY'S DINNER THEATRE

Baltimore & Columbia - 5625 O'Donnell Street / 5900 Symphony Woods Rd. 21224. Web: www.tobysdinnertheatre.com Phone: (866) 998-6297 or (800) 888-6297. Toby's offers Broadway musicals, live orchestras and service while you choose from 7 main entrée buffets, 7 salad bars and make-your-own sundae bar. Kids like the variety of food (and desserts) and are usually good about then sitting through a lively musical production like: Footloose, Buddy or It's a Wonderful Life.

HARBORPLACE

Baltimore, Inner Harbor - Inner Harbor (Light Street and Pratt Street) 21201. Phone: (410) 332-4191. Web: www.harborplace.com

Indoor and outdoor eateries, shopping (many souvenirs related to Crabs and sports) and live entertainment on the waterfront.

Try PHILLIPS SEAFOOD on the edge of the harbor serving extensive seafood menus, plus sandwiches, beef and chicken entrees. A wide

something for everyone here...

variety of offerings and friendly staff make this busy Baltimore institution a great place for first-time visitors to get acquainted with the city's number one culinary attraction: the Blue Crab. The tasty crustaceans are served in many forms: Crab Imperial, crab dip, crab cakes. Authentic Maryland Style Seafood is a tradition at Phillips so come prepared to feast! Festival Buffet. (**www.phillipsfoods.com**). Work off some of the extra treats you ate by taking a stroll on the water - in Dragon Boats called CHESSIES. They're actually elaborate pedal boats (regular pedal boats are available to rent also) that are too cute and festive. Either that, or ED KANE'S WATER TAXI (**www.thewatertaxi.com**) can provide water transport to more than 30 attractions and neighborhoods. Look for the blue and white boats. One price for all-day, unlimited on-off service.

BIG BUS COMPANY OF BALTIMORE

Baltimore, Inner Harbor - (departs from 401 Light Street, Inner Harbor West Shore) 21202. Phone: (877) BALTIMORE. Admission: $20.00 adult, $10.00 child (4-12), $17.00 senior and student. Fares are good for 24 hours. Tickets available on bus, at visitor's center and at hotels throughout city. FREE parking at the Zoo and B&O Railroad.

See all of Baltimore from the top of an authentic open-top London double-decker bus. Transportation to 16 attractions is provided while on-board tour guides highlight Baltimore's history and attractions along the way. This hop-on, hop-off service runs on a 90-minute loop that begins at the Baltimore Visitor Center at the Inner Harbor and loops through downtown to the east, north, west and south. Venues on the route include Harborplace, Flag House, Port Discovery, the Maryland Science Center, Baltimore Museum of Art, the Maryland Zoo, the Baltimore & Ohio Railroad Museum and dozens of other attractions and places of interest.

LADY BALTIMORE OR BAY LADY HARBOR CRUISES

Baltimore, Inner Harbor - 561 Light Street 21202. Web: www.harborcruises.com Phone: (410) 727-3113 or (800) 695-LADY. Miscellaneous: 60 Minute Sightseeing Tours on the Prince Charming - "Sea More Baltimore" - April – October - Departing at: 11:30am, 1:00pm, 2:30pm and 4:00 pm. Adult $11.00 Child (3-10) $9.00.

They cruise just about everyday with lively lunch, dinner and special event cruises. Also, a one-hour scenic, narrated tour is offered. An original Baltimore cruise line, they offer the most themed tours in Maryland. Basic lunch menus include: Caesar Salad, Herb Roasted

Boneless Breast of Chicken, Roasted Red Potatoes, Green Beans Almondine, Dinner Rolls with Butter. Decadent Chocolate Cake, Coffee, Tea, Decaf, Soft Drinks and Juices. Basic Dinner Menus include: Hospitality Table with Vegetables, Dip, Cheese and Crackers, Caesar Salad, Maryland Crab Soup, Maryland Crab Balls, Fried Oysters, Top Rounds of Beef in Gravy, Chicken Marsala, Pasta ala Chesapeake, Green Beans Almondine, Kicking Kernel Corn, Dinner Rolls and Butter, Delicious Layer Cakes, Seasonal Fruit, Coffee, Tea, Decaf, Soft Drinks and Juices. If you love Maryland blue crab, try their weekend Crab Fest cruises. Or, for the kids, Easter Brunch with Bunny or Christmas Brunch with Santa.

NATIONAL AQUARIUM IN BALTIMORE

Baltimore, Inner Harbor - 501 East Pratt Street, Pier 3, Inner Harbor (I-95 to I-395 to Pratt Street, turn right) 21202. Web: www.aqua.org Phone: (410) 576-3800. Hours: Daily until 5:00pm and Fridays until 8:00pm with seasonal extended morning and evening hours. Admission: $21.95 adult, 20.95 senior (60+) and $12.95 child (3-11). Miscellaneous: for safety, strollers must be checked; free front-and backpacks are available to carry babies.

Take a short walk across the promenade from the World Trade Center to the National Aquarium where stingrays (look for butterfly rays), sharks and sea turtles will greet you on the first level to start your

adventure…up close! You might visit during a feeding of sharks. Each exhibit brings new surprises, including a blackwater Amazon River forest with schools of dazzling tropical fish, giant river turtles, dwarf caimans, and pygmy marmosets - the smallest species of monkey in the world. And in the Upland Tropical Rain Forest, keen observers may spot colorful birds, golden lion tamarins (monkeys), two-toed sloths, red-bellied piranhas, iguanas and even poison dart frogs, as they wander on pathways through the dense tropical foliage. The 8-minute intro film in Australia Animal Planet is very helpful for kids to learn differences in extreme geography. Australia Wild Extremes has fish that shoot water from their mouths, encounters with the Outback's deadliest snake and relaxing sounds of a 35-foot cascading indoor waterfall. And don't forget the shark ring or giggling at the dolphin show at the adjoining Marine Mammal Pavilion. Trek across Maryland's varied terrain in the Waterfront Park outdoors.

RIDE THE DUCKS

Baltimore, Inner Harbor - 25 Light Street (boards at Light St. Pavillion at HarborPlace) 21202. Web: www.baltimoreducks.com Phone: (410) 727-3825. Admission: $24.00 adult, $23.00 senior (55+), $14.00 child (3-12).

Begin the day with a narrated tour on Ride the Ducks, where you'll hit all the harbor highlights on land and water - from the same amphibious vehicle. The journey begins with an exploration of area neighborhoods and landmarks, including the Washington Monument, Fells Point, Little Italy and Oriole Park at Camden Yards. Why were Fells Point streets built with ballast blocks from boats? How and where did the big fire of 1904

Part boat, part bus... It's Quack-tacular !

start and end after 2 days of burning. Quack along with your Captain as you rock n' roll through town. Then "splashdown" into the harbor for a historical overview of Baltimore's waterfront communities. Yes, that's right, your "bus" turns into a boat and the kids have to quack hard to be sure it stays afloat. While on tour, you can see what sites look most interesting and then visit them later - cause you know you won't be able to do it all!

USS CONSTELLATION

Baltimore, Inner Harbor - *301 E. Pratt Street, Pier 1, Inner Harbor 21202. Phone: (410) 539-1797.* **Web: www.constellation.org** *Hours: Daily 10:00am-4:30pm. Extended to 5:30pm (May-October). Admission: $8.75 adult, $7.50 senior (60+) and military, $4.75 child (6-14).*

Nearly 200' long and 300 crew aboard... it was a 19th Century floating city!

Built in 1854, this is the last all-sail warship built by the U.S. Navy and the only Civil War era naval vessel still afloat. It sits boldly in the harbor. History comes "alive" with hourly hands-on demonstrations and self-guided audio tours. Using a "Youth" or "Adult" number system, you follow a modern girl through the ship. Discover how sailors lived on board - officers in their own cubbies and shipmen on hundreds of hammocks hanging from the ceiling - no, not for naps - for good, swaying sleep before the next watch. What's a Powder Monkey? How was this mighty sailing machine powered, propelled and controlled? What technology did they have and what did they eat? Interactives include steering the ship or ringing the loud ship's bell to tell time. Listen for the cannon firings! Excellent for grade-schoolers and older - especially the audio and interactives.

WORLD TRADE CENTER "TOP OF THE WORLD"

Baltimore, Inner Harbor - *401 E. Pratt Street (World Trade Center, 27th floor) 21202. Phone: (410) 837-VIEW.* **Web: www.bop.org** *Hours: Wednesday-Sunday, 10:00am-6:00pm. Longer summer hours. Admission: $3.00-$5.00 (ages 3+).*

Start your visit to the city at the Top of the World Observation

Level, where the beauty of the resurgent city will unfold before you - from all sides - harbor and downtown. Enjoy a spectacular panoramic view of Baltimore's skyline, as well as photo-map guides featuring local attractions, hotels and neighborhoods. It's a good place to get a sense of the city. The observation level also contains

"Top of the World" to ya...

exhibits about Baltimore and its economic renaissance. The World Trade Center is the tallest pentagonal building in the world. You will have a wonderful view of the city from an elevation of 423 feet.

CLIPPER CITY TALL SHIP

Baltimore, Inner Harbor - *(Inner Harbor pier, near Harborplace) 21230. Phone: (410) 837-6700 or (410) 539-6277. Web: www.sailingship.com*
Admission: $15.00-$30.00 adult, $7.50-$15.00 child.

Baltimore's tall ship, topsail schooner sails regularly from Harborplace for the general public offering 2 hour public cruises most every day during the sailing season. Help hoist the sails and learn how they steer. The staff are very easy to talk to. The scenery is quiet and reflective.

"The first-mate and the skipper too..." - get to really be part of the crew...

MARYLAND SCIENCE CENTER

Baltimore, Inner Harbor - *601 Light Street (a couple of blocks from Inner Harbor) 21230. Phone: (410) 545-5927.* **Web:** *www.mdsci.org Hours: Monday-Friday 10:00am-5:00pm, Saturday 10:00am-6:00pm, Sunday 11:00am-5:00pm. Closed Mondays in the fall and winter. Admission: $14.50 adult, $13.50 senior (60+), $10.00 child (3-12).*

Dinosaurs. Planet Earth. The Human body. Outer space. Chesapeake Bay life. The Kids Room (under age 8 play area). Science Sir Isaac Newton never imagined. Real time connections to real time science. So much to see and do—all in a Please Touch environment. Live Maryland crustaceans and their fellow Chesapeake citizens inhabit the Blue Crab water exhibit. A kinetic, energetic, hands-on exhibit powered by you and looking at space by 3-D or satellite image.

BALTIMORE MARITIME MUSEUM

Baltimore, Inner Harbor - *802 S. Caroline Street (Piers 3 & 5) 21231.* **Web:** *www.baltomaritimemuseum.org Phone: (410) 783-1490 or (877) NHCPORT. Hours: Daily 10:00am - 5:00pm. Extended Hours in the Summer. Admission: $8.00 adult, $6.00 senior, $4.00 youth (age 6-14).*

The US Coast Guard Cutter Taney, US Submarine Torsk, Lightship Chesapeake, and the Seven Foot Knoll Lighthouse tell a story of American power and technology. Over sixty years ago, two of the ships of the Baltimore Maritime Museum were involved in events that changed the history of the world. US Coast Guard Cutter Taney was an amphibious command ship for the Battle of Okinawa, one of the bloodiest battles in US Naval history. Taney was called to battle stations ninety-nine times in forty-five days and was at the center of some of the fiercest action in this crucial campaign. By virtue of her 50 year career, she is the last surviving warship afloat today from the December 7, 1941 Japanese attack on Hawaii. Many can sense the somberness of an event that occurred on the other side of the nation - just looking at it.

On August 14, 1945, the USS Torsk fired a torpedo which hit home, sinking a Japanese coastal patrol vessel. This dramatic moment was to become the last naval action of World War II, as the Cease Fire was declared the next day.

The US Lighthouse Service first assigned Lightship 116 to the Fenwick Island Shoal (DE) Station from 1930-33; after that assignment she marked the entrance to Chesapeake Bay. Crew accommodations included two-man staterooms for the enlisted men, a crew's mess, and an electrically powered galley and refrigerator unit (a major advancement for 1930). The Seven Foot Knoll Lighthouse, the oldest surviving screw-pile lighthouse, was built as an aid to navigation on the Chesapeake Bay.

A Lighthouse Ship?

All of these actual pieces of history are docked together at the Inner Harbor - a convenient way to witness early 1900s sea life on the Chesapeake and American ocean waters.

HISTORIC LONDONTOWN

Edgewater - 839 Londontown Road   21037. Phone: (410) 222-1919. Web: www.historiclondontown.org

Discover new remnants of colonial merchant town life circa 1693 on the South River. The "lost town" was a major port of call in the 1730s for ships taking tobacco to Britain and bringing African slaves, indentured workers, and convicts to Maryland. The town's most prominent figure, James Dick, imported slaves on a large scale and used slaves in his ropewalk and other businesses. Slaves also manned the South River Ferry. By the 19th century, London Town was abandoned except for the brick mansion used as a colonial tavern and home. The mansion and gardens are open for tours but we'd recommend starting at the orientation Visitors Center. The educational facility interprets on-site archaeological finds on the property. Why is a large portion of the center underground?

SMITHSONIAN ENVIRONMENTAL RESEARCH CENTER

Edgewater - *647 Contrees Wharf Road (Follow Central Ave. (Md. 214) east to stoplight at Md. 468 (Muddy Creek Road). Turn right (south). Proceed about 1 mile) 21037. Phone: (443) 482-2200. Web: www.serc.si.edu Hours: Monday-Saturday 9:00am-4:30pm, except National holidays. Admission: Walking trails are free. Many programs and canoe tours require a minimum fee (~$10.00).*

Pick up your trail map at the Reed Education Center when you sign in and explore our two self-guided nature trails: the Discovery Trail and the Java History Trail. The Java History Trail is a 1.3-mile walking path through field, forest and marsh that deals with the history of the land and the people who lived and worked on it. Using the interpretive panels along the path, this is a self-guided walk through local history. Visitors are encouraged to call in advance of their arrival. Family Programs are offered each month. Families and individuals of all ages will enjoy creating animal track castings, designing plankton, night-time owl searches and Saturday canoe tours of Muddy Creek.

ENCHANTED FOREST & CLARKLAND FARM

Ellicott City - *10500 Rte. 108, Clarksville Pike (Rte. 29 to Rte. 108 west 2 miles) 21042. Phone: (410) 730-40409. Web: www.clarklandfarm.com Hours: Daily 10:00am-4:00pm (April-November). Admission: Petting Zoo & Enchanted Forest $4.50 per person. Additional $2.00 for hayrides or pony rides.*

Once upon a time, there was a wonderful storybook park in Ellicott City called The Enchanted Forest. Opened in 1955, it thrilled and delighted generations of families from far and wide throughout the next 30 years. Sadly, it closed to the public in the late 1980s. The folks on this farm are slowly finding and restoring many of the Storybook characters back to display park quality. Look for Mother Goose and her Gosling, the Black Duck, the six Mice that pulled Cinderella's Pumpkin Coach (and the big pumpkin coach!), Papa Bear, the giant

Mushrooms, the bell-shaped Flowers, two giant Lollipops, a number of Gingerbread Men, a large Candy Cane, the Little Red Schoolhouse, the Crooked House and the Crooked Man, the Easter Bunny's House, the Beanstalk with the Giant at the top and the beautiful Birthday Cake. You can now also see Snow White, Sleeping Beauty, Robin Hood, the Three Little Pigs' straw, stick and brick houses, the Rainbow Bridge, and Little Boy Blue, the Old Woman's Shoe and the Three Bears House. Once finished, it will feel like you're walking thru the Nursery rhymes from childhood. The scenes are woven throughout the petting farm area and into a forested area.

The Enchanted Forest lives on...

The Clark family has been farming in Howard County since 1797. Come and visit the 540-acre farm and see a wide variety of animals: goats, sheep, donkeys, pigs, alpacas, calves, horses, ponies, turkeys, ducks, chickens, bunnies, and turtles. You can feed the animals and visit the Barnyard area where you can touch and pet them. They offer hay rides through the storybook farm fields and a number of play areas for the children. Pony rides are available all day, every day that they are open. Too cute!

ELLICOTT CITY B&O RAILROAD STATION MUSEUM

Ellicott City - 2711 Maryland Avenue (I-675 exit 13 on MD 144 toward Catonsville. Travel 4 miles, cross over the Patapsco River bridge and into town. Museum is corner of Main and Maryland) 21043. Phone: (410) 461-1944. Web: www.ecborail.org Hours: Wednesday-Sunday 11:00am-4:00pm. Admission: $5.00 adult, $4.00 senior (60+), $3.00 (2-12). Miscellaneous: The Thomas Isaac Log Cabin is nearby on the corner of Main Street and Ellicott Mills Drive. This is one of the earliest dwellings in Ellicott City and the site of various living history events.

This 19th-century museum profiles the oldest terminus for the first 13 miles of track of the first commercial railroad in America! Walk through history from the 1830s thru the Civil War up to the great flood. See the cluttered Agent's Living Quarters as the first items transferred by rail were products, not people. People came later. Notice the ladies and gents had separate waiting rooms upstairs. Folks dressed in period costume inform you about each room. Exhibits include the fascinating 40-foot HO scale teaching railroad and audio-visual presentation. Only ten minutes long, the movie quickly tells you who and why the railroad was built and this is followed by a light show of the path the B&O rails took.

The "climb aboard" outside caboose is fun for play and photos. The  adorable old downtown of Ellicott City is just footsteps away - with quaint shops and cafes making this stop a perfect day trip for every member of the family. Kids will love the Museum gift shop and the toy stores downtown.

PATAPSCO VALLEY STATE PARK

Ellicott City - 8020 Baltimore National Pike (I -95 take I-195 to Rt. 1 (Exit 3) toward Elkridge to South St. Turn right) 21043. Phone: (410) 461-5005. Web: www.dnr.state.md.us/publiclands/central/patapscovalley.html Hours: Daily 9:00am-dusk.

The park extends along 32 miles of the Patapsco River, with 14,000 acres and five developed recreational areas. The Avalon Visitor Center houses exhibits spanning over 300 years of history along the Patapsco River. Housed in a 19th century stone dwelling in the Avalon Area, the center includes a re-creation of a 1930's forest warden's office. View the Thomas Viaduct – world's longest multiple-arched stone railroad bridge or hike the Grist Mill Trail – A 1.5 mile paved and accessible trail for the disabled along the river. (Avalon Area) Walk across the Swinging Bridge – a 300 foot suspension walkway over the river or hike to Bloede's Dam – world's first internally housed hydroelectric dam. (Orange Grove Area) Visit the Daniels Area fish ladder to learn about Maryland's first barrier free river to shad and herring migrations. Recreational opportunities include hiking, fishing, camping (primitive and cabins), canoeing, horseback and mountain bike trails, as well as picnicking for individuals or large groups in the park's many popular pavilions.

NATIONAL CRYPTOLOGIC MUSEUM

Fort George G. Meade - Colony Seven Road (I-95 to Rte. 32 east/Ft. Meade, exit Canine Rd. Turn left at Colony Seven Road) 20755. Phone: (301) 688-5849. Web: www.nsa.gov/museum Hours: Monday-Friday 9:00am-4:00pm; 1st and 3rd Saturdays from 10:00am-2:00pm. Closed Sundays and Federal Holidays. Admission: FREE Miscellaneous: Vigilance Park outside is home to actual spy planes used for secret missions. Once home, follow the CryptoKids characters with online stories and games.

Codemakers and Codebreakers. Located adjacent to NSA Headquarters, the Museum collection contains thousands of artifacts of the cryptologic profession - the most secret organization in the United States. Catch a glimpse of some of the most dramatic moments in history, using cryptology machines and techniques. Learning past secrets, some events in American and world history may take on a new meaning. Peek into a once secret world - the cracking of enemy codes and the protection of American communications. Look at Union code books

ssshhhh...it's all a "esrcet" here!
Figure it out...

and Confederate cipher cylinders. Learn about Code Talkers - Native Americans who used their own language and terms in radio transmissions - they NEVER made mistakes and codes were NEVER broken! Check out the world's only remaining Enigma - the German encrypting machine that Allied intelligence cracked to glean knowledge that assisted in winning the Battle of the Atlantic and facilitated the ending of WWII. And, look at everyday life applications. Government and top security level companies use Biometrics - human fingerprints or eye scans as password IDs - machines and technology developed from military security needs. Even the post office uses cryptology. Metered mail uses a 2D bar code encryption system. There are several areas where parents might want to watch movies while the kids use their free cipher disk and activity book to try to decode messages and win a small prize. This place is so secretive and so interesting!

CONCORD POINT LIGHTHOUSE

Havre de Grace - *(Lafayette & Concord Streets) 21078. Phone: (410) 939-1498. Hours: Weekends 1:00-5:00pm (May-October).*

The Concord Point light is one of the oldest lighthouses in continual use on the East Coast. It was part of a navigational improvement effort to enhance the safe flow of goods down the Susquehanna River to the ports of Baltimore and Philadelphia. Kids love the giant iron key used to open the lighthouse door. There are only about 35 steps up to the top where there is a great view of the Chesapeake Bay. Wander around the light keepers house on the property. Learn about the first keeper who was also a quirky hero of a self-prompted "battle" between British ships and one man, John O'Neill, on shore. When he ran out of cannon balls, he began to use potatoes instead - the first potato gun! On the grounds behind the lighthouse is one of the cannons used by John O'Neill in his near solitary-attempt to defend the town.

HAVRE DE GRACE DECOY MUSEUM

Havre de Grace - *215 Giles Street (on the waterfront near Tydings Park) 21078.* **Web: www.decoymuseum.com** *Phone: (410) 939-3739. Hours: Monday*

- Saturday, 10:30am-4:00pm. Sunday, Noon-4:00pm. Admission: $6.00 adult, $5.00 senior (65+), $2.00 youth (9-18). Miscellaneous: Each Saturday and Sunday, local carvers provide carving demonstrations to the public in the R. Madison Mitchell Shop, located behind the museum's main facility. Stop by to

A "coffin box" duck hunter

observe some of the techniques involved in the traditional folk art of decoy-making. This exhibit is included in the price of admission.

Located on the banks of the historic Susquehanna Flats, the Havre de Grace Decoy Museum houses one of the finest collections of working and decorative Chesapeake Bay decoys ever assembled. Not only exhibits, but tours and demonstrations are regularly scheduled. The newer areas, by the entrance, have many hands-on exhibits for kids. The museum's main gallery features "What is a Decoy?" A look at the dozens of decoys in this gallery demonstrates that the appearance of any decoy depends upon the species of animal being imitated, the purpose of the decoy, the region in which the decoy is carved, and the unique approach of the carver. "What is a Decoy?" also features a popular diorama that

A "please touch" exhibit greets you...

freezes in time a gathering of prominent carvers during an afternoon in the early 1940s. Look for the two-headed duck decoys (part of the scavenger hunt sheet kids can ask for). Compare different styles and see a recreated workshop setting. "Gunning the Flats"

Why a two-headed decoy?

explores the history of waterfowling on the Susquehanna Flats, an area long noted for its bounty of waterfowl. What is a body Booting? Or a sinkbox? The town's waterfowling traditions truly make Havre de Grace the "Decoy Capital of the World!"

HAVRE DE GRACE MARITIME MUSEUM

Havre de Grace - *100 Lafayette Street (on the waterfront, near Tydings Park) 21078.* **Web:** *www.hdgmaritimemuseum.org* Phone: *(410) 939-4800. Hours: Daily 11:00am-5:00pm (summer); Daily except Tuesday and*

Thursday (rest of year). Admission: $1.00-$2.00 per person.

The museum tells the story of the region's rich maritime heritage. Changing exhibits on boating are the mainstay. They have a boat building school on the premises where you can observe or tour (Tuesday night is live boat building). Ring the ships' bell or play with real 19th century boating tools. Try using these 200 year old tools to "caulk" the boat cracks yourself. Try casting nets, too.

"Trust me Jenny... I've got a good aim?"

On the North side of the Yacht Basin are the entries to the city's Promenade, a half-mile boardwalk that follows the shoreline and overlooks the confluence of the Susquehanna River and the Chesapeake Bay. A quaint surprise.

SKIPJACK MARTHA LEWIS

Havre de Grace - *121 N Union Avenue (boat berthed at Tydings Park) 21078. Phone: (410) 939-4078.* **Web:** *www.skipjackmarthalewis.org* Admission: $20.00 adult, $10.00 child (under 10). Special themed cruise run $15.00-$30.00+ per person. Miscellaneous: Martha's Treasure Hunters: There's treasure in them their waters! Children 6-10 will read a map and help find sunken treasure in the Susquehanna Flats. Each camper will be given the opportunity to take the helm as the Marta Lewis is navigated around the Flats in search of the prize. Captain, crew along with the other mates will be on a constant watch for pirates lurking to steal the bounty. Cost $15.00*

MARTHA LEWIS is a V-bottom, two sail bateau (skipjack). She is one of the few remaining working dredge boats, that make up the Chesapeake Bay oyster fleet -- the last to fish commercially, under sail, in the United States of America. There was a time when hundreds of wind driven vessels called "Skipjacks" sailed the Chesapeake Bay in search of oysters. Crews were hard working men, pushed to the limits of their endurance, competing for a share of the harvest---challenging the elements while dredging under sail. Those days are gone, some say never to return! However, a rare opportunity exists to experience life aboard a WORKING skipjack. On the public cruises, help the crew as you hear calls like: "Ready on Deck?", "Heave!", and "Helm's A-lee." On Thursday evening cruises, watch the sailboat races. Learn about how fast they dredge, the oyster

All together now...hoist up the sails...

harvesting peak years, and what a spat is. Even the Chesapeake Bay had Pirates - Oyster Pirates!

SUSQUEHANNA MUSEUM OF HAVRE DE GRACE LOCK HOUSE

Havre de Grace - 817 Conesteo Street (follow signs into town) 21078. Phone: (410) 939-5780. Web: www.lockhousemuseum.org Hours: Friday-Sunday 1:00-5:00pm (May-October). Admission: Donations accepted.

Why is a lockhouse right next to a river? The canal was built as a water staircase because the river was too shallow for large cargo boats. Why did they use a leather scoop on board? Where was the parking lot for boats ready for shipping? Listen to a 160 year old xylophone and secret birthday music box. In the kitchen, learn how to make an old fashioned snow ball treat. Look for the high chair that turns into a stroller. Why is it better to have rounded travel trunks vs. a flattop. At the end of the tour, make sure the kids

Help move a 4000 lb. pivot bridge..with just a push...

help move the pivot bridge. You just moved 4000 pounds! Fun things to learn in every room - and you get to touch most items.

SUSQUEHANNA STATE PARK / ROCKS STATE PARK

Havre de Grace (Jerrettsville) - 3318 Rocks Chrome Hill Road (off Rte. 155, on MD 24, eight miles north of Bel Air) 21084. Phone: (410) 557-7994. Web: www.dnr.state.md.us/publiclands/centra/susquehanna.html

This day-use park is located on land bordering Deer Creek. A popular feature of the park is the throne-like rock formation called "The King and Queen Seats," where, according to legend, Indian Chieftains once sat in tribal council. Rock climbing, picnicking, hiking, tubing, wading, canoeing, fishing, bow hunting and photo ops are plentiful. The Falling Branch area of ROCKS STATE PARK is located about 5 miles north of the main part and features a 17-foot scenic free-falling waterfall - the second highest vertical falls in the state. Historical sites include the ROCK RUN GRIST MILL, Archer Mansion and Jersey Toll House. The stone mill is open on weekends all summer operating using a 12-ton water wheel, which runs on a limited basis.

STEPPINGSTONE MUSEUM: Visitors can spend the afternoon

touring the sites of a once-working Harford County farm. The farmhouse, furnished as a turn-of-the-century home, charms the visitor as a guide invites you to share the daily life of the period. With no electricity, what did kids do for fun? Tours include the

See the many fancy tomato case labels...

formal sitting room, sleeping quarters, and kitchen with its wood burning stove and ice box. Can you find the toaster? In the other buildings, maybe watch a woodworker, blacksmith or weaver. Our favorite building is the recreated tomato cannery. Kids did this as a summer job. They begin by scalding the fruit to loosen the skin and peel. Then they pack (on a giant wheel conveyor!), cap, cook, label and store the canned product. They even have equipment to make Catsup. Very interesting and well displayed processes in here! **www.steppingstonemuseum.org** (888) 419-1762. (weekends 1:00-5:00pm, $3.00 - ages 13+).

GUNPOWDER FALLS STATE PARK / JERUSALEM MILL

Kingsville - 2813 Jerusalem Road 21087. Phone: (410) 592-2897. Web: www.dnr.state.md.us/publiclands/central/gunpowder.html

Gunpowder Falls State Park features numerous scenic areas on 18,000 acres in the Gunpowder River Valley. The park features over 100 miles of trails, trout streams and the historic Village of Jerusalem, an 18th century grist mill company town. A Visitors Center Museum in the town displays artifacts and there's a blacksmith shop and gun factory on the premises. Seasonal Revolutionary and Civil War era living history demonstrations and encampments are held here (**www.jerusalemmill.org** or 410-877-3560). Nearby NORTH POINT STATE PARK (in Fort Howard, off Rte. 20, 410-477-0757) features the Defenders' Trail used during the War of 1812. Other park areas include a rail trail, swimming beach, and a marina. Guided trips with local outfitters are available for flatwater and moving water kayaking, canoeing, fishing, catamaran sailing, windsurfing and natural history walks.

HISTORICAL ELECTRONICS MUSEUM

Linthicum - 1745 W Nursery Road (Route 295 South (Baltimore Washington Parkway). Take West Nursery Road exit, turn left at light) 21090. Phone: (410) 765-0230. Web: www.hem-usa.org Hours: Monday-Friday 9:00am-3:00pm, Saturday 10:00am-2:00pm. Admission: FREE

You can learn about TVs, radios, cell phones, and even see a working original Edison cylinder phonograph. The museum houses the first American radar ever built (used in Pearl Harbor to detect incoming Japanese planes), a lunar camera just like the one used to photograph Neil Armstrong's moon landing, and the SCR 584 - a giant radar unit that visitors can enter and explore! The educational gallery features hands-on exhibits. Use their hands on equipment to generate electricity and experiment with magnetism. Learn how electromagnetic waves power our cell phones, cook our food, and help us see into space. Become part of a human battery. Take a look at an operational amateur radio station capable of worldwide communications by voice, Morse code, digital modes, and television. See the type of radar that detected the attack on Pearl Harbor on December 7, 1941. Learn how radar led to the household microwave oven or try a hands on demonstration of phased array beam steering. Go under the sea in an Interactive demonstration of passive and active underwater sounds and then go to a room where you can see yourself in infrared.

FIRE MUSEUM OF MARYLAND

Lutherville - 1301 York Road (I-695 exit 26B, one block north) 21093. Phone: (410) 321-7500. Web: www.firemuseummd.org Hours: Saturdays 10:00am-4:00pm (May-December). Tuesday-Saturday (June-August). Closed July 4th and Christmas. Admission: $7.00 adult, $6.00 senior (62+) and firefighters, $4.00 child (2-12).

This nice, active museum still exhibits operational hand pumps, steam engines and water tower - something from each era. In the Discovery Room, pull an old fire alarm in your 1800s neighborhood, then run to the telegraph station and punch in the message to dispatch units to the fire. Climb aboard a real engine cab and turn on the siren or flash the lights.

LADEW TOPIARY GARDENS

Monkton - 3535 Jarrettsville Pike (I-95 take Exit 74 to MD Route 152. Follow MD Route 152 northwest to the dead end at MD Route 146 (Jarrettsville Pike) and go left) 21111. Phone: (410) 557-9466. Web: www.ladewgardens.com Hours: Monday thru Friday 10:00am - 4:00pm. Saturday and Sunday 10: 30am - 5:00pm (April-October). Admission: $8.00-$10.00 adult, $2.00 child for Garden & Nature Walk. Home tours extra. Miscellaneous: Ask the Admissions desk for the Kids Scavenger Hunt sheet before you walk the gardens. Garden storytimes each week - nature story and craft. Ladew Café for lunch.

The most outstanding topiary garden in America features 15 different themed flower and hedge gardens on 22 acres. What is "topiary"? The art of trimming and training shrubs or trees into unnatural ornamental shapes. See bushes shaped like swans, trophies or simple rows of boxes and triangles. A topiary of two riders atop horses and a pack of hounds pursue a cunning green fox across the front lawn. A caterpillar crawls through a whimsical garden. Make a game of who can identify the shape first. There's also a yellow garden (everything with a yellow cast) or the White Garden or the Pink Garden (you get the idea). How about the Garden of Eden (look for the apple tree) or a real Secret Garden or the Keyhole Garden - only one small hidden door in and out.

See the hunter (jumping the fence) and the two dogs ahead in hot pursuit...

Browse or cool off in the historic manor house, café, or gift shop. The Manor Tour begins with the poodle and dog house topiary near the front porch. Inside, notice all the stirrup cups shaped like many things. Why is the staircase called a glide? Why the coin in the bannister? Our favorite room was the oval room built around an oval desk with a secret passageway to outside. The Nature Walk at Ladew is a 1.5 mile trail through the woods and fields of the Ladew property. In addition to educational stations along the trail, there is a short boardwalk through wetland forest and marsh. Look for frogs and fish in the ponds.

DAY BASKET FACTORY

North East - 714 South Main Street (I-95 North, to Exit 100, MD-272 South. Proceed 2.4 miles) 21901. Web: www.daybasketfactory.com Phone: (410) 287-6100. Hours: Monday-Wednesday, 11:00am-5:00pm, Sunday 1:00-5:00pm. Extended weekday/end hours June thru Christmastime.

This local industry makes hand-made white oak baskets. Shortly after the end of the Civil War in 1876, Edward & Samuel Day came to North East from Massachusetts. Edward was an experienced basket maker. The brothers, who had been supplying the southern market with baskets, set-up shop in the North East - partly to save on transportation costs, also because the forests along the Susquehanna River were full of White Oak, the best kind of wood for baskets. Craftsmen carefully select and split each piece of oak used by skilled weavers, who produce baskets using techniques passed down by generations for over 128 years.

On tour: After the sides are woven, the weaver wraps an outside hoop around the inside hoop and nails through both hoops with brass nails. These nails automatically crimp themselves when they strike the steel band on the form, saving an extra step. Next, yokes if needed, are laced under the fillers from the bottom of the basket for reinforcement. Some baskets are also fitted with handles of different types. How do they get the wood to bow like that? The production of a basket is a three to four day process. After drying overnight the basket is trimmed, sanded and finished. The completed Day Baskets have hundreds of uses and come in a variety of sizes and styles. Four different sizes of market baskets, round farm baskets with bentwood handles or rope handles, picnic baskets with lids, laundry baskets, fish or firewood baskets, berry baskets, picking baskets with drop handles, and eel pots (yes, a popular waterman activity around these parts!).

SOLDIER'S DELIGHT NATURAL ENVIRONMENTAL AREA

Owings Mills - *5100 Deer Park Road, near the Liberty Reservoir (I-795N to exit 7B on Franklin Blvd, west. Turn right on Church Road, left on Berrysman Lane, then left on Deer Park Road) 21117. Phone: (410) 922-3044. Web: www.dnr.state.md.us/publiclands/central/soldiers.html Hours: Sunrise to sunset. I-795N via exit 19 toward Owings Mills/Reisterstown. Take exit 7B on Franklin Blvd. west. Turn right on Church Road, left on Berrysman Lane, then left on Deer Park Road.*

The area supports over 39 rare, threatened or endangered plant species, as well as, rare insects, rocks and minerals. Visitors will enjoy hiking on the trails or stopping by the visitor center to enjoy interpretive exhibits (find out what a serpentine barren is?). Trails are only open to hikers. Equestrians and cyclists are not permitted due to the sensitive nature of the area.

Serpentine Trail (2.5 miles) - Visitors will traverse a large section of the serpentine barren while hiking this trail. This area consists mainly of grassland, but also passes through wetland areas and an oak forest.

Choate Mine Trail (1.1 miles) - Hikers will pass by the historic Choate Mine. This chrome mine was operated from 1818 to 1888. It was briefly reopened during World War I for ore extraction. This loop trail connects to the Red Run Trail and Dolfield Trail.

Red Run Trail (0.9 mile) - Hikers will travel through sections of serpentine grasslands as well as the oak forest. This trail offers the only "stream side" hiking opportunity at Soldiers Delight as visitors hike along the banks of Red Run.

HAMPTON NATIONAL HISTORIC SITE

Towson - 535 Hampton Lane (I 695) eastbound or westbound: Take Exit 27B, Dulaney Valley Road northbound) 21286. **Web: www.nps.gov/hamp** *Phone: (410) 823-1309. Hours: VISITOR CENTER OPEN: 9:30am-4:00pm daily except Thanksgiving, Christmas, and New Year's Day. Admission: FREE*

The self-guided tour of this farm and grounds includes original slave quarters that tell the story of the family who lived here for more than 150 years, as well as slaves and indentured servants. Scenes from Hampton's past include a colonial merchant shipper amassing thousands of acres of property along Maryland's Chesapeake shore; indentured servants casting molten iron into cannons and ammunition for the Revolutionary army; and enslaved people loading barrels of grain, iron, and timber onto merchant ships bound for Europe that would return with luxury goods.

SUGGESTED LODGING AND DINING

CHICK & RUTH'S DELLY - **Annapolis**. Daily for breakfast, lunch and dinner. Old fashioned milk shakes, ice cream, too. 165 Main Street. (410) 269-6737 or **www.chickandruths.com**. Their menu takes a while to look over as there are tons of things to order. Ask for Delly homefries with breakfast - yum. Now, Ted, the 2nd generation owner is the ambitious one flitting about performing impromptu magic tricks tableside. The best part of breakfast here is their nickname: "Flag'n Eggs" cause each morning as the crowded restaurant is on their second cup of coffee - everyone in the place, customers and employees alike, gets up in unison and recites the Pledge of Allegiance. An act of spontaneous patriotism? No, it's an Annapolis tradition that dates back more than three decades. The Pledge is recited every day at 8:30am (Monday through Friday) and 9:30am Saturday and Sunday. What a great way to start your journey around the historic state capital!

HERRINGTON HARBOUR INN. Chesapeake Beach (Rose Haven) - 7161 Lake Shore Drive, Rte 261. www.herringtonharbourinn.com (410) 741-5100. Beautiful beachfront Caribbean style lodging, featuring fantastic Bay views, chickee huts and palm trees. Each of the "cottage-style" rooms offers a coffee maker, microwave, mini-fridge, and some have private patio hot tubs surrounded by colorful tropical murals. The suites offer full kitchens with a living area. Have tropical slushies on the patio overlooking the Olympic-sized resort pool, or jump in and enjoy. Better yet, enjoy the private beach and play in the Bay. Other resort amenities include a game room, Peddle Boats, Kayaking (Both one and two-person boats.), Playground, Volleyball, Croquet & Tennis Court, Shuffleboard Area, Picnic Facilities (grills available) on the water's edge. Rentals available for all sports activities. Homemade Continental breakfast included with some awesome muffins and coffee cake plus cereal, fresh fruit, bagels, various fruit juices, etc. Rates begin around $100.00 per night (peak), hovering around $200 for suites and weekend hot tub rooms. Mangos restaurant on premises with Kids Menu (~$5.00). Why go all the way to Florida when these folks have the cozy tropical feel on the popular Bay coast. We used it as a haven to rest and relax after day trips to neighboring sites.

PIRATE'S COVE RESTAURANT. Galesville. 4817 Riverside Drive (on the West River, end of Rte. 255). (410) 867-1861 or www.piratescovemd.com. Boat Races on Tuesday/Wednesday nights (summer). Pirates Cove Restaurant & Marina is the place to enjoy fine classic seafood dining the year round with the scenic charm of the West River. They highly recommend the Broiled Seafood Platter (~$25) or their Crab Imperial. The Children's Menu has variety. Fried shrimp, steak, spaghetti, chicken, hamburger and grilled cheese (~6.00-$8.00). Lunch/Dinner/Sunday Brunch.

CARROL'S CREEK CAFÉ. **Annapolis (Eastport)** - 410 Severn Avenue. (410) 263-8102 or **www.carrolscreek.com**. Located on the famous Restaurant Row in the Eastport section of Annapolis, Carrol's Creek is tucked in the Annapolis City Marina. A short stroll over the Spa Creek Bridge, the restaurant has a great view of the Wednesday night sailboat races. With a stunning view of the historic skyline and harbor, they feature regional American dishes with an emphasis on seafood and outside dining is available. Lunch serves gourmet style sandwiches and plates ($7.00-$15.00 average). Their Maryland Cream of Crab Soup rich with jumbo lump crabmeat and a touch of sherry, was judged Maryland's Best.

BUDDY'S CRABS & RIBS. **Annapolis**. 100 Main Street. (410) 626-1100 or **www.buddysonline.com**. Family-owned and operated with 22 windows overlooking Main Street and the City Dock. Specializing in steamed crabs, baby back ribs, seafood, steaks, chicken, salads, daily buffets (seafood lunch $12.00, dinner $20.00). All kids ten and under eat free (from the kids menu) with each full priced adult entree ordered. Free Balloons, Free Coloring pads. They find themselves different from most other restaurants because they cater to families with kids. Their slogan says it all... "WE LOVE KIDS!!" This was the site of Michele's FIRST blue crab training with mallet and knife! We'd recommend the fresh and flavorful buffet with a side of blue crab to "dissect" if you dare. Not for the seafood squeamish, those crabs. A hoot for Michele!

ANNAPOLIS ICE CREAM COMPANY. **Annapolis**. 196 Main Street. (443) 482-3895 or **www.annapolisicecream.com**. For the freshest, in-store-made ice cream look for their Penguins on Main Street. 100% natural and gourmet ice cream plus seasonal favorites like homemade hot cocoa. They make ice cream fresh nearly every day. During the summer, you can pretty much be sure that the ice cream you are eating today was made within the last 24-36 hours! With more than 35 homemade ice cream selections (like coffee, oreo, apple pie, and peanut butter vanilla!), Annapolis Ice Cream Company caters to every unique ice cream palate - and every flavor is so "on" because they use real ingredients mixed in (ex. Real coffee, real apple pie, peanut butter) - it makes the difference. And, a grand banana split is only around $6.00! So-o-o very good.

HYATT REGENCY BALTIMORE. Baltimore. 300 Light Street, Inner Harbor. (410) 528-1234 or **www.hyattregencybaltimore.com** Perfectly located, this Four-Diamond Inner Harbor hotel offers a luxurious haven in the midst of the city's premier attractions with many rooms providing an excellent Harbor View. Stroll to Camden Yards, the National Aquarium or a skywalk to HarborPlace, and then return to the downtown Baltimore harbor hotel to enjoy features like pillow top beds, flat screen TVs, summer sundeck and outdoor pool, tennis, or shoot some hoops on a rooftop deck. Several styles of restaurants are on the premises.

HILTON COLUMBIA. Baltimore (Columbia). 5485 Twin Knolls Road, off Rte. 175, just west of I-95. **www.columbia.hilton.com** (443) 539-1119. Situated in a park-like setting, this place offers standard guest rooms that are welcoming with warm, yet vibrant color scheme and modern decor. All rooms include complimentary high-speed wireless internet services, complimentary use of the indoor pool, jacuzzi, exercise facilities and sauna. Morgan's restaurant serves great chicken (Frangelico) and steak (Cajun) dishes as well as Maryland crab. The children's menu runs $4.00-$5.00 and offers so many well-portioned kids foods.

VANDIVER INN. **Havre De Grace** - 301 South Union Avenue. (800) 245-1655 or **www.vandiverinn.com**. The Vandiver Inn is an 1886 Victorian mansion located two blocks from the Chesapeake Bay in historic Havre de Grace, Maryland. What a nice treat! The owner greeted us on the front porch where we later sat during a heavy rainstorm. The kids were apprehensive at first - being in such an old mansion, but soon eased and began exploring all the nooks and crannies. One night, our family, some staff and the owner's son, Jack, watched a movie in the parlor - "Movies at the Mansion." All the staff are gracious but not at all pretentious. Breakfast and the amenities weren't so "foo-foo" that our kids wouldn't enjoy - no mile-high, lime infused cheese french toast here - more like homemade eggs or pancakes with oodles of blueberries. It is surrounded by historic homes, museums, golf, shopping, antique stores, marinas and water-oriented activities. As you walk towards downtown - you'll notice many other friendly neighbors waving from their adorable restored homes. Since the "downtown" is only one mile long, you can walk to everything. You'll love the charming streets and people. The Vandiver Mansion has nine elegant rooms, many with fireplaces. The adjacent Murphy & Kent Guest Houses provide an additional eight rooms. This Country Inn really tries to cater to family getaways, family reunions (take over the mansion!) and weddings or corporate meetings. Girls love that every room is decorated differently. All rooms are air conditioned and four of their new suites feature luxury Jacuzzi tubs. ALL of their rooms offer private in-room baths, full breakfast every morning, cable TV, phones w/data ports, high speed wireless internet, voice mail, hair dryers, irons and many other amenities. (rates around $100-$150 per night). So many "pictures" captured in our memory bank...

MACGREGORS RESTAURANT. **Havre De Grace**. 331 Saint John Street. (410) 939-3003 or **www.macgregorsrestaurant.com**. Originally a bank built in 1924, all tables here have a water view. The two-tiered all glass upscale casual dining room features lunch ($8.00-$12.00), dinner (around $20.00), lite fare and Sunday Brunch. We have to highly recommend the award-winning Rockfish and their garlic chive mashed potatoes! Mild gourmet sauces are served and fit each entrée perfectly. Children's Menu (everything from potato skins to burgers to corn dogs - most around $5.00-$6.00), balloons and coloring books.

LAURRAPIN GRILLE. **Havre De Grace**. 209 North Washington Street. 410-939-3663 or **www.laurrapin.com**. Where Northern California meets the Chesapeake Bay. Items like spring rolls, muffalattas or crab on the same menu. The newbie kid gourmet will enjoy their meatloaf and steak and potatoes, too! Lunch around $10 and dinner around $20.

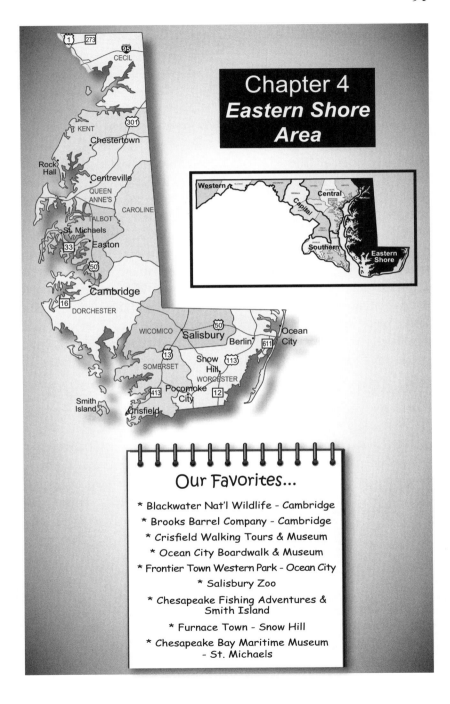

Chapter 4
Eastern Shore Area

Our Favorites...

* Blackwater Nat'l Wildlife - Cambridge
* Brooks Barrel Company - Cambridge
* Crisfield Walking Tours & Museum
* Ocean City Boardwalk & Museum
* Frontier Town Western Park - Ocean City
* Salisbury Zoo
* Chesapeake Fishing Adventures & Smith Island
* Furnace Town - Snow Hill
* Chesapeake Bay Maritime Museum - St. Michaels

ASSATEAGUE ISLAND NATIONAL SEASHORE & STATE PARK

Berlin - *7307 Stephen Decatur Hwy (from OC, take Rte. 50 bridge west, turn left onto Rte 611 south) 21811. Phone: (888) 432-2267. Hours: Visitor Center 9:00am-5:00pm daily. Admission: $10.00 per vehicle for 7 day park pass.* **Web: www.dnr.state.md.us/publiclands/eastern/assateague.html**

Begin your Maryland visit to Assateague Island National Seashore in the family-oriented Barrier Island Visitor Center, located at the end of Rte. 611, just prior to crossing the bridge to the island. Pick up a park map, enjoy the aquariums, or watch a film about the island. Cross the bridge to Assateague and explore the barrier island. Short, self-guided walks or bike trails run through the park (trail is 3.5 miles long). View magnificent marshlands, beautiful beaches and miles of water. The island is home to the wild ponies made famous in the novel "Misty of Chincoteague." The name Assateague comes from a Native American word thought to mean "the marshy place across." The island is ideal for camping (primitive), fishing, clamming, crabbing, canoeing and kayaking. Bring your own car-top boat or rent a canoe at the Bayside Picnic Area (daily during summer and on spring or fall weekends).

BLACKWATER NATIONAL WILDLIFE REFUGE

Cambridge - *2145 Key Wallace Drive (Rte. 16 south) 21613. Phone: (410) 228-2677.* **Web: www.friendsofblackwater.org** *Hours: Refuge open Dawn to dusk. Visitors Center open Monday-Friday 8:00am-4:00pm, Weekends 9:00am-5:00pm. Admission: $3.00 per vehicle. Miscellaneous: Orientation video is*

about 20 minutes long. Then pick up a Wildlife Drive Map and head on the driving path. Want to make this a game? Ask the ranger for a waterfowl checklist and see how many you can find.

This is a prime resting and feeding area for migrating waterfowl. Huge flocks of ducks, geese and swans migrate through in November and December. As a major stop on the Atlantic Flyway, Blackwater is a vital haven for waterfowl, as well as a sanctuary for the threatened American bald eagle and the endangered Delmarva fox squirrel. These squirrels are much less active - we saw one taking a nap! The largest nesting population of bald eagles on the East Coast hang out here each year. What makes the refuge attractive? Why do they farm corn and soybean?

The endangered Fox Squirrel... taking a nap on a log...(see just above)

Why do they drain the pond in summer? If you decide not to venture into the refuge, you'll find a rapidly growing Butterfly and Beneficial Insect Garden. And if you look out the window at the rear of the building, you will see their Osprey Cam platform off in the distance. The second floor contains a bird-watcher's observatory overlooking the marsh. You never have to leave the building to catch some great views of wildlife (especially helpful if the weather isn't cooperating).

BROOKS BARREL COMPANY

Cambridge - 5228 Bucktown Road (Rte. 50 east, right onto Bucktown Road) 21613. Phone: (410) 228-0790. Web: www.brooksbarrel.com

One of the last remaining slack cooperages operating in the U.S. and the only one in Maryland. What is a cooperage? They're important to people all over the world - IGA, Cracker Barrel, even *Pirates of the Caribbean* movie sets. Biggest reason, because they do it the old-fashioned way. Their barrels are handcrafted just like in the

Handcrafted in America...they make it look so easy...

colonial days using top quality pine logs. They take those logs through many exact processes to form barrels, kegs, planters and tubs. Durable steel hoops hold the position and complete the authentic rustic appearance. The whole process can be seen as it is all done in-house in a giant "shed." How do they get the barrel-sliced wood? (a barrel saw, of course - now, they use more modern saws). You'll love the funny looking expander machine (circa 1905) - looks like an octopus. We really enjoyed this short tour watching modern folks using age-old equipment and techniques. You don't find many of these left...

CAMBRIDGE LADY CRUISES

Cambridge - Cambridge Municipal Marina, A Dock 21613. Phone: (410) 221-0776. Web: www.cambridgelady.com Admission: Fees vary by tour. Call for rates.

CAMBRIDGE WATERFRONT TOUR - A one and a half hour scenic cruise along the Cambridge waterfront on the Choptank River takes you past homes from the 17th century as well as new waterfront estates. Hear the story of how this once agricultural community became a leading commercial seafood processing center on the Chesapeake Bay. They'll take you past historic Hambrooks Lighthouse and the former home of Francis DuPont at Horn's Point.

MICHENER'S CHESAPEAKE TOUR - Depart aboard The CAMBRIDGE LADY for a narrated cruise based on James A. Michener's experiences while writing this world renowned novel. The novel was set in the 10 square mile area between the two historic towns of Cambridge and Oxford. Using your map, follow along as your guide tells the story of local residents, from plantation owners to watermen, whose experiences were the source of Michener's 300 year tale of these waters. Begin your tour in Cambridge on Historic High Street with homes dating to the 17th and 18th centuries. Dock in Oxford and enjoy lunch at the historic Robert Morris Inn, built prior to 1710 as a home of one of the most prominent families of the town. Here author James Michener declared he had the "Best Crab Cakes on the Eastern Shore." After lunch take a Walking Tour of this quaint village. One of the oldest towns in Maryland, Oxford was one of the only two ports of entry on the Chesapeake Bay during Colonial times.

RICHARDSON MARITIME MUSEUM & BOATWORKS

Cambridge - *401 High Street, downtown 21613. Phone: (410) 221-1871. Web: www.richardsonmuseum.org Hours: Wednesday, Sunday 1:00-4:00pm. Saturday, 10:00am-4:00pm. (closed Wednedsay, November-February)*

Walk into the Museum and step back into the rich history of Dorchester County's influence on Chesapeake Bay traditional wooden sailing vessels. Bordering the Bay, bounded by broad rivers and laced with countless waterways, the County has been home to hundreds of boatyards since its early settlement. Chesapeake bay ship models and waterman artifacts honor the craftsmen and culture of Eastern Shore boat building. Just down the street, watch traditional wooden boat building in action at the Boatworks (Corner of Maryland Avenue & Hayward Street).

SKIPJACK NATHAN OF DORCHESTER

Cambridge - *526 Poplar Street (All Public Sailings depart from Long Wharf) 21613. Phone: (410) 228-7141. Web: www.skipjack-nathan.com*

Skipjack boat sailing cruises on the Choptank River. Help raise her sails or take a turn at the helm, and hear stories of the working watermen. One of the last skipjacks built, it is meant to preserve the nautical heritage of the county and a way of life.

C & D CANAL MUSEUM

Chesapeake City - *815 Bethel Road 21915. Phone: (410) 885-5622. Web: www.nap.usace.army.mil/sb/c&d.htm#attractions Hours: Monday-Friday 8:00am-4:00pm (except government holidays). Admission: FREE Miscellaneous: a full-sized replica of the 30-foot Bethel Bridge Lighthouse is nearby. The original was one of the many wooden light-houses used to warn vessels of locks and bridges in the days before the 1927 canal changes made it sea level. The lighthouse is located on Corps property, a short walk from the museum.*

The Chesapeake and Delaware Canal is listed on the National Register of Historic Places and is designated as a National Historic Civil Engineering and Mechanical Engineering landmark. The canal is unique as the sole major commercial navigation waterway in the United States built during the early 1800s still in use.

The C&D Canal Museum - provides visitors with a glimpse of the canal's early days. The waterwheel and pumping engines remain in the original pumphouse (now the museum). These steam engines are the oldest of their type in America still on their original foundations. Other artifacts and exhibits in the museum detail and illustrate the canal's history. New exhibits include interactive videos and a television monitor which gives visitors up-to-the minute locations on ships as they travel through the canal.

CHESAPEAKE FARMS

Chestertown - 7319 Remington Drive 21620. Phone: (410) 778-8400. Web: www.dupont.com/ag/chesapeakefarms/tour.html

Chesapeake Farms is a showcase for advanced agriculture and wildlife management. The guide-booklet leads you through the Farms and points out or explains many of the agricultural and wildlife practices being applied there. Some of these techniques you might use on your own land when you get home. There are 16 stops on the driving tour. Each stop is marked by a sign bearing a number. The tour begins at the Farms' main waterfowl rest area and passes many areas of interest such as: Sunflowers, Farm ponds, Deer food plantings, Nesting structures and a Cottontail rabbit habitat.

SCHOONER SULTANA

Chestertown - 105 S Cross Street, dock at end of Cannon Street (Rte. 213 for about 20 miles to the Chester River Bridge. Go over the bridge and into Chestertown. Turn left at the first traffic light onto Cross St) 21620. Phone: (410) 778-5954. Web: www.schoonersultana.com Miscellaneous: Public sails also available. Passengers are encouraged to help raise the sails, steer using Sultana's 7-foot long tiller and explore the authentically reproduced crew's quarters below-decks. Sultana offers two-hour sails far families ($15.00-$30.00 per person, must be age 6+). Reservations please.

Schooner Sultana, school-ship of the Chesapeake, sails the bay to teach bay ecology and Colonial maritime history to thousands of students each year. Activities include but are not limited to: Raising sails and steering the schooner; Using maps, charts and electronic equipment to examine the geology, hydrology and physical characteristics of the

Chesapeake and its watershed; Collecting and examining live fish, crabs and oysters to study their life cycles and physical adaptations; Collecting and examining zooplankton and phytoplankton with the use of a high powered video microscope while discussing the concept of food chains/webs; Performing water quality tests, including: turbidity, salinity, dissolved oxygen, phosphorous, nitrogen and pH; Employing reproduction 18th century navigational equipment to determined speed, depth and latitude; Using historic maps and charts to explore 18th century geopolitics and to discuss the Atlantic triangular trade route; Exploring Sultana's authentic below decks area, including the surgeon's cabin and galley, to learn about everyday life in 18th century America.

CONOWINGO HYDROELECTRIC PLANT

Conowingo - 2569 Shurs Landing Road (I-95 south to Rte. 222 North toward Craigtown. At Rte. 1, turn west, cross river to Plant) 21034. Phone: (410) 457-5011. Admission: FREE

The Conowingo Dam on the Susquehanna River, constructed in 1926, is 4,468 feet long and 100 feet high. It impounds 105 billion gallons of water in a 14 square mile lake. At full capacity, water flows at more than 38 million gallons per minute. The power generating station is one of the nation's largest hydroelectric installations featuring eleven generators. It contributes 1.7 billion kilowatt-hours of electricity to its service area and takes only minutes to start or shut down. The flood gates close and open controlling the amount of water flowing. Water flow allows for electricity to be generated. Visitors can tour the dam and hydroelectric plant for a giant physics experiment - to get a first-hand view of the operation of an important power source.

CRISFIELD WALKING & TROLLEY TOURS

Crisfield - 3 Ninth Street (depart from Crisfield Visitors Center, Somers Cove Marina) 21817. Web: www.crisfieldheritagefoundation.org Phone: (410) 988-2501. Hours: Center open daily 9:00am-5:00pm (summer). Closed Sundays rest of year.

While visiting the "Crab Capital of the World", why not really get some insights into what gave the area that title? Did you know this town was built on top of oyster shells? Now that oyster and crabbing are dwindling, what is the town's new market - tourism and condos.

WALKING TOUR: The Port of Crisfield Tour takes each patron through the port area of the city. One of the highlights of the tour is

a visit to a modern crab and oyster processing facility where you can see, first hand, how the products of the Chesapeake are made ready for market. (small fee, Monday-Saturday at 10:00am)

A classic example of a waterman's boat

TROLLEY TOUR: the Crisfield Heritage Tour takes each group on a trolley ride that includes a narrative overview of the town's history with a stop at the workshop of Lem and Steve Ward, founders of the art form known as decoy carving and painting. (Monday-Saturday at 1:00pm, $2.50-$3.00 per person)

JANES ISLAND STATE PARK

Crisfield - 26280 Alfred Lawson Drive (MD RT 13 to Westover; RT 413, approximately 11 miles to Plantation Road) 21817. Phone: (410) 968-1565. www.dnr.state.md.us/publiclands/eastern/janesisland.html Miscellaneous: Janes Island is part of the Beach to Bay Indian Trail. This trail recognizes travel patterns established by the American Indians and later followed by the first European settlers. For more information about the trail, contact Somerset County Tourism at (800) 521-9189. Janes Island State Park is a Chesapeake Bay Gateway, one of over 100 special places to experience the Chesapeake. Visit www.baygateways.net to find more Bay Gateways.

Janes Island State Park is nearly surrounded by the waters of the Chesapeake Bay and its inlets. It has rental cabins, camping and miles of isolated shoreline and marsh areas. Historic artifacts that can be found along the shoreline of Janes Island provide evidence of activities by primitive man, from hunting mammals to shucking oysters. In a sense, native people living on Janes Island were practicing a lifestyle very similar to the modern watermen surviving off the bounty of the Chesapeake Bay. If you are looking for a few hours of tranquil canoeing or kayaking in a natural paradise with few signs of civilization, you'll find it at Janes Island State Park. The approximately 2,900 acres of marsh, beach and high land offers paddlers an outdoor adventure through small waterways within the island. Most of the waterways are protected from wind and current providing ideal conditions for the novice as well as the experienced canoeist. Features: Boat launch, boat rental, fishing and crabbing, swimming, and a visitor's center.

TAWES, J. MILLARD, HISTORICAL MUSEUM

Crisfield - 3 Ninth Street, Somers Dove Marina 21817. Phone: (410) 968-2501. Web: www.visitsomerset.com/TAWES_MUSEUM.HTML Hours: Monday-Friday 9:00am-4:30pm; Weekends 10:00am-3:00pm (Memorial Day-October). Closed weekends (rest of year). Admission: $2.50 per person (over age 12). Miscellaneous: Pop over to Gordon's for a cheap bite or ice cream. Linger there a while and listen in on the local watermen's chatter.

The museum traces the history of the Lower Shore with exhibits on the beginnings of the Chesapeake Bay, the influence of the Native-Americans on the early colonists, seafood harvesting and processing, and the evolution of that truly American art form, decoy carving and painting. The Ward Brothers only had a fourth grade education but they learned to turn scrap wood into useful decoys and then works of art commanding huge amounts of money. Learn about how the Indian inhabitants showed colonists how to build eel pots, tong for oysters and most importantly, how to build the famous Chesapeake Bay Log Canoes. Wonder who brings the seafood you love to the table? Those hardy Chesapeake watermen harvest oysters and crabs by the millions. The museum tells their story and the story of the processing and marketing of seafood throughout the United States and the world. Learn how to use crab pots and look at pictures of ladies crab picking. Compare this to the different methods of soft shell crabbing and floating peelers.

SMITH ISLAND CRUISES & SMITH ISLAND

Crisfield - 4065 Smith Island Road (depart from Somers Cove Marina) 21824.
Phone: (410) 423-2771. Web: www.smithislandcruises.com/daycruise.html
Hours: Center: Daily Noon-4:00pm (May-October). Wednesday and
Saturday only (weather dependent, rest of year).

Join Captain Tyler for a delightful cruise across the Tangier Sound to Smith Island. Enjoy looking around Smith Island on a self-guided

walking tour, or rent a golf cart or a bicycle. There are gift shops to browse in, the SMITH ISLAND CENTER (20846 Caleb Jones Road, 410-425-3351 or **www.smithisland.org**), and plenty of narrow streets to stroll and meet native islanders.

Piles and piles of crab pot
marker buoys...

Smith Island is Maryland's only inhabited island accessible exclusively by boat. There are three separate villages on the island and an Interpretive center about the island community where lifestyles change slowly with time. While wandering around, notice dozens of cats. Why? They love the crab scraps!

<u>SMITH ISLAND CENTER</u>: A small museum ($2.00 admission ages 12 and older) with permanent exhibits related to the history of the Island, working on the water and the interaction of people and the Chesapeake Bay. It explores the role of women in Island life, and distinctive speech patterns which have developed on the Island. Do you know what "peelers" or "Christmas Give" means? The Film, "Land and Water, People and Time" runs about 20 minutes and shows the history of the land and its people, their life on the water and in the community...a good way to hear some of their typical stories. The Center really gives you the "feel" of the Island - how the people work, cope & eat. Can you figure out what is most important to them? Food, family & church. So real.

Smith Island Cake...
so yummy!!

PICKERING CREEK AUDUBON CENTER

Easton - 11450 Audubon Lane   21601. Web: www.pickeringcreek.org
Phone: (410) 822-4903. Hours: Monday through Friday 8:30am- 5:00pm
and Saturday 10:00am- 4:00pm.

The four-hundred acre farm and science education center features 2 lab classrooms (including live reptiles and amphibians); Nature Trails; One mile of shoreline; Freshwater Pond; Children's Imagination Garden; 100 acres of hardwood forest; a Canoe fleet; Live Reptile and Amphibian Displays; Mounted Bird and Mammal Displays and an Eastern Shore Tool Museum. They have Tiny Tot and Fishing programs each month for families.

CHESAPEAKE BAY ENVIRONMENTAL CENTER

Grasonville - 600 Discovery Lane   21638. Web: www.wildfowltrust.org
Phone: (410) 827-6694. Hours: Daily 9:00am-5:00pm. Admission: $5.00
adult, $4.00 senior (55+), $2.00 youth (5-8).

The Wildfowl Trust of North America operates the Chesapeake Bay Environmental Center, a 500 acre preserve surrounded by the waters of the Chesapeake Bay and comprised of several distinct habitats. Visitors can explore over 4 miles of wetland and woodland trails, collections of live waterfowl and non-releasable raptors, an aviary and visitors center. Rental canoes are available for exploring the surrounding waters and wetlands. Monthly programs called Marsh Muckers and Creepy Crawlers are held for specific, naturalist led, hikes and exploration (small fee). The Center is an excellent place to see the Chesapeake's wintering population of waterfowl including: Canvasback, American Black Duck, Shoveler, Ruddy Ducks, Redhead, Canada Goose and Tundra Swan. Shorebirds make a strong showing in May and late summer, when hundreds can be seen.

CHOPTANK RIVERBOAT COMPANY

Hurlock - 6304 Suicide Bridge Rd 21643. Web: www.choptankriverboat.com
Phone: (410) 943-4775.

The Choptank River Boat Company operates The Dorothy & Megan and The Choptank River Queen. They are reproductions of authentic 80-foot turn-of-the-century paddlewheeler river boats. Fully enclosed with heating and air conditioning. Savor the scenery along the Choptank River on a sightseeing cruise or enjoying a delicious lunch or dinner prepared by the Suicide Bridge Restaurant, the home harbor and embarkation point of their river-boat cruises. Dine on the area's seafood as you watch the waterfowl dine with you. You may also see watermen returning, aboard their workboats, with their daily catch of fish, crabs or oysters fresh from the Choptank River.

ELK NECK STATE PARK AND FOREST

North East - *4395 Turkey Point Road (10 miles south of the town of North East on MD 272) 21901. Phone: (410) 287-5333. Admission: $3.00 per person (weekends and holidays); $3.00 per vehicle weekdays. Add $1.00 out of state.* **Web: www.dnr.state.md.us/publiclands/central/elkneck.html**

Sandy beaches, marshlands and heavily wooded bluffs comprise the peninsula formed by the North East and Elk Rivers, and the Chesapeake Bay, where this park is located. Several trails meander through the diversified topography, revealing the great variety of plant and animal life. An easy walking trail to Turkey Point Lighthouse (www.tpls.org) provides a view of the Elk River and the Chesapeake Bay. Features: Boat launch, cabins, campfire programs, campsites, campstore, fishing, flatwater canoeing, hiking trails, historic interest, swimming, and visitor center.

ASSATEAGUE ADVENTURE

Ocean City - *(Talbot Street on the Bay, downtown) 21842. Phone: (410) 289-3500.* **Web: www.talbotstreepier.com/boatrides/adventure.html** *Admission charged. Miscellaneous: Sodas and Bottled Water Available.*

A great way to visit Assateague Island when you don't want to overnight and camp. The ride over and back is comfortable and you can leisurely observe the fishing boats go by and learn about the area's ecosystem. Once you land on the Island, everyone disembarks to explore. Search for Wild Ponies or dredge for clams. They even do a hands-on crab and crab pot demonstration.

JOLLY ROGER AMUSEMENT PARKS

*Ocean City - 30th Street & Coastal Hwy or the Boardwalk 21842. Phone: (410) 289-4902. **Web: www.jollyrogerpark.com** Hours: Summers open daily 11:00am-1:00am. Admission: per ride or purchase wristband. FREE admission and parking.*

With 35 rides for the whole family, Ocean City's largest family entertainment center includes SPLASH MOUNTAIN WATER PARK and SPEEDWORLD, plus miniature golf, traditional boardwalk rides, games and concessions. Don't forget to ride the World Famous Wild Mouse Coaster.

OCEAN CITY BOARDWALK

*Ocean City - 21842. Phone: (800) OC-OCEAN. **Web: www.ococean.com** Miscellaneous: Just one block off the boardwalk is the OCEAN CITY TRAIN GARDEN (109 Dorchester St, **http:utzjr.home.mchsi.com**) open most Friday and Saturday afternoons in the spring and summer, plus Sundays during summer school break. Free. Bayside at 65th Street is the SLIDE N' RIDE water and dry amusements (**www.slidenride.com**) Admission.*

Be sure to visit Ocean City's world-famous Boardwalk during your stay at the beach. From the tiny train that chugs along the three-mile promenade to the antique carousel that dates back to 1902, visitors realize the charm of the traditional wood walkway. An early morning bicycle ride (only until 10:00am in summer, till noon off-peak seasons) along the Boardwalk is a great way to start every day in town. Numerous bicycle rental shops are conveniently located to get you on your way. Next, splash in the surf, boogie board (excellent here), or sit back and watch the waves roll in. Paddle a canoe or kayak. Fly a kite or build a sandcastle. Cast a line

The Ocean Gallery...an art store oddity

from one of several fishing piers or from the beach (rentals available). Although we suggest walking the beach/boardwalk during the day, a small fee boards a tram anywhere on the strip. Enjoy browsing through the Boardwalk shops for that perfect souvenir. Bring your appetites along with you. Boardwalk eateries serve a delicious

assortment of treats. Eastern Shore seafood including crab cakes, Maryland fried chicken, pit beef barbeque (Boogs), and famous french fries (Thrashers) are just a few of the offerings. Satisfy that sweet tooth with saltwater taffy, caramel popcorn, frozen custard swirl (Kohrs), funnel cakes, cotton candy, and creamy

See the incredible sand carvings of Randy Hofman...what an inspiration!

fudge. Children (of all ages) enjoy the Boardwalk's amusements and arcades. Get a bird's eye view of the barrier island from atop the Ferris wheel. Then take a seat on a bench overlooking the inlet and watch the boats come and go or listen to the nightly street musicians. Near 2nd Street, you can't miss two works of art - the OCEAN GALLERY folkart store where you have free admission to a spectacle (really, the fun art to look and PLEASE TOUCH is on the outside wall of the shop) and Randy Hofman's amazing Biblical sand sculptures (www.randyhofman.com). They get your attention! Each summer, they offer free family activities like evening Bonfires and Sundaes in the Park plus many free concerts on the weekends.

OCEAN CITY BOAT TOURS

Ocean City - 21842.

SEA ROCKET - Wicomico Street & the Bay Downtown at Bahama Mamas. (410) 289-5887 or **www.searocket.com**. Enjoy safe, affordable family fun onboard Ocean City's original and largest speedboat. Music and frequent encounters with playful dolphins. Children 12 and under are free (one per paying adult). $16.00 adults, $12.00 seniors. 50 minute tour leaves two to six times each day (seasonally).

SEA ROCKET ADRENALINE - same contact info as Sea Rocket. Experience high speed, exhilarating rides onboard the new, cutting edge custom designed speedboat. Age and height restrictions apply. 35 minute tour leaves several times each day (Memorial Day - September). $32.00 all passengers.

OC ROCKET - Talbot Street Pier. **www.talbotstreetpier.com**. (410) 289-3500. Leaving two-eight times per day each summer, this is OC's fastest speed boat ride. They claim to see the most dolphins and have raised, comfortable cushion seating for the best ride. 50 minute tour.

DUCKANEER - Talbot Street Pier. Same contact info as OC Rocket. The call is out to brave treasure hunters of all ages. Ye best be ready for a magical pirate journey with buccaneer battles (water guns) and sunken treasure (everyone gets some). Plan to get wet in the heat of battle. Weekends (May & September), several times daily in June, July & August.

RIPLEY'S BELIEVE IT OR NOT!

Ocean City - Wicomico Street & Boardwalk 21842. Phone: (410) 289-5600. Web: www.ripleys.com/oceancity/ Hours: Daily, 10:00am-5:00pm , longer hours summer. Weekends, March, October, November. (Admission: $10.95 adult, $7.95 child (6-12).

Discover the museum full of the bizarre and exciting objects you won't see in any other museum. 14 theme galleries showcase everything from a rock from Mars to shark attack stories. Look for the world's only 40 foot animated shark crashing through the pier building. From shrunken heads to modern weirdness, always unusual. Probably best for the older kids in your party.

WHEELS OF YESTERDAY

Ocean City - 12708 Ocean Gateway (Rte. 50) 21842. Phone: (410) 213-7329. Web: www.wheelsofyesteryear.com Hours: Daily 9:00am-9:00pm (June - early September). Closes at 5:00pm (rest of year). Admission charged.

Antique, classic, and special interest cars are the feature here. Over 30 exhibits featuring Jack Benny's Overland, a 1928 Lincoln passenger touring car, an 1830 rural mail delivery wagon and a 1930 racing car. See Joe Morgan's 1950s service station, too. Just pulling into the parking lot is interesting - the items displayed lure you inside.

OCEAN CITY LIFE-SAVING STATION MUSEUM

Ocean City - *813 S. Boardwalk 21843. Web: www.ocmuseum.org Phone: (410) 289-4991. Hours: Daily 11:00am-10:00pm (June-September). Only open until 4:00pm (rest of year). Admission: $1.00-$3.00 per person. Miscellaneous: To engage your children in learning some history of the beach (instead of just the amusements, food and surf fun), try doing the Scavenger Hunt worksheet. If your child completes it, they receive a prize.*

Shipwrecks, Life-Saving & Rescue, History, Swimwear, Sealife, & More! This very building once housed the surfmen charged with rescuing shipwrecked mariners from the sea, and later, the U.S. Coast Guard. One room is devoted to lifesaving stories and techniques. Notorious keepers give written and verbal accounts of heart-breaking rescues. The Beach Room houses a large collection of bathing fashions, beach toys, and accessories worn by Ocean City beach goers during the

Learning rescue techniques of the past...

past century. Look for the Paper Blend Bikini available in vending machines in 1971. Kids think this room is very funny. The Aquarium Room contains two 250 gallon saltwater aquariums and several smaller tanks filled with interesting creatures indigenous to the Ocean City waters. Sands From Around the World is a unique collection of over 200 samples of sand collected by friends of the museum. Can you find sand from your region of the country? Davey Jones' Locker - always wondered what it is? Deep-sea divers share with you unusual objects that have been recovered from the shipwrecks off of Ocean City and the surrounding area. Another room is dedicated to Mermaids. Several unique dolls' houses depict the once gracious hotels and notable businesses of Ocean City's past. Hear Sal laugh (an animated mannequin from Jester's Fun House). You'll catch yourself laughing outloud, too. Isn't it crazy how much has NOT changed!

FRONTIER TOWN WESTERN PARK

Ocean City, West - *(Rte. 611 west) 21811. Web: www.frontiertown.com Phone: (410) 641-0057. Hours: Daily 10:00am-6:00pm (mid June to Labor Day). Admission: Packages for Western Park, waterpark, other rides. See website for current packages. Waterpark & mini-golf run $11.00-$13.00 per person. Frontier Town park alone is the same. Many discounts offered in OC coupon books. Miscellaneous: FREE parking, waterpark changing rooms and lockers. Miniature golf course.*

No place for evil in this town...

"C'mon down folks"...to this replica western town circa 1860 situated alongside of Frontier Town Campground (sites rented with reservations). Return to them days of yesteryear and live a day in the life of a rootin' tootin' cowboy, an earth-poundin' Indian Chief or a high steppin' Can Can gal. Most young deputies want to spend their allowance purchasing cap guns and cowboy apparel to pretend shootin' at the OK Corral (before and after the show). Besides the dispersed schedule of live shows, try to take in a steam train ride, stagecoach ride, pan for gold, paddle boats, trail rides and such. Be careful the outlaws don't get you out on the trail.... The Waterpark has a western theme, too. Slide down Red Bird's Mountain, a giant water slide, and splash into the catch pool. Their Lazy River will have ya wishin' you'd "growed fins instead of feet". Designed for kids (with parents in mind) The Waterin'

Hole, a family activity pool, features a huge shallow wadin' pool with covered wagon mini-slides, cactus fountains, water sprays and more.

OC JAMBOREE

Ocean City, West - *(Rte. 611 & 12600 Marjan Lane) 21811. Phone: (410) 213-7581. Web: www.ocjam.com* *Shows: Open year-round at 8:00pm. Some matinees, too. All seats reserved. Admission charged depending on show & age.*

Ocean City's only live music theater presents brand new shows each year. Their high energy productions take you and the family on a whirlwind tour of memorable music, laughs, and patriotic pride. Country, pop, 50s or gospel music themes. The rustic styled theater has intimate seating. Country Christmas Memories each December.

STURGIS ONE ROOM SCHOOL HERITAGE HOUSE

Pocomoke - *209 Willow St. 21851. Phone: (410) 957-1913. Hours: Wednesday & Saturday from 1:00-4:00pm (May-October). Admission: Donations.*

Sturgis One Room School Museum, formerly known as Sturgis School, is the only African American One Room School in Worcester County retaining its original integrity. It is a small structure built about 100 years ago on Brantley Road on land that was purchased by William Sturgis in 1888. Sturgis One Room School operated as a school for 37 years. Grades 1 - 7 were taught by one teacher until it closed its doors in 1937. Next door is a Heritage House used to display local artifacts.

TUCKAHOE STATE PARK

Queen Anne - *13070 Crouse Mill Road 21657. Phone: (410) 820-1668. Web: www.dnr.state.md.us/publiclands/eastern/tuckahoe.html*

Tuckahoe Creek, a quiet country stream bordered for most of its length by wooded marshlands, runs through the length of the park. A 60-acre lake offers boating and fishing. The park offers 20 miles of scenic hiking, biking and equestrian trails, flat water canoeing, hunting, picnicking, as well as a recycled tire playground for children. The ADKINS ARBORETUM (410-634-2847, 12610 Eveland Road, daily 10:00am-4:00pm) encompasses 500 acres of park land and almost three miles of surfaced walkways leading through the tagged native species of trees and shrubs through meadows and woodlands. The park offers activities and special events on a seasonal basis. Activities include day camps, Scales & Tales Program, and canoe trips.

WYE ISLAND NATURAL RESOURCES MANAGEMENT AREA

Queenstown - *632 Wye Island Road (Route 50 and turn right onto Carmichael Road. Travel 5.1 miles on Carmichael Road until you cross the Wye Island Bridge) 21658. Phone: (410) 827-7577. Hours: Dawn to dusk.* **Web: *www.dnr.state.md.us/publiclands/eastern/wyeisland.html***

Privately owned and farmed for more than 300 years, now the island's 2,800 acres are managed for some agriculture but mainly a habitat for wintering waterfowl and native wildlife. Wildlife viewing and hiking are the most popular activities on Wye Island's six miles of trails. The School House Woods Nature Trail takes you through a mature hardwood forest while the Ferry Landing Trail leads beneath a canopy of Osage Orange Trees. Wye Island also houses a Holly Tree that is more than 275 years old. Follow the Holly Tree Trail to visit this long-time resident. Other activities include boating, fishing, biking, equestrian trails, canoeing and kayaking.

PLUMPTON PARK ZOO

Rising Sun - *1416 Telegraph Road (10 minutes off I-95 and 5 minutes off Route 1) 21911. Phone: (410) 658-6850.* **Web: *www.plumptonparkzoo.org*** *Hours: Open daily 10:00am-4:00pm (March-September), weather permitting. Admission closes 1 hour prior to closing. Admission: $10.95 adult, $9.95 senior (60+), $6.95 child (2-12). Miscellaneous: Concession Stand, vending machines available for animal feed.*

Exotic animals are displayed in a pastoral country setting, including giraffes, bears, tigers, monkeys, deer and kangaroos. Other unusual adoptions are pot-bellied pigs and bearded dragon. Most of these animals come here from threatened or abandoned situations.

EASTERN NECK NATIONAL WILDLIFE REFUGE

Rock Hall - *1730 Eastern neck Road (At the blinking red light in Rock Hall, turn left onto Rt. 445. Follow Rt. 445 about 6 miles out) 21661. Phone: (410) 639-7056.* **Web: *www.fws.gov/northeast/easternneck*** *Hours: Daily sunrise to 1/2 hour after sunset. Admission: FREE*

Eastern Neck National Wildlife Refuge, located at the confluence of the Chester River and the Chesapeake Bay, is a 2,285-acre island refuge and a major feeding and resting place for migratory and wintering waterfowl on Maryland's Eastern Shore. It is especially noted as a staging area for tundra swans. The refuge is also home to the endangered Delmarva fox squirrel and the threatened southern bald eagle. Nearly six miles of roads and trails are open to visitors most of the year. Four wildlife trails and a handicap-accessible boardwalk and observation tower are available for those who wish to observe the varied habitats of the refuge. Trails vary 1/4 mile - 1½ miles.

ROCK HALL MUSEUM

Rock Hall - 8 Main Street, Municipal Bldg. 21661. Phone: (410) 639-2296. Web: http://rockhallmd.com/museum Hours: Weekends 11:00am-3:00pm (March-December). Admission: FREE, donations accepted. Miscellaneous: DURDING'S STORE (5742 Main Street, intersection of Main and Sharp, 778-7957) is in nearby Sailing Emporium waterfront area. Have a real milkshake from a real soda fountain! Over in the corner, the old wooden telephone booth still stands...and works.

The Rock Hall Museum collection includes representative examples of equipment used in the early years of harvesting the Bay, such as oyster bed charts, ice buoys, a drift net lantern, a hand-winder mast and boom oyster rig with patent tongs, a shucking box, a grass shrimp net and a number of other commonly used tools. While guns and dogs played a critical role in Rock Hall's preoccupation with hunting waterfowl, nothing was quite so important as a good string of working decoys. Hand-carved at first, working decoys eventually evolved into plastic mass-produced lures in more recent years, adding significant worth to the surviving early crafted models. Rock Hall still has some decorative carvers. The Rock Hall Museum features a re-created carving shop, featuring original tools, furnishings, patterns and partially carved decoys.

WATERMAN'S MUSEUM

Rock Hall - 20880 Rock Hall Avenue 21661. Phone: (410) 778-6697. Web: www.havenharbour.com/hhwatmus.htm Hours: Daily 10:00am-4:00pm, except major holidays. Admission: FREE. Donation box.

Locals have put together assorted artifacts on Chesapeake Bay crabbing, fishing, and oyster tonging. Crab pots, eel traps, dinghies, anchors, oarlocks, nets, buoys and knots everywhere. In winter, watermen often lived for lengthy periods of time in tiny one room shanties mounted on flat bottomed boats. Moored out on the partially or totally frozen bay, these shacks provided just enough space for a man, a few critical belongings, a potbellied stove, a bunk, a table, a chair, and of course, his dog…see a real-life sample of this. Another exhibit space details a realistic oyster harvesting station.

DELMARVA SHOREBIRDS BASEBALL

Salisbury - 6400 Hobbs Road (Arthur Perdue Stadium) 21802. Phone: (888) BIRDS-96. Web: www.theshorebirds.com

The single A affiliates for the Baltimore Orioles play home games at this modern ballpark. Come see Sherman the Shorebird and the future stars of the major leagues. While you're there, take the kids on the carousel and playground, speed-pitch machine, enjoy an all you can eat buffet or occasional post-game fireworks.

PEMBERTON HALL PLANTATION

Salisbury - (take Salisbury Bus. Rte 50 to Rte. 349, Nanticoke Rd, for 1/4 mile. Turn left on Pemberton Drive) 21802. Phone: (410) 548-4900. Web: www.dnr.state.md.us/baylinks/27.html Miscellaneous: The 262-acre park boasts 4.5 miles of self-guided natural trails, hardwood forests, meadows, wetlands and fresh water ponds.

Pemberton Hall, as the plantation house is known, was built in 1741 for Colonel Isaac Handy and his wife Ann. It is one of the earliest dated brick gambrel roofed houses in Maryland. The park features a historic Eastern Shore plantation house, a visitor's center, a small museum with artifacts from the plantation, and several miles of nature trails spread throughout the 207 acre property. Settlers discovered that Maryland's Lower Eastern Shore offered many advantages: level expanses of sandy soil favorable for growing tobacco, grain and other crops; abundant streams to power mills; and protected inlets and coves suitable for boat landings from which plantation goods could be shipped overseas. Along with viewing the house and enjoying the trails and property, participate in organized educational programs.

SALISBURY ZOO

Salisbury - 755 S Park Drive (City Park, Rte 50 into town, left on Civic Avenue, right at end, next left onto Memorial Plaza) 21802. Phone: (410) 548-3188. Web: www.salisburyzoo.org Hours: Daily 8:00am-4:30pm. Open until 7:30pm in summer. Closed Thanksgiving and Christmas. Admission: FREE

Long touted as one of the finest small zoos in America, the zoo houses more than 400 species of animals and wildfowl native to North, Central and South America. From bears hanging out in a hammock

to curious prairie dogs or elegant flamingos. Unusual Cavys look like a sort of kangaroo deer. Spider Monkeys like to play. Over by the sloth, try hanging upside down like the sloth. Because they're in the middle of decoy art country, they have a wonderful display of live

just hangin' around with friends...

wildfowl. Compare it to the decoys you've seen around town. Set inside City Park, located on the Wicomico River, the area also offers sport courts, paddle boat rentals and more than three miles of trails. The park also has a large, sturdy "Castle" playground and a huge misting station to cool off.

SALISBURY PEWTER OUTLET

Salisbury - 2611 N. Salisbury Blvd. (Rte. 13 north) 21804. Phone: (410) 546-1188. Hours: Monday-Friday 9:30am-5:30pm, Saturday 10:00am-5:00pm. Some Sundays. Admission: FREE.

The company continues the tradition of handcrafted American products. Watch a short video of the process - then see them do it, live! Look directly into the factory from an observation window to watch items being made. They start with a thin pewter disk or flat and model

metal art...

and shape it around a form on a lathe. As it's spinning, the crafter uses hands and old tools to scrape, shape, shave and sink designs into the pewter piece. Another window reveals the ladies polishing and engraving. Then, browse in the elegant showroom featuring gift items of pewterware at factory seconds and overrun savings. This is a great tour as you don't have to worry about safety, noise or reservations.

WARD MUSEUM OF WILDFOWL ART

Salisbury - 909 S Shumaker Drive 21804. Web: www.wardmuseum.org Phone: (410) 742-4988. Hours: Monday-Saturday 10:00am-5:00pm, Sunday Noon-5:00pm. Closed major winter holidays. Admission: $7.00 adult, $5.00 senior, $3.00 student or college, $17.00 family rate. School group tours are $3.00-$4.00 per person. Miscellaneous: Classes on elementary carving (with soap) for kids are held often with master carvers assisting. A beginners decoy painting kit is available in the gift shop, too. The Nature Trail is 2 miles long and hooks up with the zoo. Plaquards along the way detail flora and fauna.

This museum has the largest collection of bird carvings in the world! Antique decoys and modern carvings are displayed along with waterfowling history interpretations and development of decoy carving. By now, you've probably heard of the Ward Brothers who started this new art form. The Ward Brothers Workshop is a stylized recreation of their workshop and contains examples of their carving, painting and poetry used as work or inspiration. Begin in The Decoy in Time Hall which focuses on the history of the decoy as a hunter's tool. In the gallery, see the interesting progression of variations of theme over the last 100 years. The Habitat Theatre takes a detailed look at natural wildfowl environments. To  engage the kids interest, ask for an Activity Sheet to complete. Look for decoy ducks from your state/area; birds nesting in a tennis shoe; American Indian primitive decoys and the many ways hunters hide to trick the waterfowl.

CHESAPEAKE FISHING ADVENTURES

Smith Island (Tylerton) - (Pier B, Slip 4, Somers Cove Marina dock departures in Crisfield) 21866. Phone: (410) 968-8175. Web: www.cfadventures.com Admission: Fares run $200 - $349+ per day, per adult including all daily activities. Kids ages (3-14) are discounted depending on activity level. Most want to fish but you can substitute sight-seeing or lighthouse cruises.

Hosts Chris & Sharon Marshall of CFA are located on the uniquely beautiful piece of land called Smith Island, which is the only inhabited offshore island accessible only by boat in Maryland. Their packages

offer some of the best fishing that the Chesapeake Bay has to offer as well as a glimpse of the past in this peaceful island setting that has been home to the hardy handful of residents for over 300 years. Once you set foot on the soil of the island, it is

Off to Smith Island...

hard to believe that such a place exists only a few hours' drive from major cities. CFA Basic Fishing package includes: (a) transportation from Crisfield, Maryland, to Smith Island and back to Crisfield at the end of your adventure; (b) Guided fishing on their boats with a fully licensed captain with all rods, bait and tackle provided; (c) Overnight waterfront lodging in their spacious guest quarters along with use of the pier facilities including gas grill, fish cleaning station as well

docking the Capt. Marshall

as refrigeration for your catch. Another package provides all three meals - cooked for you. Sharon is a very good cook! She uses age-old Island recipes making homemade Crab Imperial (best ever had), corn pudding, whole crab, assorted meat and potatoes and Smith Island Cake for dessert. Homemade breakfast is just as good. For your convenience and enjoyment, with all of the package choices, they provide all linens so there is no need to bring items such as bedding, towels, etc. nor is there a need to bring cooking utensils as their kitchen facilities and utensils are available for your use. You only have to bring your personal items and food as determined by the package you select. For the non-fisherman, they also offer island and lighthouse tours,

delicious waterfront dining...

island exploration and just plain old get-away-from-it-all relaxation packages. Limit six people in one group.

Exploring on your own? The "street" around the island is only 1/3 mile! Begin at the Drum Point Market - home of the enormous half-pound crab cake and assorted snacks and souvenirs. Locals pick up

Exploring Tylerton...only 1/3 mile!

grocery items at the small market. Towards dinnertime, you have to visit the Smith Island Crabmeat Co-op. For generations these ladies used to work picking crabs at home. Then, they formed the co-op. The ladies' fingers fly while picking Maryland Blue

Crabs. If you are lucky and ask nicely, maybe they will sing an old hymn or two. What an awesome scene and beautiful sound! (found out later the ladies are in the church choir). Nearby, Waverly Evans has a home-spun art shop down at the boat harbor. He is a retired waterman who makes neat old-fashioned toys. Whether you are reeling in a trophy rockfish, enjoying freshly steamed crabs, or just relaxing on the screened in sunset

crab pickin' at its best...

deck complete with hammock, your time on Smith Island will be an experience you'll never forget! Be sure to savor each moment...

FURNACE TOWN LIVING HERITAGE MUSEUM

Snow Hill - 3816 Old Furnace Road (SR 12, 14 miles south of Salisbury) 21863. Phone: (410) 632-2032. Web: www.furnacetown.com Hours: Daily 10:00am-5:00pm (April-October). Admission: $2.00-$4.00 (age 2+).

This is an iron manufacturing village from long ago located in Pocomoke Forest. The interpretive program at Furnace Town is an

effort to bring to life the daily life activities of this 19th century village. Highlights of the self-guided tour include: the organ playing in the old church; the Charging Ramp (imagine filling the carts and then hauling them up the ramp to pour into a 3000 degree furnace hole!); and artifacts found

up and down the charging ramp...

on the property displayed in the museum (many you can touch). Also, artisans recreate the various crafts and professions that were part of Furnace Town during its life. We met the town weaver and a kitchen gardener harvesting peanuts. The 35' high furnace was designed to smelt bog ore found in the swamp just behind the structure. Later, it had a heating element added to make pig iron. Pig iron bars were sold and melted to make iron artillery, stoves, nails, well pumps, skillets, etc. Their models of an iron furnace are the best interpretation we've seen anywhere.

inside a furnace...

MT. ZION ONE-ROOM SCHOOL MUSEUM

Snow Hill - 117 Ironshire Street (Ironshire and Church Streets) 21863. Phone: (410) 632-0669. Hours: Tuesday-Saturday 1:00-4:00pm (mid-June thru 1st week of September). Admission: $0.50-$2.00 per person.

The Mt. Zion One Room School House was used as a school until 1931. Years later, a school superintendent moved and restored the school and it has since demonstrated to students and visitors how their forebears were taught in the days of one room schools. McGuffy readers, quill pens, inkwells, slates and a water bucket are in place just as if the students had been dismissed yesterday.

POCOMOKE RIVER STATE PARK & FOREST

Snow Hill - 3461 Worcester Hwy   21863. Phone: (410) 632-2566. Web: www.dnr.state.md.us/publiclands/eastern/pocomokeriver.html

The scenic Pocomoke River is the setting for the Pocomoke River State Forest and Park, Shad Landing, and Milburn Landing areas. (Note: Shad Landing is on the south side of the Pocomoke River off Route 113. Milburn Landing is on the north side of the river on Route 364. It is a 25 minute drive between the two areas of Pocomoke River State Park). With 14,753 wooded acres in the Southwestern section of Worcester County, between Snow Hill and Pocomoke City, the state forest is famous for its stand of loblolly pine and for its cypress swamps which border the Pocomoke River. Pocomoke means black water, and there is good fishing in these waters. The river originates in the Great Cypress Swamp in Delaware and flows southwesterly 45 miles to the Chesapeake Bay. Recreation features include: biking trails, boat launch, boat rental, camp fire programs, camp sites, camp store, fishing, flat water canoeing, hiking trails, picnic shelters, swimming pool (seasonal) and visitor center.

PURNELL MUSEUM

Snow Hill - 208 West Market Street   21863. Phone: (410) 632-0515. Web: www.purnellmuseum.com Hours: Tuesday-Saturday 10:00am-4:00pm, Sunday 1:00-4:00pm (April-October). Admission: $2.00 adult, $0.50 child (5-12)

The Julia A. Purnell Museum offers interpretive exhibits of many aspects of the lives of Snow Hill and Worcester Countians. A time-line parallels the history of Worcester County with the history of the United States. Kitchen and hearth exhibits show visitors the utensils and methods used to keep a happy home during the 18th and 19th centuries. A "general merchandise" welcomes browsers back to a time when communities were built around the local general store. The Victorian era is also represented, complete with clothing, jewelry and everyday items made of silver and exquisitely carved ivory. Machines and tools show the many "modern" improvements Mrs. Purnell experienced. Kids like the display of toys, games and bicycles.

CHESAPEAKE BAY MARITIME MUSEUM

St. Michaels - *Waterfront Park, St. Michaels Harbor, Navy Point (Rte. 50 to Easton, right on Rte. 322, right on Rte. 33) 21663. Phone: (410) 745-2916.* **Web: www.cbmm.org** *Hours: Daily 10:00am-6:00pm (summer); until 5:00pm (spring/fall); until 4:00pm (winter). Admission: $10.00 adult, $9.00*

senior (62+), $5.00 child (6-17). Miscellaneous: Lighthouse Overnights for groups and families (run around $35+ per person) can be arranged. Museum admission is included. Bring picnic foods and coolers - a campout in a real lighthouse!

Chesapeake Bay Crabs don't give up easily!

Situated on the harbor in historic St. Michaels, the Chesapeake Bay Maritime Museum brings to life the story of the Bay and the people who have lived and worked around it. Explore its many exhibit buildings, the world's largest collection of traditional Bay boats, and its fully restored 1879 Hooper Strait Lighthouse. Try on some daper yacht clothes and then climb on board a cruiser and pretend to drive. Listen in on advice at the tackle shop or oyster boat. Young kids may want to "Rub-a-dub-dub" at rubbing stations or read a storybook "My Life as an Oyster." Meet local crafters; pull up crab pots and nipper for

"Thor" was a sunken old workboat, now a playground...how cool!

oysters; and enjoy interactive exhibits exploring the Bay's role in our nation's history: the sport and art of Chesapeake decoys, the golden age of steamboats, and oystering on the Chesapeake. Unlike most museums, the Chesapeake Bay Maritime Museum offers you the real thing: people who actually live the story they tell. In the Museum's working Boat Yard, you can watch the restoration of the Bay's traditional vessels and go talk with the shipwrights, apprentices, or a visiting captain or boat builder. Lots to do and see. Nicely done, plan on a few hours here.

CHESAPEAKE SAILING CRUISES & TOURS

Tilghman Island - Tilghman Harbor docks 21671.

DOCKSIDE EXPRESS (Tilghman Island, Rte 33 and Phillips Wharf): Explore the Chesapeake Bay aboard the Express Royale. Families mostly gravitate to the Tilghman Island Sampler, sunset, environmental or historic tours. (888) 31-CRUISE or **www.docksidexpress.com**. Cruise under the Narrows Bridge, watch watermen in action, and learn the history of the tiny fishing village of Tilghman Island. Learn of John Smith's explorations, the War of 1812, and the restlessness during the Civil War. Seasonally (spring-fall), Friday thru Tuesday mornings and afternoons. $10.00-$15.00 (age 3+). Tours include FREE admission to Phillips Wharf. Before you sit down to a mouth full of Blue Crab, learn about the life cycle of the crabs and handle them and their crustacean friends in the touch tank.

CHESAPEAKE SKIPJACK (Tilghman Island, Sailing Charters departing Daily from the Crab Claw Restaurant, Dogwood Harbor). (410) 745-6080 or **www.oystercatcher.com**. To sail aboard the H.M. Krentz is akin to stepping back in history, which is ever present on the Eastern Shore - home of the last fleet of working sailing vessels in North America. There are no winches, just manpower and blocks and tackle along with the luck of a good breeze to set time back in motion. Experience the life of the waterman; help pull up the sails and dredge some oysters. Relax and enjoy the sounds of wind and water; see osprey and waterfowl; observe undeveloped waterfront and historic towns; learn about the ecology of the incredible Chesapeake Bay. Public Tours (2 hours) scheduled 3 times daily during season. $15.00 child (under 12) or $30.00 adult.

WYE GRIST MILL AND MUSEUM

Wye Mills - (Rte. 662 off Rte. 50) 21676. Phone: (410) 827-6909. Web: www.historicqac.org Hours: Thursday-Sunday 10:00am-4:00pm (April-November). Grindings the 1st and 3rd Saturday of the month.

General George Washington and his troops owed a debt of gratitude to Wye Mills. During the Revolutionary War, the Wye Grist Mill supplied flour to the Continental army - helping this area earn the reputation as the "breadbasket of the Revolution." Today, the 1681 mill operates as a living museum and houses an exhibit titled, "Wheels of Fortune," which tells the story of the Shore's agricultural history. Every other Saturday, the mill comes to life when volunteers demonstrate how the massive steel water wheel, the grinding stones, and maze of chutes and elevators were used to grind wheat and corn. Did you know this Mill is the beaten biscuit capital of the world? Leavening agents were rare in Colonial times so bakers discovered that biscuits would rise if the dough was beaten for thirty minutes with a hammer or back of an axe. The Orrell family mill in town has been making the round, dense biscuits and today operates the world's only commercial beaten biscuit business. Stop by for a bag to go.

SUGGESTED LODGING AND DINING

HYATT REGENCY CHESAPEAKE BAY RESORT. **Cambridge**. - 100 Heron Blvd @ Rte. 50. (410) 901-1234 or (800) 233-1234 or **www.chesapeakebay.hyatt.com**. Discover an authentic Chesapeake Bay experience in a spacious 350-sq.-ft. room featuring neutral decor reflective of the area's maritime past. Luxurious amenities include step-out balcony, two plush double beds, refrigerator, coffeemaker, generous work area, wireless high-speed Internet access, marble bath with Portico products, vanity mirror, and cozy robes. Many of the 400 luxury rooms face the river. A focal point of the resort, the 150-

slip River Marsh Marina offers guests a variety of activities. Pirate's Cove offers a fun-filled activities program where kids can make new friends and learn new skills and crafts. Parents... head off on your own adventures (golf) or enjoy some quiet time (spa) while your kids learn and discover experiences only found here on the Eastern Shore (avail. Summers, holidays and weekends for a fee). Daily activities are offered poolside like water games, crafts, contests and fireside smores. The Winter Garden area pool is open year-round in a climate-controlled, glass-enclosed area. Large outdoor swimming pools include the Activities Pool with waterslide (a little on the cold side), a children's pool and Infinity Pool. Several restaurants, snack bars and grill for dining. Johnny Venture Kids Menu has a wide variety of kids favorites ($5.00-$6.00).

THE ISLAND GRILLE. **Taylors Island**. 514 Taylors Island Road. (410) 228-9094. Casual waterfront dining with a varied menu including salads, chargrilled hamburgers and steaks, homemade soups and desserts, hand-cut fries, and seasonal seafood specialties. Anything named Island Grill or Jerk Chicken is wonderful. Most everything is under $7.00 for lunch. Nice local atmosphere and service. The old building used to be a tomato picking house and a general store.

COMFORT INN. Salisbury. 2701 North Salisbury Blvd., US 13 north. (410) 543-4666 or **www.comfortinnsalisbury.com**. Two room family suites and deluxe complimentary continental breakfast are nice features for a fair price. Every room has a small frig and microwave. Only minutes from downtown attractions and 20 miles from Ocean City. Located right in the middle of a huge shopping complex.

BAYSIDE INN. **Smith Island**. Bayside Inn restaurant is a favorite lunch spot. Order individual entrees or family-style meals. Most seafood lovers order the meal ($19.00) with crab cakes, clam fritters, baked ham, green beans, corn pudding, macaroni salad, coleslaw, stewed tomatoes and the famous Smith Island Cake. (8-10 thin layers of moist, creamy cake between layers of fudge icing). Their soup is really good, too. No matter what you order, you must try the Smith Island Cake!

PRINCESS ROYALE RESORT HOTEL. **Ocean City** - 9100 Coastal Avenue (91st Street on the Ocean). (800) 4-ROYALE or **www.princessroyale.com**. The all-suite hotel (separate bedroom and living room and kitchenette) is in a quieter part of the "strip" yet right on the beach and just minutes away from the busy boardwalk area. Besides being right on the waterfront, families also love the four-story oceanfront glass atrium with olympic-sized indoor pool, hot tub, and arcade games. Up on the roofs you can pay a small fee to play tennis, deck tennis or mini-golf - on the roof! Schooners restaurant and Atrium Café serve food and entertainment and in-house, they have a convenience store and gift shop. A grocery store is across the street for other supplies as you have a small kitchen in your suite for cooking or reheating leftovers. $100-$300 per night depending on season and number of bedrooms.

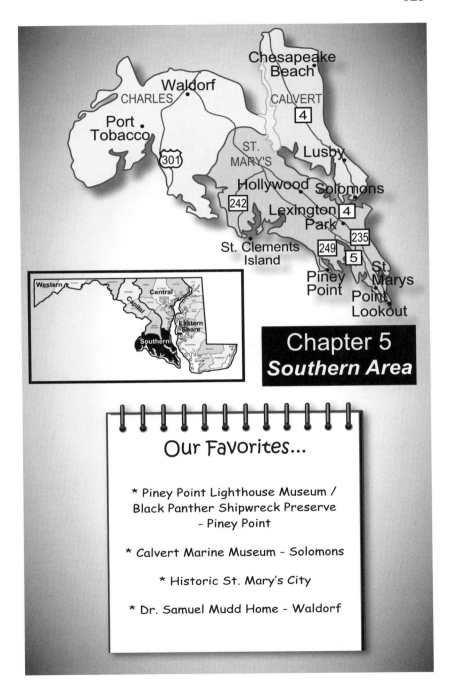

Chesapeake Beach

Waldorf

CHARLES

CALVERT

4

Port Tobacco

301

ST. MARY'S

Lusby

Hollywood

242

Solomons

Lexington Park

4

235

St. Clements Island

249

5

Piney Point

St. Marys Point

Lookout

Western

Central

Capital

Eastern Shore

Southern

Chapter 5
Southern Area

Our Favorites...

* Piney Point Lighthouse Museum / Black Panther Shipwreck Preserve - Piney Point

* Calvert Marine Museum - Solomons

* Historic St. Mary's City

* Dr. Samuel Mudd Home - Waldorf

BREEZY POINT BEACH

Chesapeake Beach - *Breezy Point Road (Rte. 4 south to MD 260 to Chesapeake Beach. Right on MD 261) 20732. Phone: (410) 535-0259. Web: www.co.cal.md.us/ccpr Hours: Daily daylight hours May - October. Admission: $6.00 adult, $4.00 child (under 12).*

A bayfront park featuring swimming, fishing, picnicking and seasonal camping. Explore the beach, swim in the Bay (nettle nets provided), fish for your dinner or picnic in the shade.

CHESAPEAKE BEACH RAILWAY MUSEUM

Chesapeake Beach - *4155 Mears Avenue (next to parking lot of resort area) 20732. Phone: (410) 257-3892. Hours: Daily 1:00-4:00pm (May-September), Weekends only (April and October). Admission: Small fee charged seasonally. Miscellaneous: Summer Children's Programs and evening concerts on summer Thursdays.*

Opened in 1900, this building was the station for a standard gauge railway operating between the District line and Chesapeake Beach. The station service ended in 1935. The site now houses a museum of bay resort and railroad memorabilia. Some rail cars are parked outside and open to look through. Because this is right in the midst of the "action" attractions of town, it's an easy stop to fit into your visit.

CHESAPEAKE BEACH WATERPARK

Chesapeake Beach - *4079 Gordon Stinnett Avenue (Rte. 261, right on Gordon Stinnett) 20732. Web: www.chesapeake-beach.md.us Phone: (410) 257-1404. Hours: Weekends May-September. Daily 11:00am-7:00pm, when County school is out. Weather permitting. Admission: $16.00-$18.00 (age 2+). Good discounts for county and city residents.*

Eight water slides, fountains, waterfalls, a lagoon, kids' activity pool, water volleyball area, and more treat everyone to a cool time. The adjacent recreational center houses a gym for casual games of basketball or dances, a game room with pool table, meeting rooms with windows over-looking the water, and much more.

ST. CLEMENTS ISLAND MUSEUM

Colton's Point - *38370 Point Breeze Road (Rte. 5 to Morganza and turn west onto Rte. 242. On the mainland overlooking the island) 20626. Web: www.stmarysmd.com/recreate/museums/stclementsisland.asp* *Phone: (301) 769-2222. Hours: Monday- 9:00am-5:00pm; Weekends Noon-5:00pm (spring/summers) and Wednesday-Saturday Noon-4:00pm (fall/winters). Admission: $1.50-$3.00 (age 6+).*

The museum rests on the east shore of the Potomac River overlooking ST. CLEMENTS ISLAND STATE PARK, the "Birthplace of Maryland." The Museum itself focuses on the English history

An early colonist

that preceded the voyage to Maryland - mostly for political and religious issues. Discover the vision of George Calvert, the First Lord Baltimore, to begin a colony of religious tolerance and his sons' implementation of this plan (he died before they set sail). Learn about the voyage of the Ark and the Dove departing from the Isle of Wight in England on the feast day of

The Birthplace of Maryland

St. Clement, the patron saint of mariners. Dress up in Colonial clothes to pose with Lord Baltimore. You'll view a priest's written account of the voyage and landing on the Island - even the early negotiations with the Native Americans for a permanent settlement. How was the yucca plant used as detergent? The Potomac River portion shares the heritage of industries in hunting, crabbing, fishing and oystering.

a huge punt gun mounted on a boat for duck hunting

Also on the grounds, the Little Red Schoolhouse is an authentic 19th century one-room school for viewing, set up as if students were out on recess. A dory boat watercraft is on display and the fishing dock outside lures many fishermen. Look for unusual marine life like skate and jelly fish – or maybe try to catch the infamous blue crab swimming by.

GREENWELL STATE PARK

Hollywood - (Rte. 245 to Steerhorn Neck Road) 20636. Phone: (301) 373-9775. Web: www.dnr.state.md.us/publiclands/southern/greenwell.html

The park consists of land along the Patuxent River and features ten miles of hiking, equestrian and cycling trails, as well as a fishing pier. The focal point of the park is Rosedale Manor House with spectacular river views. The Francis Knott Lodge offers overnight accommodations for groups. There's a beach and swimming.

SOTTERLEY PLANTATION

Hollywood - 44440 Sotterley Wharf Road (Rt. 4 to Solomons, cross the Thomas Johnson Bridge, go to Rt. 235 and turn right heading north 4-5 miles to Rt. 245) 20636. Phone: (301) 373-2280. Web: www.sotterley.org Hours: Tuesday-Saturday 10:00am-4:00pm, Sunday Noon-4:00pm. (May-October). Admission: $5.00-$8.00 per person (age 6+).

Located on the banks of the Patuxent River, this very early 18th - century Tidewater Plantation features an architecturally significant manor house of unique post-in-ground construction and fine Georgian woodwork. Sotterley was home to generations of prominent families including that of the third Governor of Maryland, and later, that of financier J.P. Morgan. It was also home to hundreds of anonymous slaves. The 90-acre site includes gardens with panoramic views of the river, a smokehouse, a "necessary", a 1757 Customs Warehouse, a rare extant slave cabin and nature trails.

ST. MARY'S RIVER STATE PARK

Leonardtown - (Rte. 5 to Camp Cosoma Road) 20634. Phone: (301) 872-5688. Web: www.dnr.state.md.us/publiclands/southern/stmarysriver.html Hours: Dawn to dusk.

Situated at the north end of the St. Mary's River watershed, evidence indicates that Indians lived in the region dating back to 3,000 BC.

Arrowheads, axe heads, and pottery can still be found along the stream banks. In 1634, English settlers founded the first colony, named St. Mary's City, near the mouth of the St. Mary's River. At the time of the industrial era, the nearby town of Great Mills relied on the river for power. Birding, fishing and trails are on the developed side of the land.

PATUXENT RIVER NAVAL AIR MUSEUM

Lexington Park - *22156 Three Notch Road (intersection of Rte 235 & Pegg Road, Gate 1 of the Warfare Center) 20653. Phone: (301) 863-7418. Web: www.paxmuseum.com Hours: Tuesday-Sunday 10:00am-5:00pm. Admission: FREE*

This is the only museum in the USA dedicated to preserving the rich heritage of the research, development, test and evaluation (RDT&E) of Naval Aircraft. Indoor exhibits specialize in aircraft models, propulsion systems, the development of the helmet and simulator flight trainers. Kids especially like the history of the ejection seat display. The Flight Deck outside displays actual modern aircraft - so many familiar planes lined up, it looks like a movie scene. With names like Hornet, Tomcat and Stallion, your kids may want to guess names or create new ones. If you wonder what they really do here - the process of testing new equipment is broken down for you. Some tests are ground-based and some are in-flight activities. A trained Navy or Marine Corps test pilot, who has graduated from the US Navy Test Pilot School at Patuxent River, is assigned to fly the test missions. The test team plans for, collects and evaluates Test Data. Not as glamorous inside, the outside display is probably the most fun for kids to look at.

CALVERT CLIFFS STATE PARK

Lusby - *9500 HG Trueman Hwy (Rte 4 south, 14 miles south of Prince Frederick look for the park sign off HG Trueman Hwy) 20657. Web: www.dnr.state.md.us/publiclands/southern/calvertcliffs.html Phone: (301) 743-7613. Hours: Daily sunrise to sunset. Admission: $3.00 donation requested. Miscellaneous: Don't want to hike the trail and hunt for fossils? An indoor replica exhibit is at the Calvert Marine Museum.*

A hike through this wooded state park brings you to the majestic Calvert Cliffs on the Chesapeake Bay. Formed in ancient times, the cliffs contain more than 600 species of fossils. The park is ideal for hiking and walking, picnicking, fishing, and fossil hunting. At the entrance there is a wonderful tire park for children and a pond for fishing. There is a 45-minute walk one-way (two miles) to the beach. Fossil collecting can still be done along the open beach near the cliffs. The beach area is small and you need to be watchful of falling clay from the cliffs - especially after heavy storms.

FLAG PONDS NATURE PARK

Lusby - (N. Solomons Island Road, Rte. 2 & 4 south, 10 miles past Prince Frederick) 20657. Phone: (410) 586-1477. Web: www.calvertparks.org Hours: Daily 9:00am-6:00pm, weekends until 8:00pm (summer). Weekends only (rest of year). Admission: $4.00-$6.00 per vehicle.

Visitors frequently find ancient fossils deposited from the Calvert Cliffs. Several miles of trails lead you through a variety of habitats from upland forest, wooded swamps, open marshes and to the beach dune community typical of the Eastern Shore or the Carolinas. The half-mile walk to the beach takes you past relics of a pound net fishery operation from the early 1950s. The Museum has a Pound-Net Fishing Exhibit interpreting the fishery camp. A fisherman's shanty, the "Buoy Hotel No. 2," clearly demonstrates the camp. From there a "Fisherman's Trail" leads to other historical sites in the park.

SMALLWOOD STATE PARK

Marbury - 2750 Sweden Point Road, off MD 224   20658. Phone: (800) 784-5380. Web: www.dnr.state.md.us/publiclands/southern/smallwood.html Hours: Sunday 1:00-5:00pm (May-September).

This is the site of General William Smallwood's Retreat home. Smallwood was a Revolutionary War officer and fourth governor of Maryland. Guided tours by costumed docents or attend a Military exhibition. Marina has great access to the Potomac River. Nearby is the PURSE STATE PARK (Rte. 224 on Riverside Road, 301-743-7613) where fossilized sharks teeth, bones and shells are often found along the water's edge during low tide. The beach is basically nonexistent during high tide. Be sure to venture out during low tide.

PINEY POINT LIGHTHOUSE MUSEUM & THE BLACK PANTHER SHIPWRECK PRESERVE

Piney Point - 44701 Lighthouse Road (SR 5 south to Waldorf, thru to Calloway. Turn right on Rte. 249, then right at the lighthouse) 20674. Phone: (301) 769-2222. Web: www.stmarysmd.com/recreate/museums/ppl.asp Hours: Museum open Friday-Monday from Noon-5:00pm. Shipwreck preserve for diving open Friday-Monday only (May-October). Admission: $1.50-$3.00 (ages 6+).

Due to Hurricane Isabel a few years ago, the museum exhibits and building had to be replaced or moved. Exhibits now focus on the construction and operation of the lighthouse, the role of the United States Coast Guard, and the attraction of the Piney Point area as a get away for the social elite. Divers are interested in the story of the Black Panther U-1105 German submarine sunk in the Potomac that now serves as Maryland's first historic shipwreck dive preserve. Also

a huge bell, and a rubber hammer...who could resist?

on campus is the building that houses the collection of four historic wooden vessels: a skipjack, a bugeye, a log canoe, and a Potomac River dory boat - all used on this River over time. Exhibits focus on the life of the watermen who sustained a livelihood working the waters of the Potomac for crabs, fish and oysters. The Lighthouse grounds and pier are designed for exploring and the lighthouse itself is open to climb during museum hours. Perfect time to come and wander the grounds is near sunset. Known as the "lighthouse of Presidents", James Madison, Abraham Lincoln and Theodore Roosevelt were among the Presidents who visited Piney Point in its days as a resort for Washington dignitaries.

AMERICAN CHESTNUT LAND TRUST

Port Republic -   20676. Phone: (410) 586-1570. Web: www.acltweb.org
Hours: Dawn to dusk.

Fifteen miles of serene hiking trails open to the public in two locations. Port Republic (South Trail) and Prince Frederick (North trail). Much of this land was once rich tobacco and crop farming acreage. The cash crop was supplemented by hunting, trapping, and fishing that was easily supported by nearby woods, marshes, and waterways. Guided canoe trips are on the beautiful Parker's Creek, spring through fall. FREE.

THOMAS STONE NATIONAL HISTORIC SITE

Port Tabacco - 6655 Rosehill Road 20677. Web: www.nps.gov/thst Phone: (301) 392-1776. Hours: Wednesday-Sunday 9:00am-5:00pm. Daily each summer. Admission: FREE

Ranger-Led tours of Haberdeventure, Thomas Stone's home, are offered as insight into the sacrifices of a signer of the Declaration of Independence. In 1770, when Thomas Stone began the construction of his home, he was a modest family man with a career as a lawyer and local political figure. Haberdeventure, which literally translates as a "dwelling place of or in the winds", was built by Thomas Stone to be the home he would raise his family in.

But, in 1776, Thomas Stone's world changed, no longer just a country lawyer, by signing the Declaration of Independence he had literally written himself into American History. Thomas Stone spent the rest of his life in public service which necessitated moving his family to Annapolis. The home remained in the family. Visitors are also welcome to experience the park at their own pace to stroll across the park grounds amidst the farm buildings or travel old farm trace roads and imagine the past. The park contains the restored home of Thomas Stone, outbuildings and family cemetery. Both Stone and his wife are buried here. A Visitor Center features exhibits, an orientation film, sales area and restrooms. Admission to the park is free.

BATTLE CREEK CYPRESS SWAMP SANCTUARY

Prince Frederick - Grays Road (Rte. 4 south, right on Sixes Rd (MD506), turn left on Grays Rd, 1/4 mile on right) 20678. Phone: (410) 535-5327. Web: www.calvertparks.org Hours: Tuesday-Saturday 10:00am-5:00pm, Sunday 1:00-5:00pm (April-September). Closes at 4:30pm rest of year. Admission: FREE

This unique ecological area is the northernmost naturally occurring stand of bald cypress trees in America. A sub-tropical tree found mostly in the Carolinas and Southeast, cypress stands are unusual this far north. This stand is believed to have established itself sometime in the last 10,000 years. Early settlers in the county, especially boat builders, discovered that cypress wood does not break down readily from bacterial or fungal infection and is virtually rot resistant underwater. A 1/4 mile elevated boardwalk trail meanders through the 100-foot canopy of trees that can reach an age of over 1,000 years. Such swamps were prevalent during the age of mammoths. The Nature Center contains live animals and exhibits about their environment. Live animal demonstrations are often offered.

POINT LOOKOUT STATE PARK

Scotland - (junction of Chesapeake Bay & Potomac River, Rte. 5) 20687. Web: www.dnr.state.md.us/publiclands/southern/pointlookout.html Phone: (301) 872-5688. Hours: Dawn to dusk. Admission: $3.00-$4.00 per vehicle.

Point Lookout lies at the tip of the county peninsula at the confluence of the Potomac River and the Chesapeake Bay. In addition to its historic Civil War Museum (Point Lookout sponsors historic programs and demonstrations throughout the year) and a Nature Center, the park offers abundant recreational opportunities for canoeing, kayaking, and boating, fishing and crabbing, beaching and swimming, cycling and hiking. The site offers camping and cabins for rental.

LIGHTHOUSE & CIVIL WAR MUSEUM: Point Lookout served as a watch post to warn of British ships traveling the Chesapeake Bay during the Revolutionary War and the War of 1812. Point Lookout Lighthouse was built in 1830 to aid in navigating the Chesapeake Bay (access to the lighthouse is very limited). During the Civil War, Point Lookout served as a Union hospital and a prison camp for captured Confederate soldiers. The site features a Civil War museum and the remains of Fort Lincoln.

ANNMARIE GARDEN

Solomons - 13480 Dowell Road (Rte. 4 south, left on Dowell Rd. at Solomons Firehouse) 20688. Phone: (410) 326-4640. Web: www.annmariegarden.org Hours: Daily 9:00am-5:00pm. Pets allowed except during special events. Admission: FREE. Small fee during some events.

This garden is a 30-acre public sculpture park featuring an inviting paved path through the woods past works of outdoor sculpture. Notice the seasonal changes reflected in outdoor art. Some sculptures are gates or ramps. Two favorite works, The Council Ring and A Surveyor's Map invite the guest into the art to walk on, touch, read, and explore how art and nature complement each other. The Tribute to the Oyster Tonger piece is a local heritage favorite. Many families like biking, picnicking or walking the trails. Look for the Garden of Lights in December.

CALVERT MARINE MUSEUM

Solomons - 14200 Solomons Island Road (Rte 4 south, take the right lane exit just before the Bridge, go left at the stop sign and drive 1/2 block) 20688. Phone: (410) 326-2042. Web: www.calvertmarinemuseum.com Hours:

Daily 10:00am-5:00pm. Admission: $7.00 adult, $6.00 senior (55+), $2.00 child (5-12) - Museum and outdoor exhibits. $7.00 adult and $4.00 child for boat ride. Oyster House viewing is FREE. Miscellaneous: The COVE POINT LIGHTHOUSE is accessible via a shuttle bus from the Museum, or a drive a few miles north. Tour a piece of history at the oldest continuously working lighthouse in Maryland. Built in 1828, the forty-foot brick tower is surmounted by an iron lantern containing a fourth-order lens. In addition to the light tower and keeper's house,

buildings at the station include a 1901 fog signal building, a brick generator/
fog signal building and a two-bedroom cottage. Tours seasonally are $3.00
per person. Self-guided tours are free. Groups can overnight here.

The rich maritime history and diversity of life found in the Bay come alive in this wonderful museum set on land and water. Inside the museum, you'll find boats, models, woodcarvings, oysters and crabbing history, fossils and the incredible Skates and Rays exhibit. Do you know what a Mermaid's Purse is? See live skate embryo in various stages of development inside the purses and a new baby skate, too! Another "Wow" area is the Paleo Hall! The prehistoric skeleton of a shark greets you

Learning sailors' knots

as you try to place clues together to determine how the animals died. The Treasure From the Cliffs area is where trained scientists (and volunteers) are working on current specimens for display. If you're interested, they may invite you into their lab to help. A "hands-on" Discovery Room for children of all ages (preschool to adult) features a touch tank housing creatures from the Chesapeake Bay. The plumbing and systems required to operate the tank

It was scary just standing by this mouth..

and keep the creatures alive are in plain view, allowing interpreters to explain how they work to mimic the natural environment. One of the exciting features in the Discovery Room is a model of the Cove Point Lighthouse. Visitors are able to climb inside to activate the light, or dress as lighthouse keepers and enter the

Discovering fossilized clues of the past...

keeper's cottage. A boat made especially for kids is here for children to practice their

voyaging skills as they climb aboard, raise and lower the sail, or steer the tiller. In the paleontology zone, a segment of the Calvert Cliffs will emerge from the mural that decorates the entire wall. At the foot of the cliff, visitors can search for fossils in the beach box and then take their treasures to a fossil identification station to learn about the creature it came from in prehistoric times. And the best part, you get to take your fossil find home as a souvenir!

Outdoors find a boat basin, River Otter habitat, and a recreated salt marsh, complete with a boardwalk over to DRUM POINT LIGHTHOUSE. Climb up through the hatch of the Lighthouse constructed in 1883 at Drum Point to mark the entrance to the Patuxent River. This screwpile, cottage-type light is one of only three remaining that once served on the Chesapeake Bay. Beautifully restored, complete with furnishings of the early 20th century, it has become a popular attraction . . . probably because the keeper's house is actually part of the

A unique lighthouse... and a very loud bell..!

tower. By far, this is the most family-friendly maritime museum we have ever visited!

CHESAPEAKE BIOLOGICAL LAB VISITORS CENTER

Solomons Island - Charles Street (Rte 4 south, take the right lane exit just before the Johnson Bridge. Left at stop sign, right at MD 2) 20688. Phone: (410) 326-7443. Web: www.cbl.umces.edu Hours: Tuesday-Sunday 10:00am-4:00pm. (mid-April to mid-December). Admission: FREE

Founded by a zoologist, now a part of the UM Center for

Environmental Science, its mission is to educate college students and the community about the ongoing exploration of the natural world. Experience the true scientific atmosphere of the research facility, learn about the ecology and resources from the Chesapeake Bay and the important discoveries of CBL scientists. The Visitors center is at the end of the island, overlooking the bay. A Welcome Video briefly recounts the history of CBL's founding, introduces the exhibits in the Center, and reviews the basic principles of Chesapeake Bay ecology. A series of both permanent and changing displays highlight Ongoing Research Projects. An Oyster Reef Community Display and Aquarium illustrates marine life associated with oyster reefs. A station devoted to BAYPULSE, illustrates some of the new remote sensing and electronic technologies upon which today's scientists depend. A Research Fleet & GEAR Display focuses on an exhibit of traditional and historical sampling equipment and there's an Oyster Bar Reconstruction and Seagrass Replenishment Display.

J.C. LORE & SONS OYSTER HOUSE

Solomons Island - 14430 Solomons Island Road (just south of the Calvert Mairne Museum) 20688. Web: www.calvertmarinemuseum.com Phone: (410) 326-2042. Hours: Daily 10:00am-4:30pm (June-August). Weekends and holidays (May and September). Admission: FREE

Visit this restored 1934 seafood-packing house and learn about the boom and decline of the region's commercial seafood industries. The orientation film is made from actual pictures from the mid-1900s. Can you believe all of those shells lying around?? Imagine yourself as a shucker paid by the gallon. Now, stand in the actual workroom. We learned they liked to sing as they worked. In realistic settings, you'll see the tools and gear used by local watermen to harvest fish, soft-shell clams, eels, crabs and oysters. The boat building exhibit, located on the second level of the Oyster House, portrays the present traditions of wooden work-boat building in the region. The dock outside is teeming with boats and sea critters that summer here - jellyfish, oysters and crab. Quite interesting.

HISTORIC ST. MARY'S CITY

St. Marys City - (SR 5 & Rosecroft Road, south of Leonardtown) 20686. Phone: (240) 895-4990. Web: www.stmaryscity.org Hours: Wednesday-Sunday 10:00am-5:00pm (mid-March thru November). Closed Thanksgiving Day. Admission: $10.00 adult, $8.00 seniors (60+) and student, $3.50 child (6-12). Audio tour rentals are an additional $3.00. Miscellaneous: Hands-on activities are offered at most sites. Special events occur on weekends - kids have the chance to work alongside pro archaeologists (they're currently working on rebuilding original sites for a chapel and print shop), churn butter, watch a militia drill, or shoot a bow and arrow.

At Historic St. Mary's City, colorful costumed interpreters appear in recreated 17th-century settings to tell stories about Maryland's first

years, when St. Mary's was the colony's capital. You're encouraged to interact with the first person "characters" as you discuss the 1600s and talk to colonists eager to share advice for surviving the seasons and making a new home in the Americas.

Splitting logs for fence slats...

Outdoor exhibits include the reconstructed State House of 1676, Smith's Ordinary (find out what colonists did for entertainment), and the Godiah Spray Tobacco Plantation, a working colonial farm. The wonderful plantation tour treats you, the guest, as a new colonist in this fair land. Tobacco - why was it so cool back then? - more popular than coffee or chocolate. Reenactors use the children to split logs, properly greet one another, pick herbs, or use balm as furniture polish. At the village's Woodland Indian Hamlet, visitors discover how Maryland's native population interacted positively with English Colonists.

Sailors' stories of the tobacco trade and immigration resound across the deck of the Maryland Dove, a replica square-rigged ship. What was it like? Where did you sleep? What did they eat? The site offers 5 miles of wooded and waterside trails, too. Did you know St. Marys City was the location of the first printing press in the south and the first Catholic chapel in English America? Ghost and recreated structures are forever appearing on the property. Very interactive, professional docents make this attraction a must family day trip.

Viewing the Maryland Dove...

PISCATAWAY INDIAN MUSEUM
& TRADING POST

Waldorf - 16816 Country Lane 20601. Web: www.PiscatawayIndians.org Phone: (301) 372-1932. Hours: Sunday from 11:00am-4:00pm. Miscellaneous: American Indian Pow-wow is held annually the first week in June.

Exhibits that offer a look into the history and culture of the Piscataway and other native people of the U.S. are found in the Piscataway Indian Museum. Each exhibit contains historical and contemporary artifacts from the Eastern Woodlands, Plains, Northwest, and Southwest, while demonstrating how location influenced tribal structure, art and lodging. Other items on display reveal the importance of animals and plants in Piscataway life. A major attraction of the museum is the full-scale reconstruction of a longhouse, the very type of home used by the Piscataways when first contact was made with the Europeans. Found inside the longhouse are items that would have been common at the time of European contact, such as deer and fox pelts, tobacco leaves, bow and arrows, and medicine pouches. During your visit, you are encouraged to stop by the Piscataway Trading Post, a gift shop that includes a variety of native arts and crafts. Did you know this land was once sacred hunting ground?

DR. SAMUEL MUDD HOME

Waldorf (Beantown) - 3725 Dr. Samuel Mudd Rd (SR 5 South, off Poplar Hill Rd) 20601. **Web: *www.somd.lib.md.us/museums/mudd.htm*** *Phone: (301) 645-6870. Hours: Wednesday, Saturday & Sunday 11:00am-4:00pm, last tour begins at 3:30pm. (April - late November) Admission: $5.00 adult, $1.00 child (6-16).*

After leaving the Surratt tavern, Booth arrived early the morning of April 15 at the Mudd's house. Dr. Mudd set Booth's broken leg, had crutches made and sent Booth and his friend, Herold upstairs to a bedroom to sleep. Mudd had met Booth on several occasions before - some say discussing Confederate matters, others claim they were social or business-related meetings. Docents at the house, now a museum, stress Mudd's side of the story. Mudd didn't recognize Booth in the dim lighting and didn't know of the assassination until

a house with so much important history...

later. The original red plush couch where Booth first sat in the parlor and the bedroom where he slept can be seen on the tour. Booth left the Mudd property by horseback down a plantation road, which you can still see behind the house. At his trial, Mudd was convicted of aiding in the death of Lincoln and received a life sentence at Fort Jefferson Prison (see *Kids Love Florida*). Articles made by Dr. Mudd while incarcerated at the Dry Tortugas prison are on view throughout the house. The game table, secretary table, and jewelry boxes (made with shells and wood from the deserted island). President Andrew Johnson pardoned Mudd in 1869, after Mudd helped save the lives of prisoners and guards during a yellow fever epidemic. Mudd returned home to his wife and they had more children.

SUGGESTED LODGING AND DINING

HAMPTON INN. **Lexington Park** - 22211 Three Notch Road, Route 235. (301) 863-3200 or **www.hampton-inn.com**. The Hampton Inn Lexington Park hotel is located across from the Patuxent River Naval Air Station Gate 1 in Lexington Park, Maryland. The hotel is about one mile north of the Central Business District and 8 miles southwest of Solomon's Island. Clean, spacious rooms and wonderful beds. Guests also enjoy the following complimentary items: On the House™ hot breakfast, Hampton's On the Run™ breakfast bags (Monday-Friday), high speed internet access in every room, wireless internet access in the lobby. Their breakfast bars are so fresh and plentiful! Outdoor pool, too.

EVANS SEAFOOD. **St. George Island** - Route 249. (301) 994-2299 or **www.evansseafood.com**. Serving local homemade favorites for 40 years. Locals and visitors can drive, walk or boat up to the fishing pier for good seafood with a nice river view. Seafood, steaks, and chicken. Their sides are OK but save your appetite for some awesome seafood. Crab is best here. Lunch/Dinner on weekends. Dinner weekdays, except closed on Mondays.

LINDA'S CAFÉ. **St. Mary's County** - Lexington Park, Route 235. (301) 862-3544 or Leonardstown Town Square, Rte. 245, (301) 475-5395. Home cooked meals - their specialty is an 8 oz. Hamburger smothered with onions and gravy. Good homemade soups, too. Lots of flavor. Very fair pricing and large servings. Breakfast all day. Lunch and dinner.

STONEY'S KINGFISHERS SEAFOOD HOUSE. **Solomon's Island**. 14442 Solomons Island Rd. **www.stoneysseafoodhouse.com** (410) 394-0236. On the water in a favorite marine side town is a nice place to walk to/from the Calvert Marine Museum. Try a Crabcake or Baby Crabcake. Babies are the size of baseballs, regular, the size of softballs - literally! Also liked the Broomes Island Crab Soup. The Kids Menu has PB&J plus shrimp or grilled cheese plates. Watching the boaters come in is a favorite pasttime while waiting for your food.

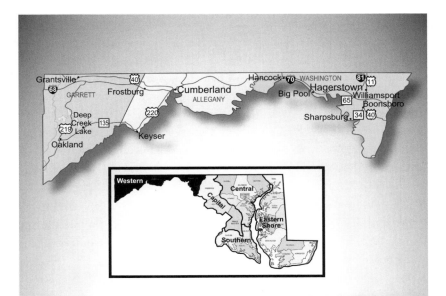

Chapter 6
Western Area

Our Favorites...

* Canal Place Heritage Area - Cumberland
* Husky Power Dogsledding - Deep Creek Lake
* WISP Resort - Deep Creek Lake
* Deep Creek Lake Area
* Hagar House & Hagerstown City Park
* Sideling Hill - Hancock
* Swallow Falls State Park - Oakland
* Simon Pearce Glassblowing - Oakland
* Antietam Battlefield - Sharpsburg

FORT FREDERICK

Big Pool - *11100 Fort Frederick Road (18 miles west of town - one mile south of I-70 (Rte. 56 exit 12) 21711. Phone: (301) 842-2155. **Web:** www.dnr.state.md.us/publiclands/western/fortfrederick.html Hours: Daily 8:00am-sunset (April-October). Monday-Friday 8:00am-sunset; weekends 10:00am-sunset (November-March). Closed major winter holidays. Admission: $3.00-$4.00 per person. Weekends in April, May, September, October. Daily Memorial Day-Labor Day. Miscellaneous: Programs include a Memorial Day weekend anniversary reenactment and Colonial Children's Day in June - probably the best time to visit.*

The massive stone fort, Fort Frederick, was built by the colony of Maryland in 1756 to protect the frontier settlers during the French and Indian War. It also served as a prison camp for Hessian soldiers during the Revolutionary War. Union troops used it during the Civil War as a post. Later, for several generations, the fort was farmed by a family of free-African Americans. The nearby C&O Canal runs through the park. The visitor center offers a 10 minute orientation film, "Legacy of Fort Frederick," upon request. Exhibits highlight aspects of the park's history. Summertime and weekends, costumed interpreters orient and answer questions about life with the fort walls during 4 different time periods or wars. The park also features a boat launch, cross country skiing, camp sites, camp store, food and beverage, fishing, flat water canoeing, hiking trail, historic interest, picnic, playground, shelters, and visitor's center. The Wetlands Trail, 1/3 mile in length, passes along a wetlands area behind the campground.

CRYSTAL GROTTOES CAVERNS

Boonsboro - *19821 Shepherdstown Pike, Rte. 34 (one mile south of Alt. Hwy 40, six miles from Antietam) 21713. Phone: (301) 432-6336. Hours: Daily 9:00am-6:00pm (April-October); Weekends only 11:00am-4:00pm (November-April). www.goodearthgraphics.com/showcave/md/crystal.html Admission: Call for current rates.*

Maryland's only commercial underground caverns feature many pure white-colored stalactites and stalagmites; natural sculptures and other formations that can be seen from illuminated walkways, including 'Old Father Time,' 'The King on His Throne,' and the cathedral ceiling chandelier in the 'Crystal Palace' room. The Lake Room contains a reflecting pool that shows off stalactites on a 16-foot ceiling that is out of the visitor's line of view. Well-informed guides explain the history, formations, and geological aspects of the caverns on a 40-minute tour. The walkways are dry with only a few stairs and a graded ramp at the exit, making Crystal Grottoes one of the easiest show caves to visit.

GREENBRIER STATE PARK

Boonsboro - 21843 National Pike (I-70 exit 42, Rte. 17 north thru Myersville. Turn left onto US 40 for 3 miles) 21713. Phone: (301) 791-4767. Web: www.dnr.state.md.us/publiclands/western/greenbrier.html Hours: Daily 8:00am-sunset. Admission: $3.00-$4.00 per person (summers); $3.00 per vehicle (rest of year). Out-of-state residents add $1.00 to all day use service charges.

Located in the Appalachian Mountains, this state park offers many recreational opportunities. The man-made freshwater lake offers swimming, sunbathing, boating and fishing opportunities. There are also hiking trails which meander through a variety of wildlife habitats and afford a view of the area's geological history. Picnic tables and grills and playgrounds are available in the day-use area.

SOUTH MOUNTAIN STATE BATTLEFIELD

Boonsboro - Park Office is at Alt.40 at Turners Gap @ Washington Monument (the battlefield stretches for 7 miles along the back of South Mountain between Washington & Gathland State Parks) 21713. Phone: (301) 791-4767. Web: www.dnr.state.md.us/publiclands/western/southmountain.html Hours: Daily 8:00am-4:00pm, weather permitting. Admission: FREE

Maryland's first battlefield! Fought September 14, 1861, the Battle of South Mountain was the first major battle of the Civil War to be fought in Maryland, three days *before* Antietam. The battle was the turning point of Lee's Maryland campaign with over 6,000 casualties falling in the long, one-day battle. Hiking (along part of the Appalachian Trail) and picnicking are available.

WASHINGTON MONUMENT STATE PARK

Boonsboro - *(four miles east of Boonsboro and 1 1/2 miles north of Alternate Route 40 on Monument Road) 21713. Phone: (301) 733-0462. Hours: Daily 9:00am-sunset.* ***www.dnr.state.md.us/publiclands/western/washington.html***

Sitting atop South Mountain, this park is home to the first monument built in honor of George Washington. Locals built it from "blue stones" in the area and it is said to be a monument built with "the purest of intentions." In addition, the park offers camping for youth groups, picnicking, and shelters for a rental fee.

GATHLAND STATE PARK & TOWNSEND MUSEUM

Burkittsville - *(junction of Gapland & Arnoldstown Roads, one mile east of MD 67, 1 mile west of town, off MD Route 17) 21718. Phone: (301) 791-4767.* ***Web: www.dnr.state.md.us/publiclands/western/gathland.html*** *Hours: Park open year round; museum open weekends Noon-5:00pm (April-October). Admission: FREE Miscellaneous: Gathland State Park sponsors Civil War living history events featuring individual reenactor units on weekends throughout the year. The annual Civil War weekend, the largest living history event, features artillery firing and infantry demonstrations and is held on the second weekend in September each year.*

Gathland stands atop South Mountain at Crampton's Gap, one of three gaps involved in the Battle of South Mountain in September 1862, two days before the fateful battle of Antietam. George Alfred Townsend, youngest Civil War Correspondent, author and columnist, built a unique estate on the site in the late 1800s and erected a large stone arch in memory of his fellow correspondents, artists and photographers. The museum chronicles Townsend's life and touches on artifacts and replicas of Civil war weapons and uniforms. The Appalachian Trail traverses the park and nature lovers are offered picturesque hiking trails and many picnicking sites.

CANAL PLACE HERITAGE AREA

Cumberland - *Western MD Railway Station, 13 Canal Street (I-68, exit 43C, left at bottom of ramp, then straight) 21502. Phone: (301) 724-3655 or (800) 989-9394.* ***Web: www.canalplace.org*** *Hours: Daily 9:00am-5:00pm. Some* *aspects closed on Monday and Tuesday in winter months. Miscellaneous: Kramers Deli offers quality cold cuts, homemade salads, as well as steaks and specialty sandwiches. Whether you are in the mood to indulge in something new or just want to enjoy some old favorites, Kramer's is open seven days a week for lunch and early dinner, to eat in, take out or order for delivery. (www.kramersdeli.com)*

ALLEGHENY HIGHLANDS TRAIL OF MARYLAND is the 21 mile local section of an interstate hiker/biker trail starting in Pittsburgh and ending in Cumberland. (**www.ahtmtrail.org** or phone 301-777-2161)

C & O CANAL NATIONAL HISTORICAL PARK VISITOR CENTER: Newly-opened, the park features an orientation area with park maps, brochures, and general C&O Canal information. Visitors enter the main exhibit area through a re-created Paw Paw Tunnel (this is a really cool illusion and a great way to get you in the mood). Once inside the main exhibit hall, kids can play in and interact with exhibits related to boat building at the Cumberland boatyards, the Alleghany County coal industry that shipped on the canal and the significance of Cumberland,

inside the giant canal boat...

Maryland as a transportation center. The highlight exhibit is the giant, full size replica Canal Boat (look for the kitchen table, even!) If the kids don't understand how canal lock and dams work, they have an easy video along with mini-diorama to explain it simply. Lots of stations have talking phones that make it fun for kids, too. Great job on display content. (**www.nps.gov/choh** or (301) 722-8226)

CUMBERLAND FULL SCALE C & O CANAL BOAT REPLICA: Located along the Trestle Walk at Canal Place, guides in period clothing discuss the history of the C&O Canal and daily life aboard a canal boat. Visitors can tour the mule shed, hay house, and furnished Captain's cabin. Stand at the tiller and picture yourself on the historic

C&O Canal with a load of coal bound for Georgetown. See how families lived and worked on the canal.

SHOPS AT CANAL PLACE: The Shops at Canal Place offer a unique shopping experience, featuring one-of-a-kind gifts and souvenirs, delectable treats, and fabulous dining. The Shops include Awesome Gifts & Collectibles, Arts at Canal Place, Queen City Creamery, The Crabby Pig, Timeless Treats, Tree House Toy Shop, Wild Mountain Cafe, and Simply Maryland. Hours of individual stores vary.

GEORGE WASHINGTON'S HEADQUARTERS: Riverside Park at Greene Street. One room cabin used by a young George Washington while aiding General Braddock. Built in 1754-55, it is the only remaining structure of Fort Cumberland. (301-777-5132)

CUMBERLAND THEATRE

Cumberland - 101-103 N Johnson Street 21502. Phone: (301) 759-4990. Web: www.cumberlandtheatre.com

Western Maryland's only regional professional theater presents musicals, comedies and dramas, June - December. Most shows are Wednesday-Saturday nights or Wednesday and Sunday afternoons. Tickets run $20.00 per person.

GORDON-ROBERTS HOUSE

Cumberland - 218 Washington Street 21502. Phone: (301) 777-8678. Web: www.historyhouse.allconet.org Hours: Tuesday-Saturday 10:00am-5:00pm. Tours on the hour. Miscellaneous: The Allegheny County Historical Museum is also downtown and open every day but Monday and holidays. Best to visit during special events.

Visitors are welcomed by costumed tour docents that escort them along three floors of the home illustrating the lifestyle of an upper-middle class family of the late 1800's. During Tea Socials, enjoy a soothing cup of tea served by an elegantly costumed server. This 1867 home was built for Josiah Gordon, a President of the C&O Canal. The second family to live in the home was the W. Milnor Roberts family who lived in the home for sixty years and added modern conveniences such as indoor plumbing and an elevator which ran between the first and second floor. A Museum-Explorer tour is offered to school-age children. This tour offers children the opportunity to use clues to find specific items in the house and highlights how people lived, worked, and played in the 1800s. Victoria Mouse House Tour- young visitors will meet Victoria Mouse, The Gordon-Roberts House puppet, and help her gather items to pack for a trip. Items Victoria will need for her trip are pictured on a handout allowing young visitors to look for those items as they tour the museum.

WESTERN MARYLAND SCENIC RAILROAD

Cumberland - 13 Canal Street (2nd floor of Canal Place) 21502. Phone: (301) 759-4400 or (800) TRAIN 50. Web: www.wmsr.com Admission: Basic 3 1/2 hour tours cost around $23.00 for adults and about half price for kids.

The restored early 20th century train steams on a 32-mile round trip through the mountains between Cumberland and Frostburg. Enjoy three centuries of transportation history on scenic excursions or special events (Day out with Thomas week). The scenery is beautiful any time of year and they stop for a short layover in Frostburg to stretch and purchase a treat. We also recommend you purchase or bring coloring books/crayons; travel games and a deck of cards to do along the way (unless the excursion is a themed one with entertainment on board). The Western Maryland Scenic Railroad departs at 11:30am, Thursday-Sunday (May-December).

HUSKY POWER DOGSLEDDING

Deep Creek Lake (Accident) - 2008 Bumble Bee Road (I-68 exit 14A to US 219 south 10 miles to McHenry. At Mosser Road, turn left bear right and then bear left onto Bumble Bee for 2-3 miles) 21520. Phone: (301) 746-7200. Admission: See website for tours. Web: www.HuskyPowerDogsledding.com

Dogsledding is a very popular recreational sport in many northern states, and now can be enjoyed in Maryland all year round! Depending on the time of year (cooler is better), make your arrangements with the enthusiastic and commanding couple who operate this unique business. Why do these dogs prefer cold temperatures? Siberian and Alaskan Huskies love the cold! As you pull down the driveway and they see visitors, they yelp, almost yelling with glee - showing you how excited they are to pull today! An adorable doggy playground! Equally exciting are the yelps and expressions of glee from your kids when they see the beautiful dogs by their individual kennels.

As everyone quickly stumbles out of the vehicle, Linda will begin to describe certain characteristics of the dogs, show you a video about the dogs and their love for mushing, and how they train them to obey commands. All done with the dogs yelping for more hugs, fresh water, or the first chance to be on the pull

Now here's a sign we don't see everyday...

team! The dogs are so healthy and each is adorable with different colored hair, eyes, paws. Each and every dog is named, too. Often the names fit their personality. Zsa Zsa is the female dominant dog of the whole lot - a pampered queen, she gets attention first to show the rest

of the team she's top dog. How do the dogs get chosen for lead, pull or wheel positions (clue: it has to do with how smart they are)? The command "Gee" means what? How about "straight on"? Now, the most memorable part: dog sledding or carting. No Snow? - they still go out on the "Dogsled-on-Wheels" - a specialized cart mushers use to train their dogs when there's no snow. Once the dogs are tied onto the line, they can't wait to be released

The dogs LOVE to run... hang on Jenny!

and pull. Once off, it is peacefully quiet, the only sounds are those of the snow or brush crunching under you, the panting of the dogs eager to run, and the musher's strong calls. You just hold on and relax. Once back at base, the dogs are anxious to be served hearty compliments, hugs and fresh water. What an unforgettable treat!

SMILEY'S FUNZONE PIZZERIA

Deep Creek Lake (McHenry) - (1/2 mile north of Deep creek Bridge on Rte. 219) 21541. Phone: (301) 387-0059. Web: www.smileysfunzone.com Hours: Daily afternoons until 9:00pm or later. Schedule changes seasonally. Admission: FREE. All amusements operate on tickets ($6.00 generally) or an all day wristband (miles of smiles, $30.00).

Whether you're a kid or a kid at heart, you'll love Smiley's. Start outside with Frontier Adventure Golf with greens, traps and water hazards. Or, one of three go-cart tracks, batting cages or Splash & Crash bumper boats. We loved the fact that each activity is monitored by roaming managers and cameras for safety and prevention of rowdy youth acting up. Heading indoors, try Lazer

The race was won by a nose... but who won?

Tag or Lazer Target (ex. Duck hunting), two arcade buildings (with the latest video and redemption games) or Old Time Photography (dress in old time western wear or contemporary magazine cover scenes). After you're exhausted from the activities, re-energize with a snack or a meal. Try Mindy's Monster (almost everything on this pizza) or Smile'n Supreme pizza. They have wings voted the best on the lake and for hot buffalo wings, we agree. Also, soups and salads, appetizers like cheese fries or onion rings or maybe some wonderful homemade spaghetti and meatballs. Sandwich and wraps, too. Their kid's menu has 10 items to select from - all under $4.00.

WISP RESORT AT DEEP CREEK LAKE

Deep Creek Lake (McHenry) - 290 Marsh Hill Road (US 219) 21541. Phone: (800) 462-9477. Web: www.wispresort.com   Admission: Rates as low as $99.00 per night. Adventure Packages as low as $200 for a family (several activities included).

This casual resort has almost too many activities to choose from. Most rooms come with continental breakfast which you need to fill up on to have energy for your day! With energy to burn, either take a dip, play or swim laps in the huge, warm indoor pool, hot tub (the deck has warming lights to keep you cozy and dry faster), fitness center and racquetball courts. Or, venture outside for some extreme sports....

Summer: Wisp Outdoors - experience new adventures each day. Wisp offers water and land sports such as water skiing, paint ball (target or combat), whitewater rafting, rock climbing, golf, kayaking, fly fishing, and disc gulf. Weekend and some evening sunset pontoon rides, bonfires, and

All ready for paintball...

concerts, too. You'll notice many disc golf holes on your way up the scenic chairlift ride - it's long and slow enough to take in the scenery. For another fun adventure, try taking mountain bikes up the lift. With your trail map in hand, try the beginner Possom trail first. Your first ride will probably go slow and you'll use your brakes most of the time. After that, you'll know the trail and can coast more and ride faster (best for kids age 8+ with some bike riding skill). What

Ski slope mountain biking...

fun, though! Grab some lunch at Wispers and then head back out to

cool off on the Summer Tubing ramp - a slippery wet slide. Not too extreme, the whole family can tube. Don't want as much adventure? Try a leisurely pontoon boat tour on the Lake (departs from the Discovery Center). Ask the captain to point out the various restaurants to try and folks who own some beautiful lakefront homes.

Slippery Slope fun...

Winter: 32 slopes and trails of ski-able terrain that includes a new super pipe,

2 RailParks, Terrain Trails and Gardens. Ski Carpet and Tow Ropes, Chairlifts. Cross-country snowshoe and snowmobile tours, snow Tubing and snowboarding.

DEEP CREEK LAKE STATE PARK & DISCOVERY CENTER

Deep Creek Lake (Swanton) - 898 State Park Rd (off US 219 or US 495, follow signs) 21561. Phone: (301) 387-4111 or (301) 387-7067 (center). *www.dnr.state.md.us/publiclands/western/deepcreeklake.html or /discovery.html Hours: Park open 8:00am-sunset. Center open daily 10:00am-5:00pm (summers); weekends rest of year. Admission: FREE to Discovery Center. Day use charges are $3.00 per person (summertime) or $3.00 per vehicle (rest of year). Add $1.00 for out of state residents. Miscellaneous: Feeding programs - "We've got Worms" or Critter Encounter; Scales and Tales outside in the Aviary.*

This park is home to black bear, wild turkey, bobcat and one mile of shoreline along the state's largest lake, with public boat access. Besides staying on the lake and loving the outdoor adventure, the park hosts a great kid-friendly Discovery Center. Children can put their hands in a black bear paw print, touch fossils, and sneak a peek under a microscope to learn about local underwater creatures along the shores of the

lake. The huge center also displays cultural and historical items, a lighted geography map of the Lake, mounted specimens, an aviary, and children's interactive room. Daily, they show live feed video of a bird's nest or underwater fish pond. The Naturalists ("Ammo" and "Frog") love to catch creatures from the park and display them. Look for red-eye bass, American Toads, or a Monarch

This little turtle critter sure was friendly...

butterfly. The Aviary hosts raptors like hawks and the screech owl. The owl has beautiful, big eyes, doesn't he? Check their website to join a planned family hike during your visit.

GREEN RIDGE STATE FOREST

Flintstone - *28700 Headquarters Drive NE (I-68 exit 64) 21530. Web: www.dnr.state.md.us/publiclands/western/greenridge.html Phone: (301) 478-3124.*

Green Ridge is the second largest of Maryland's State Forests consisting of a 44,000-acre oak-hickory forest. The region's average annual precipitation is the lowest in the state -- just 36 inches -- creating pockets of desert-like habitats known as shale barrens. Unusual plants, like the Prickly Pear Cactus, Large Blazing Star and Kate's Mountain Clover are found here. Magnificent views of the surrounding landscape can be seen from Point Lookout, Banners, Logroll, Warrior Mountain and No Name Overlooks. Green Ridge offers a variety of camping and hiking experiences, as well as off-road recreation. Most of the trails are too long to hike completely with kids in tow but you can begin one and turn around before too long. Rich in history, the forest was once the site for the Carroll Furnace, originally built as part of a steam powered saw mill in the 1830's.

FROSTBURG STATE UNIVERSITY PLANETARIUM

Frostburg - *Tawes Hall, Frostburg State University 21532. Phone: (301) 687-4270. Web: www.frostburg.edu/planetarium Hours: Sundays at 4:00 and 7:00pm (September-May). Admission: Small*

The hour-long presentation includes a look at current evening skies and a multi-media show that changes each month.

THRASHER CARRIAGE MUSEUM

Frostburg - *19 Depot Street (I-68 exit 34, Rte. 40 to Depot Street) 21532. Phone: (301) 689-3380 or (301) 777-8678. Web: www.thrashercarriage.com Hours: Wednesday-Saturday 10:00am-4:00pm, Sunday Noon-3:00pm. Admission: $2.00-$4.00 per person (age 7+).*

Travel to a time when craftsmen practiced the art of carriage making. Visit a collection of horse-drawn vehicles representing all walks of

life. Tours led by costumed docents offer a glimpse into the world
of the elegant traveler. Imagine riding in a formal carriage or the
Vanderbilt family sleigh. Stories of the clothing, activities, and
lifestyles of Victorian Americans are interspersed with the fascinating
details of these remarkable vehicles. Special weekends, kids can
participate in hands-on activities such as scavenger hunts, carriage
wheels & whirl-a-gigs.

SAVAGE RIVER STATE FOREST/ NEW GERMANY & BIG RUN STATE PARKS

*Grantsville - 349 Headquarters Lane (US 219 south to Glendale Road,
east. Left on Rte. 495, follow signs) 21536. Phone: (301) 895-5453.* **Web:**
*www.dnr.state.md.us/publiclands/western/newgermany.html Hours: Daily
8:00am-sunset. Admission: $2.00-$4.00 per person on summer weekends,
ski weekends and holidays.*

This is the largest of the state forest and park system facilities. BIG
RUN STATE PARK is situated on the mouth of the savage River
Reservoir. With boat launches nearby, Big Run is a popular base camp
for outdoor lovers intent on fishing, hiking or hunting. Big Run is the
trailhead for a six-mile hiking trail, known as Monroe Run.

NEW GERMANY STATE PARK's lake was formed when Poplar
Lick Run was dammed for, once-prosperous, mill operation. The lake
offers a boat launch, non-motorized boat rentals, swimming, fishing,
flatwater canoeing, hiking, a nature center and cross-country skiing
(rentals available). CASSELMAN RIVER BRIDGE STATE PARK
(Rte. 40) is the namesake for the centerpiece, often photographed, 80
foot stone arch bridge - the longest single-span stone arch bridge in
the country when it was built in 1813. It was reportedly made longer
than it needed to be in hopes that the planned Chesapeake and Ohio
Canal would pass under it. A public celebration was held at the bridge
on the day that workmen removed the supporting timbers. To the
amazement of many, the bridge did not collapse. The railroad and then
modern highways replaced the well-traveled path once used crossing
the bridge.

SPRUCE FOREST ARTISAN VILLAGE

Grantsville - 177 Casselman Road (just off I-68, along the Old National Road) 21536. Phone: (301) 895-3332. Web: www.spruceforest.org Hours: Monday-Saturday 10:00am-5:00pm.

Spruce Forest Artisan Village is a non-profit living museum, where nine contemporary artists, working in restored 19th century log cabins, open their studios to the public. Visitors may also shop in the eight craft galleries, picnic along the Casselman River, and explore other historic buildings, including Stanton's working grist mill, the Miller House, Village Church, and Compton School. Artists in Residence include: metalsmith, potters, bird sculpture; slate painter, weaver, stained glass; and metal sculptor. If you're in the area for a little while, plan ahead to attend art classes.

ANTIETAM RECREATION & WILD WEST SHOWS

Hagerstown - 9745 Garis Shop Road (1-70 take Exit 29 (Route 65 - Sharpsburg Pike) past McDonalds, second left onto Wagaman Road. At the stop sign turn right onto Garis Shop Road) 21740. Phone: (301) 797-3733. Web: www.antietamrecreation.com Shows: Summer - every Saturday evening (June-August). Winter - almost every Thursday, Friday, Saturday (mid-November thru December). Admission: Chuckwagon & Show, plus Activities: $~18.00-$24.00 per person. Miscellaneous: Summer camp is a great place to enjoy swimming, riding, canoeing, kayaking, tennis, games, drama, arts and crafts, and much more. Groups rent the facility on Saturdays and school and home school groups utilize the facility during the month of May and September.

At Antietam Recreation, they specialize in providing active and educational fun in a Christian environment. Summer comes to Maryland with guns A'blazin'! The Wild West Show, featuring World Champion Roper Andy Rotz, runs every Saturday (June-August). These shows include dinner (with fried chicken, potato salad, applesauce, baked beans, rolls, cake and lemonade), followed by outdoor activities like swimming, boating, cable ride, boat slide and other activities, plus the action-packed cowboy drama. You'll see galloping horses, swishing hoop skirts, lively song-and-dance numbers, thrilling stunts, exciting fight sequences, and incredible tricks by our resident cowboy, World

Champion Roper Andy Rotz. It's a dinner theater like none other and great for kids cause they get to play around, too.

DISCOVERY STATION

Hagerstown - 101 West Washington St., downtown (across from the Washington County courthouse, metered parking on street) 21740. Phone: (301) 790-0076. Hours: Tuesday-Saturday 10:00am-4:00pm, Sunday 2:00-5:00pm. Closed Mondays, Sundays in July and August and major holidays. Admission: $7.00 adult, $5.00 senior (55+) and military, $6.00 child (2-17).

This "hands on" learning museum includes exhibits that promote science, technology and local history through displays and programs that are both educational and entertaining. Included is Hagerstown's Aviation Museum, exhibits from Maryland's Science Center, and more. Look for an actual model of a Triceratop skull, see the film

Inside a GIANT safe...

"When Dinosaurs Roamed America" and wonder at the animatronics that recreate Tyrannosaurus Rex. Or, demonstrate how the eye focuses light, how we perceive motion and color, and how the brain processes visual information into a meaningful picture. Look for angels and Cheshire cats that appear and disappear; a solar powered spacecraft or a farm exhibit where you can harvest corn or dig for veggies.

HAGERSTOWN SPEEDWAY

Hagerstown - 15112 National Pke (along US 40 near Clear Spring) 21740. Phone: (301) 582-0640. Web: www.hagerstownspeedway.com

Hagerstown Speedway features several special events throughout its season including AMA Grand National Motorcycles, monster trucks, World of Outlaw Sprint Cars & Late Models, DIRT Modified and MACS late models. The 1/2 mile, semi-banked clay oval and quarter midget track are on location. Weather permitting, the racing season opens in February and continues until the last weekend of October. Mostly Saturday evening events. Admission charged and varies depending upon the event.

HAGERSTOWN SUNS BASEBALL

Hagerstown - 274 E. Memorial Blvd. (Municipal Stadium) 21740. Phone: (301) 791-6266. Web: www.hagerstownsuns.com

The Suns have called this stadium home since 1981, but the history of pro baseball in town dates back many years beginning in the early 1900s with the Blue Ridge League. History was made in 1930 when the great Willie Mays played his first pro baseball game for the Trenton Giants in Hagerstown. Currently, the Suns play in the 14-team South Atlantic League, a long-standing Class A-league and a minor league affiliate of the New York Mets.

MARYLAND SYMPHONY ORCHESTRA (MSO)

Hagerstown - 13 South Potomac Street, downtown (most performances take place at the Maryland Theatre at 21 South Potomac) 21740. Phone: (301) 797-4000. Web: www.mdsymphony.com

The MSO provides high quality performances for the four-state region. Kids especially like the Family Concerts, Annual Salute to Independence and the Holiday Concert.

THE TRAIN ROOM

Hagerstown - 360 South Burhans Blvd. (US 11) (I-81 exit 5) 21740. Phone: (301) 745-6681. Web: www.the-train-room.com Hours: Monday & Friday 9:00am-8:00pm; Tuesday & Thursday 9:00am-6:00pm; Saturday 9:00am-6:00pm; Sunday Noon-6:00pm. Closed Wednesdays. Admission: $4.50 adult, $0.50 child (3-12).

The Train room offers model railroading enthusiasts, collectors and novice alike a completely unique experience. A large display of Lionel® model railroading items in 0.027 and standard gauge. A 20'x12' two level, four track model railroad layout which is the centerpiece. You will also see a large selection of other Lionel Products, Model planes, Geiger counters, science kits, fishing equipment, records, electric fans and hundreds of other items manufactured by Lionel® and its subsidiaries over the years. Although most of them are behind glass in showcases, everything is so colorful and nostalgic. The Science kits are especially interesting (wish you could still get some of them). Bring the grandparents along for stories of toys they loved in their youth.

HAGAR HOUSE & HAGERSTOWN CITY PARK

Hagerstown - 110 Key Street (located in Hagerstown City Park) 21741. Phone: (301) 739-8393. Web: www.hagerhouse.org Hours: Tuesday-Saturday 10:00am-4:00pm, Sunday 2:00-5:00pm. Closed Mondays and the months of January-March. Also closed during the last week of November thru the first Tuesday in December to prepare for Christmas. Admission: $1.00-$3.00 per person (ages 6+). $8.00 per family.

This is the original home of German colonist, Jonathan Hager, founder of Hagerstown. Hager was also known as the first German to make his mark in politics. Built with solid walls and foundation, it was uniquely erected over two springs, and is completely restored with period furnishings. Look for giant wardrobes; pop goes the weasel; a horse's tail fly-swatter; a broom made from one piece of wood; and actually see the cool spring running right thru the house basement. Re-enactors are present for annual Easter, Christmas and Living History Festivals each year.

HAGERSTOWN CITY PARK, nestled in the city's South End, is considered one of America's Most Beautiful. 50 acres of trees, flowers and open spaces surround three man-made lakes that are home to hundreds of ducks, swans and geese. Park facilities include a concession stand, picnic areas, grills, playgrounds, sport courts, walking trails and a restored steam engine. Engine 202 was built by the Baldwin Locomotive Works in 1912. It is the only Western Maryland road-type steam locomotive in existence. Cabooses built in town are available to board and a small museum is open for a small admission. Do you know what a velocipede is? Ask the engineer at the museum to take you up in the Engine 202.

WILSON COUNTRY STORE/ ONE ROOM SCHOOLHOUSE

Hagerstown (Clear Spring) - (Route 40 west just past the Conococheague Creek on Rufus Wilson road) 21722. Phone: (301) 582-4718. Hours: Store: Monday-Saturday 7:30am-6:00pm, Sunday 9:00am-5:00pm. Admission: FREE. Shopping is tempting, though. Miscellaneous: The schoolhouse looks as though the pupils just went to recess. Open by appointment and special events. Call ahead.

Wilson Country Store, built in the 1850s, stocks stuff that you just don't see anymore. The store sells everything from seed potatoes to three brands of liniment salve (what is it? The kids ask?). They also carry a standard assortment of modern groceries. Try some of their cheese selections, too. Locals really love their white cheddar.

C & O CANAL VISITOR CENTER

Hancock - 326 E. Main Street 21750. Web: www.nps.gov/choh/ Phone: (301) 678-5463. Hours: Daily 9:00am-4:30pm Admission: Voluntary donation. Miscellaneous: THE C&O CANAL PAW PAW TUNNEL - and engineering marvel is just south along Rte. 51, right at the Maryland/WV border, across the Potomac River. Thousands of men labored to build this dramatic portal through an entire mountain.

The Chesapeake and Ohio Canal had its beginning in 1828, when President John Quincy Adams broke ground for what was called "The Great National Project", a canal that would stretch from Georgetown, near DC and end in Pittsburgh. The canal would be used to carry goods and supplies inland and aid with the migration of people heading west to settle beyond the original 13 colonies. The estimated cost: about $3 million and would take ten years. When the canal was completed in 1850, it had taken 22 years and $13 million to build, plus it fell short of the original destination of Pittsburgh and ended in Cumberland, Maryland. Worse yet, upon completion, the canal was obsolete because of the railroad. Despite all of this, the canal remained open 74 years. Boats pulled by mules floated tons of cargo, including coal, hay, hydraulic cement and fertilizer from Cumberland to Georgetown. Inside the Visitors Center, relive the canal era through models of canal boats, pictures and memorabilia. Giant trees shade a sandy towpath between the river and the old canal bed, visited by thousands of hikers, bikers, birders, and naturalists who enjoy the spectacular scenery of the park.

SIDELING HILL EXHIBIT CENTER & WILDLIFE MANAGEMENT AREA

Hancock - (off I-68 exit Woodmount Road at the top of Sideling Hill Mountain. 5 miles west of Hancock) 21750. Phone: (301) 678-5442. Web: www.dnr.state.md.us/publiclands/western/sidelinghill.html Hours: Daily 9:00am-5:00pm, except major holidays. Admission: FREE

More than one hundred thousand people annually visit what's been called a geological marvel - one of the best rock exposures in the NW United States. In the early 1980s, a massive project began to construct a roadway. To begin this monumental task, a V-shaped wedge was blasted out of Sideling Hill. More highway construction cut through the mountain exposing almost 850 vertical feet of a textbook example syncline (exposed sedimentary rock formations). There are fossils galore! The Center, at the base of the syncline, is a large facility where trained personnel and geologists are on hand to explain  how color-coded sedimentary layers, curled in an upward swing, explain plate tectonics. It's much more interesting to study science "hands and view-on" (a giant science project). You can even touch a piece of the oldest Maryland rock! If weather permits, take a walk outside up the fenced walkway, to view the cut up close. Several geologic wayside stations help you interpret what you see. A walk over the pedestrian bridge offers good photo opportunities from the middle of the bridge, as well as from the opposite side, south of the road. Why is water and rust seeping from the rock?

Hiking opportunities abound in the Wildlife Management Area (WMA). For outdoor folks, this is a prime spot for mountain scenery and wildlife, especially in the spring when the wildflowers of the forest floor and the mountain laurel bloom. Fall foliage lovers enjoy the colors Some plants ONLY grow here, and are protected by the government. The area also offers fishing and picnicking opportunities.

WESTERN MARYLAND RAIL TRAIL

Hancock - (one mile off I-70 to Rte. 56 or parking lot one mile west of I-70 on Rte. 144 on Main St.) 21750. Web: www.hancockmd.com/wmrt/index.html Phone: (301) 842-2155. Hours: Open year round 8:00am-sunset, weather permitting. Admission: FREE

The Western Maryland Rail Trail provides a unique paved hiking and biking trail built on an abandoned railroad bed. Over 21 miles, the easy-to-access trail extends from Big Pool (near Fort Frederick) to Pearre (foot of Sideling Hill Mountain) paralleling the Potomac River and the C&O Canal. Traveling this trail, hikers, cyclists, joggers and in-line skaters experience the beauty of rolling farmland, abundant wildlife, and history of the surrounding area. Interpretive programs and special events are held throughout the year.

DANS MOUNTAIN STATE PARK

Lonaconing - 17410 Recreation Area Road (I-68 exit 34, Rte. 36 south to Midland) 21539. www.dnr.state.md.us/publiclands/western/dansmountain.html Phone: (301) 463-5487. Hours: Dawn-dusk. Miscellaneous: Dan's Rock is within the park. (left onto Paradise Street Extended, cross bridge and go to the second street (Paradise St) and turn left and go about three miles) LONACONING IRON FURNACE AND PARK is on Rte. 36. The furnace, erected in 1837, used coal and coke rather than charcoal to make iron.

This day-use park has rugged mountain terrain, and an Olympic-size pool with a waterslide. Nearby, Dans Rock is a 2,898 foot rock structure that sprawls along the brow of Dan's Mountain overlooking the panoramic Potomac Valley that stretches for twenty miles. The viewer will be delighted with the colorful foliage and the surrounding rolling mountains from the new 28 foot square observation deck with gazebo. Dan's Mountain received its name after Daniel Cresap, one of the first settlers in the area, who was killed on the mountain.

CRANESVILLE SUBARTIC SWAMP

Oakland - (Cranesville & Lake Ford Rds, just past Deep Creek Lake) 21550. Phone: (301) 387-4386. Web: www.nature.org Hours: Daylight hours

A swamp in Maryland? Walk in the footsteps of prehistoric creatures in the small piece of forest and bog remaining after the Ice Age - wild and still home to a range of species of plants usually found in the extreme northern areas of Alaska and Canada. Home to a bog that contains peat more than three feet deep, plants that eat insects, a conifer that sheds its needles in fall, and an owl that fits in the palm of a hand. Listen for the saw-whet owl's strange, tooting call. A 1,500 foot boardwalk crosses the swamp, and six trails wind through this unusual tundra region. Although all trails are fewer than two miles and not difficult to walk, hiking boots are recommended as some trails may be muddy.

HERRINGTON MANOR STATE PARK

Oakland - *222 Herrington Lane (4 miles past entrance to Swallow Falls) 21550.* ***www.dnr.state.md.us/publiclands/western/herringtonmanor.html*** *Phone: (301) 334-9180. Admission: $2.00 per vehicle, off peak and summer weekdays. $2.00-$3.00 per person summer weekends and ski season weekends. Add $1.00 for non-state residents. Miscellaneous: Summer Wednesday morning hayrides through the park into the outlying forest. $5.00 per person.*

The park features a 53-acre lake and beach for swimming and non-motorized boating (canoe and paddle boat rentals). Other activities include hiking, biking trails, interpretive programs, groomed cross-country ski trails along with ski/snowshoe rentals, and 20 log cabins available to rent.

OAKLAND HERITAGE SQUARE

Oakland - *117 E. Liberty Street (I-68 to exit 14 south 26 miles to junction of US 219 & Rte 135) 21550.* ***Web: www.garrettchamber.com*** *Phone: (301) 334-1243. Hours: Shoppe and Train Station daily 9:00am-5:00pm. Museum daily 10:00am-3:00pm. Admission: Donations accepted.*

There was a time when the train station in Oakland was the busiest place in town. Some of the famous visitors to the 1884 Train Depot were President Ulysses S. Grant and President Benjamin Harrison. President and Mrs. Grover Cleveland, William McKinley and Buffalo Bill Cody have walked through the train station, too. The first train reached Oakland in 1851. Regular passenger train service ended in the early 1970s and the station was used for a while as an office and storage

building for CSX Railways. Now, the elegant Queen Anne style structure has been restored and is the centerpiece of the Heritage Square with other buildings including a hiking/ biking trail, town park, farmer's market, community pavilion, and a handicapped accessible fishing ramp and a kayak/canoe launch. Some of the crafts made by local artisans are displayed and sold in various rooms of the station. Look for some train items, a Fidgit or a catnip play mouse. The indoor play train table and the outdoor railroad caboose are available for kids to play on.

The Garrett County Historical Society Museum (107 S. Second Street) is in an old bank building. Most rooms are decorated for different time periods such as a Victorian era and a log cabin. Ask if they have a scavenger hunt with prize available for the kids to engage. Otherwise, some rooms are a little musty and dim - not intriguing to youth.

PLEASANT VALLEY DREAM RIDES

Oakland - 1689 Pleasant Valley Road (follow 219 3 Miles South of Oakland, Turn Left On Paul Friend Road) 21550. www.pleasantvalleydreamrides.com Phone: (301) 334-1688. Looking for a great family or group activity near Deep Creek Lake Resort? The picturesque area known as Pleasant Valley is the backdrop for your horse drawn tour of the Miller Family Farm. Take a winter sleigh ride or a horse drawn carriage ride and enjoy the pastoral mountain beauty of this Amish community. Tour the agricultural facilities and learn about daily life on an Amish dairy farm. Educational hands-on experiences are included.

Tour the Farm and learn about life on an Amish Dairy Farm. Hand feed cows grain or baby calves using a bottle. No matter what time of day, they will prep a cow and allow you to hand milk it, then put the cow on the milker to demonstrate how a cow is milked today.

POTOMAC-GARRETT STATE FOREST/ BACKBONE MOUNTAIN

Oakland - 222 Herrington Lane (US 219 south to Sand Flat Road, turn east past Rte. 135, through town of Deer Park) 21550. Phone: (301) 334-2038. Web: www.dnr.state.md.us/publiclands/western/potomacforest.html Hours: Dawn to dusk.

Home to the highest point in any Maryland state forest, BACKBONE MOUNTAIN (3,220 feet). A densely forested and serene area, this is a favorite of hikers. This steep gradient has numerous fast falling brooks and streams which feed the river. Don't forget to pick up a certificate near the marker sign confirming that you made it to the highest point in Maryland. (easiest access is from WV Monongahela National Forest; head south on Rte. 219, sign will be on your left). The rest of the forest's public lands are for fishing, primitive camping, 3-D bow range, snowmobile trails and some hiking/biking trails. Activities are of a more primitive nature.

SWALLOW FALLS STATE PARK

Oakland - 222 Herrington Lane (six miles north of town) 21550. Phone: (301) 334-9180. Web: www.dnr.state.md.us/publiclands/western/swallowfalls.html Hours: Daylight hours. Admission: $2.00 per person (summer). $2.00 per vehicle (rest of year). Out of state residents add $1.00 to all service charges. Miscellaneous: Hiking, campground, fishing, picnic area, playground and nature programs (summer).

See some of Maryland's best waterfalls. This mountainous park contains some of the state's most breathtaking scenery. The Youghiogheny River flows along the park's borders, passing through shaded rocky gorges and creating rippling rapids. Muddy Creek Falls is a vivacious 52-foot waterfall surrounded by tall hemlocks and an old forest (possibly over 300 years old).

These falls are the tallest waterfalls in the state and are so accessible. Begin at the trailhead right by the small Visitors center. Walk a short distance on the path and then bear to your right for another short distance on a path lined with soaring hemlocks. Then, begin the  boardwalk portion that leads you to many easy viewing platforms. You can hear the rush of the falls as you approach. The first one is near where Edison, Ford, Firestone and friends once camped in the early 1900s. Another takes you to the top of the falls. Yet another, with wooden steps and platforms, takes you to the bottom of the falls. All observation decks have fantastic views. Once you're at the bottom, the adventure trail begins. Climb over rocks and under small cave overhangings while still on a trail. Remember to bring some water and first aid basics. Few falls are as impressive as locals will tell you - but these trails and falls are!

BROADFORD LAKE RECREATION AREA

Oakland (Mountain Lake Park) - (Rte. 135, Mountain Lake Park & Recreation Lane) 21550. Phone: (301) 334-9222. Web: www.oaklandmd.com/outdoors Hours: Daily 8:00am-sunset. Closed mid-November thru March. Admission: a few dollars per vehicle or person.

This popular family park has a lake, concession stand, picnic and beach area, volleyball, basketball, boat launch, and boat and pavilion rentals. The beach and swimming area is most popular for kids in the area.

SIMON PEARCE GLASSBLOWING

Oakland (Mountain Lake Park) - 265 Glass Drive (Rte. 219 south to Oakland downtown. Then Rte 135 and turn left on Glass Drive) 21550. Phone: (301) 387-5277 or (877) 452-7763. Web: www.simonpearce.com Hours: Daily 9:00am-5:00pm. Admission: FREE

Visitors to the site can take self-guided tours to observe the glassblowers at work. The setup includes a catwalk viewing gallery above the factory floor providing a great "birds-eye" view. Explanatory process sheets and details along the way describe the glassblowing process. Glass vessels began hundreds of years ago in wide variety. Using similar old-world techniques, clear glass is formed by melting, gathering, blowing, shaping, finishing and annealing (cooling very slowly). Art in motion...we were mesmerized! We inquired about all the movements necessary to shape the molten glass. The manager said the artists call it "the dance" - all the twisting and tooling and blowing and cooling synchronized! Did you know the first piece new glass blowers work on is a glass ice cube? Once they've successfully made several hundred, they move on to napkin holders - then the big stuff.

Don't try this at home kids...

ANTIETAM BATTLEFIELD

Sharpsburg - (along MD 34 & 65. Main entrance is off of MD 65, ten miles south of I-70) 21782. Phone: (301) 432-5124. ***Web: www.nps.gov/anti/*** *Hours: Daily 8:30am-5:00pm. Open until 6:00pm summers. Closed only major winter holidays. Admission: $4.00 per person fee or $6.00 per family. Miscellaneous: Be sure to visit the new Pry House Field Hospital Museum. This new museum is located in the historic Pry House which served as Union Commander General George B. McClellan's headquarters during the battle. The museum is sponsored by the National Museum of Civil War Medicine and is open daily 10:00am to 5:00pm.*

The Battle of Antietam on September 17, 1862, climaxed the first of General Robert E. Lee's two attempts to extend the Confederate effort into the North. This peaceful family town was the place where the slow moving giant armies exploded, leaving 23,110 dead and wounded. More men were killed

Peace at this church...

or wounded at Antietam than on any other single day of the Civil War. Visitors can still feel the profound stillness of the battlefields. Although neither side gained a decisive victory, Lee's failure to carry the effort effectively into the North produced two important results: Great Britain postponed the recognition of the Confederate government, and President Abraham Lincoln issued the Emancipation Proclamation on January 1, 1863. "Antietam Visit," an award-winning film, is shown on the hour. This 26-minute movie recreates the battle as well as President Abraham Lincoln's visit to the Union commander General George B. McClellan. Every day at 12:00 noon a

new one hour documentary about the battle of Antietam narrated by James Earl Jones is shown in the visitor center theater. The driving tour can be a little long for kids but look for interesting tidbits found on these stops: Clara Barton's visit (angel); the Dunker Church where men from both sides chatted

Walk over the famous Burnside Bridge

and had peace when not in battle; Bloody Lane where so many fell the length of a straight lane street; and the famous walk out to the Burnside bridge.

WASHINGTON COUNTY RURAL HERITAGE MUSEUM

Sharpsburg - *7313 Sharsburg Pike (Rte. 65) (I-70 exit 29, five miles south on Rte. 65 at the Washington Cty. Agricultural Education Center) 21782. Web: www.washco-md.net/public_works/parks/museum.htm Phone: (240) 313-2839. Hours: Weekends 1:00-4:00pm (April-October). Admission: Free, donations accepted.*

The museum contains more than 2,000 items, most of which are on loan from or have been donated by local residents. Upon arrival, there is a short video to introduce visitors to the museum. Exhibits include: a typical General Store (on loan from the Washington County

Historical Society); examples of Rural Living, such as a farm kitchen, parlor, and a country church; and examples of Modes of Travel, such as an original Conestoga wagon, sleighs and sleds. Other exhibits contain equipment and artifacts used by local farmers, and displays on butchering and dairying. Kids are often invited to watch crafting like broom making, grain grinding, milking and butter churning. Great time to visit is their Spring or Holiday Open House or the annual SpudFest. Ever harvested potatoes with the prize being homemade potato chips?

SUGGESTED LODGING AND DINING

SCHMANKERL-STUBE BAVARIAN RESTAURANT. **Hagerstown.** 58 South Potomac Street, downtown (US 40 west, left on Potomac, corner of Antietam St). (301) 797-3354 or **www.schmankerlstube.com**. Hagerstown's Bavarian Restaurant carries on the Old Bavarian and German traditions in a truly ethnic atmosphere: "Schmankerl" meaning a Bavarian culinary delicacy and "Stube" a cozy room. Often personally greeted by Charlie Sekula, the proprietor, or by attractively dressed waiters and waitresses in typical Bavarian dress, the guest quickly feels at home in an inviting, cozy environment. If you're not familiar with Schnitzel, Wurst and Strudels - try a sampling of each. Lunch and dinner served daily except Monday.

YOGI BEAR'S JELLYSTONE PARK. **Hagerstown.** 16519 Lappans Rd (I-81 exit MD 63/68, turn east one mile). **www.jellystonemaryland.com**. (800) 421-7116 or A fun and full day and night can be had here. They have almost hourly activities planned all day long each summer including bingo, treasure hunts, pool games, movies and such. Cabins and campsites are available huddled near attractions or off in secluded woods. Play Yogi mini-golf, pedal carts and the moon bounce. Cool off in one of two pool areas. One basic, the other Water Zone is full of interactive squirts and sprays and two new giant, twisting waterslides. Finish off the day with the Bear's Cave black light game room.

AMERICAN DELI AND NUTTER'S ICE CREAM. Sharpsburg
(Antietam Battlefield). For lunch we recommend The American
Deli (Great sandwiches and wraps). Cool off at Nutter's Ice Cream,
famous for miles around. Serving great ice cream, shakes, sundaes, all
an amazing value for those used to city prices.

PLAZA HOTEL. Hagerstown. 1718 Underpass Way (I-70 & I-81,
I-81 north exit 5A Halfway Blvd). **www.plazahotelhagerstown.com**
(301) 797-2500. Plaza Hotel - a full service hotel - provides the most
pleasing accommodations at reasonable cost - tastefully decorated,
rooms with refrigerators, coffee makers, hair dryers, satellite TV, and
more. Indoor heated pool, sauna, spa, fitness center, restaurant on
premises. Kids love being greeted by live birds and fish in the lobby.

THE THIRSTY CRAB. **Deep Creek Lake**. 567 Glendale Road,
Silver Tree Inn (1/2 mile around the corner from the Discovery
Center). (301) 387-7679 or **www.thirstycrab.com**. Daily lunch and
dinner. Entertainment most weekends. What fun and interesting food
is served here! Besides the Kids Menu with six items under $5.00
and kids playground, they specialize in Maryland Hard Shell Blue
Crabs and Crab Legs. Want something different? Maybe the Krabby
Patty (deep fried burger stuffed with jumbo lump crabmeat served
on a bun) - for real, Chicken with crab, pasta with crab, salad with
crab, mushroom with crab - you get the picture. Tired of seafood?
Their reuben sandwiches are wonderful and what about the variety of
gourmet wings. They call them wings around the world - we especially
liked the Tyler Wings, South Western Wings, or Chesapeake Wings
(you guessed, with Old Bay). Others are Mexican, Caribbean or
exotic fruit spiced. Oh, by the way, instead of rolls, they serve these
wonderful homemade Old Bay or BBQ potato chips with a special
dipping sauce.

TRADER'S COFFEE HOUSE. **Deep Creek Lake**. 1/2 mile south
of Deep Creek Bridge on Rte. 219 south, below Brenda's Pizzeria
(serving take-n-bake pizza and Dinners by the Dozen Italian entrees
prepared to serve a dozen people). **www.traderscoffeehouse.com**
(301) 387-9246. On a rainy, foggy or chilly morning, this coffee
house is a haven for locals and visitors. Freshly brewed coffee and

cappuccinos or lattes and wonderful chai tea to start. Juices and smoothies for the kids (or hot cocoa). Need some carbs for an energy breakfast? Try fresh bagels, strudels, belgian waffles, croissants, cinnamon rolls, doughnuts, quiches and muffins. They have many cozy tables and chairs to cuddle your cup. Before you leave, browse through shelves of books, mugs (we had to get one), local crafts and gift packages to take home.

FIRESIDE DELI. **Deep Creek Lake**. 2205 Glendale Road, 2 miles past State Park Rd. **www.firesidedeli-wineshop.com**. (301) 387-0083. A place more for the moms and dads to enjoy (local and around-the-world wine and exotic party and dessert cheeses plus sparkling beverages are queen here), our kids found they loved the meatball sandwich and the Chicken Parmesan. . . And Paninis, at that. Their Cuban panini is wonderful as is all of their wraps - especially anything with MaryEllen's picky selection of cheeses on top. Fresh salads and various cheeses and gourmet chips fill the plate as sides. Specialty sauces and European packaged desserts or mixes are sold, too, to take home. Open daily for lunch and most days, dinner. Sandwiches run between $6.00-8.00 and are very large portioned. Smaller appetites may want to choose half portions with salad, side or soup for the same price.

LAKESIDE CREAMERY. **Deep Creek Lake**. (301) 387-2580 or **www.lakesidecreamery.com**. Rte. 219 or inside Smiley's Funzone. Over 90 flavors are made on the premises including unique favorites like Cake Batter, Cantelope, Graham Cracker Swirl, PB&J or Cinnamon Bun flavors. Visit by car or boat.

Chapter 7

Seasonal &
Special Events

JANUARY

POLAR BEAR PLUNGE, MARYLAND STATE POLICE

CENTRAL – **Annapolis**, Sandy Point State Park. **www.somd.org**. Afternoon winter plunge into the Chesapeake Bay and freeze your "fur" off for the athletes of Special Olympics Maryland. Admission. (fourth Saturday in January)

MARTIN LUTHER KING JR. BIRTHDAY CELEBRATION PARADE

CENTRAL – **Baltimore**, MLK Jr. Blvd. And Eutaw Street. (877) BALTIMORE or **www.promotionandarts.com**. Commemorates the birth of Reverend Dr. Martin Luther King Jr. with floats, marching bands and church choirs. (MLK Jr. Holiday)

WINTERLIGHTS: A CELEBRATION OF CHESAPEAKE BAY LIGHTHOUSES

SOUTHERN – **Solomons**, Calvert Marine Museum. The bay's lighthouses are treasures. **www.calvertmarinemuseum.com**. Displays and tours of area lighthouses, book signings, and a gingerbread contest. (second weekend in January)

JANUARY / FEBRUARY

THE TRAINS OF CHRISTMAS

WESTERN – **Hagerstown** Roundhouse Museum. 300 S. Buthans Blvd (US 11). (301) 739-4665 or **www.roundhouse.org**. The visions, sounds, and snows of Christmas past and present on an "O" Gauge railroad. Admission (January & February, Friday-Sunday)

FEBRUARY

AFRICAN-AMERICAN HERITAGE WALKING TOUR

CENTRAL – **Annapolis** City Dock. **www.watermarkcruises.com**. Explore the rich African-American history of Annapolis including the Thurgood Marshall and Kunta Kinte Memorial. Admission. (second Saturday in February)

MARCH

NATION'S ST. PATRICK'S DAY PARADE

CAPITAL-DC – **Washington, DC**. **www.dcstpatsparade.com**
(March, second weekend)

MAPLE SYRUP FESTIVAL

CAPITAL – **Thurmont**, Cunningham Falls State Park, Houck Area. (301) 271-7574. See maple syrup made from sap to syrup. Enjoy a pancake breakfast and other family activities. Donation requested. (second and third weekends in March)

MARYLAND DAY

CENTRAL–Annapolis, historic sites downtown. **www.annapolis.org**. Learn about Diamondback Terrapins, Chesapeake Retrievers and other Maryland state symbols during this kid-friendly event. (March 25 or thereabouts)

MAPLE SUGARIN' FESTIVAL

CENTRAL – **Westminster**, Hashawha Environmental Center. **www.ccgov.carr.org/hashawha**. Maple syrup demonstrations, pancake brunch, taste testing, country crafts and food concessions. Small admission per vehicle. (first Sunday in March)

EAGLE FESTIVAL

EASTERN SHORE – **Cambridge**, Blackwater National Wildlife Refuge Visitor Center. **www.blackwater.fws.gov**. Festival celebrating eagles and other birds of prey, featuring live animal programs and children's activities. (second Saturday in March)

ST. PATRICK'S DAY PARADE AND FESTIVAL

EASTERN SHORE – **Ocean City**, on Coastal Hwy. (800) OC-OCEAN or **www.ococean.com**. Parade, Irish festival with dancing and food. (weekend before St. Patrick's Day)

March *(cont.)*

MARYLAND DAY

SOUTHERN – **St. Mary's City**, historic area. **www.stmaryscity.org**. Celebrate Maryland's birthday with pageantry and ceremonies marking the founding of the state in 1634. Tour the living history exhibits and fly over to the kite festival – BYOK. FREE. (March 25th or close to)

APRIL

JOHN WILKES BOOTH ESCAPE ROUTE TOUR

CAPITAL – Clinton, Surratt House Museum. **www.surratt.org**. Narrated bus tour on the trail of President Lincoln's assassin. Advance reservations required, sells out quickly. Admission. (two Saturdays in April)

FARM MUSEUM FAMILY FESTIVAL

CAPITAL–Frederick, Rose Hill Manor Park. **www.rosehillmuseum.com**. Family festival with hayrides, tractor pull, lawn games, crafts and activity relating to agricultural heritage. Admission. (last weekend in April)

SUGARLOAF CRAFTS FESTIVAL

CAPITAL – **Gaithersburg**, Montgomery County Fairgrounds, exit 11 off I-270. **www.sugarloafcrafts.com**. This exciting show features 450 artists and crafters, delicious food, craft demos and children's entertainment. Admission. (first full weekend in April)

HAYRIDE IN BUNNYLAND

CAPITAL–Germantown, Butler's Orchard. **www.butlersorchard.com**. Bring your basket, hunt for eggs, take a hayride in Bunnyland, visit Butler's Country Bunny and barnyard bunnies. Admission. (week of Easter)

MARCHING THROUGH TIME

CAPITAL – **Glenn Dale**, Marietta House Museum grounds. **www.pgparks.com**. Annual multi-period military and domestic living history encampment. 400+ reenactors representing Romans to Desert storm period merchants and food. Admission. (late April weekend)

BUNNY TRAINS

CAPITAL – **Walkersville** Southern Railroad. **www.wsrr.org**. Ride the train with the Bunny. Cookies and juice in the museum while you enjoy model trains and receive an Easter treat. Admission. (weekend before and Saturday of Easter weekend)

WHITEHOUSE EASTER

CAPITAL-DC - White House. This annual tradition dates back to 1878 and President Rutherford B. Hayes. Children ages 3 to 6 can frolic on the South Lawn searching for over 24,000 wooden eggs that have been hidden throughout the grounds. There is also an Easter celebration at the Ellipse including entertainment, music, storytelling and food giveaways for the whole family to enjoy. **www.whitehouse.gov/easter/**. FREE.

CHERRY BLOSSOM FESTIVAL

CAPITAL-DC - Washington, DC's annual National Cherry Blossom Festival is a celebration of the coming of spring and commemorates the gift of 3,000 cherry trees given to the U.S. by Tokyo mayor, Yukio Ozaki in 1912. The two-week festival includes many cultural, sporting and culinary events culminating with the Festival Parade and DC's Sakura Matsuri Japanese Street Festival, presenting over 80 organizations highlighting Japanese performances, arts, crafts and food. The Parade showcases entries from across the country and around the world, including Ringling Bros. And Barnum & Bailey circus, lavish floats, gigantic helium balloons, exciting international performance groups, marching bands and celebrity guests. Also, The Smithsonian Kite Festival on the grounds of the Washington Monument. **www.nationalcherryblossomfestival.org**. Most events are FREE. (first two weeks of April, beginning end of March)

BALTIMORE WATERFRONT FESTIVAL

CENTRAL – **Baltimore**, Inner Harbor and surrounding area. (877) BALTIMORE or **www.promotionandarts.com**. Seafood cooking demos, entertainment, maritime exhibits, sailing races, family fun and Chesapeake Bay exhibits. (last long weekend in April)

April *(cont.)*

EASTER BRUNCH CRUISE

CENTRAL – **Baltimore**, Bay Lady and Lady Baltimore, Inner Harbor. **www.harborcruises.com**. Buffet brunch, DJ for dancing, Easter treats, three-hour cruise. Admission. (Easter Sunday)

SUGARLOAF CRAFTS FESTIVAL

CENTRAL – **Timonium**, Maryland State Fairgrounds. **www.sugarloafcrafts.com**. This exciting show features 350 artists and crafters, delicious food, craft demos and children's entertainment. Admission. (last weekend in April)

SPRING CELEBRATION

EASTERN SHORE – **Berlin**, Main Street. **www.berlinmdcc.org**. Events for children and adults, breakfast with the Easter Bunny, Easter Bonnet parade, pig races, food vendors and music. (Saturday before Easter)

EASTER KIDS FAIR

EASTERN SHORE – **Ocean City**, Convention Center. Continuous events, activities and entertainment including Beanny the Easter Bunny, egg hunts, coloring tables, magic and puppet shows, clowns and contests. **www.oceanpromotions.info**. Admission. (long Easter weekend)

MARYLAND INTERNATIONAL KITE EXPOSITION

EASTERN SHORE – **Ocean City**, Boardwalk area. (410) 289-7855. Kite competition consisting of multi-level precision flying events. Internationally known kite flyers show unique displays. (last long weekend in April)

NANTICOKE RIVER SHAD FESTIVAL

EASTERN SHORE – **Vienna**, on the waterfront. **www.cbf.org**. Vendors, exhibitors, river rides, food, music, kidstown, and the famous planked shad (served at Noon). (last Saturday in April)

EASTER SUNRISE SERVICE

SOUTHERN – **Scotland**, Point Lookout State Park picnic/beach area. (301) 872-5688 or **www.dnr.maryland.gov**. Non-denominational service beginning at sunrise. Admission. (Easter Sunday)

CELEBRATE MARYLAND ARCHAEOLOGY MONTH

SOUTHERN – **St. Leonard**, Jefferson Patterson Park and Museum. **www.jefpat.org**. Learn how archaeologists study cultures at the Woodland Indian Hamlet and mock archaeology sites. Adults can learn about the actual processes used to expose archaeology in daily life. FREE. (fourth Saturday in April)

CELTIC FESTIVAL & HIGHLAND GATHERING

SOUTHERN – **St. Leonard**, Jefferson Patterson Park and Museum. **www.cssm.org**. Celtic music, dance and craft demos; Highland athletic, bagpipe, and dance competitions; re-enactments, storytellers. Admission. (last Saturday in April)

JEFFERSON PATTERSON PARK AND MUSEUM OPENING CELEBRATION

SOUTHERN – **St. Leonard**, **www.jefpat.org**. Bring a picnic and enjoy the quiet beauty of the park and museum. In the Visitors Center, see "12,000 years in the Chesapeake" and other exhibits on local culture, history and archeology. Learn about American Indian and Colonial history through hands-on activities in the Children's Discovery Room and visit the Show Barn Museum Shop. Also, kite flying and puppet shows and Calvert Spinners and Weavers demos. FREE. (Saturday in mid-April)

WORLD CARNIVAL

SOUTHERN – **St. Mary's City**, St. Mary's College of Maryland Admissions Field, Fisher Road off Rte 5. **www.smcm.edu**. One of the largest events on campus featuring cultural performances, carnival games, food vendors, craft booths, music and children's activities. (Saturday in early April)

April *(cont.)*

18TH CENTURY MARKET FAIR

WESTERN – **Big Pool**, Fort Frederick State Park. Witness the best 18th-century artisans, craftsmen, and sutlers amid a 1730-1740 encampment. **www.dnr.state.md.us/publiclands/western/fortfrederick**. Admission. (last weekend in April)

SPRING OPEN HOUSE

WESTERN – **Boonsboro**, Washington County Rural Heritage Museum. **www.washco-md.net/museum**. Children's Egg Hunt for goodies and eggs, Egg Dying using purple and brown onionskins (old-fashioned way). Donations accepted. (first weekend in April)

EASTER EGG HUNT

WESTERN – **Oakland**, Broadford Lake Park. Hunt begins at Noon-sharp. A free event for area children ages 2-10 sponsored by local media. Three different age groups hunt for thousands of Easter eggs stuffed with candy, prizes and $50 savings bonds. (Saturday before Easter)

MAY

BOWIE HERITAGE DAY

CAPITAL – **Bowie**, Belair Mansion/Stable Museum. A celebration of Maryland history and horseracing at one of Maryland's most historic homes. Free pony rides, music, tours of Railroad Museum (depot and tower) and the Radio and Television Museum (first telegraph to first TV). **www.cityofbowie.org**. FREE. (third Sunday in May)

MEMORIAL DAY PARADE

CAPITAL – **Bowie**, Belair Annex to Acorn Hill Park. Don your red, white and blue and fill the streets of Bowie with patriotism. **www.cityofbowie.org**. (Memorial Day Saturday)

CHILDREN'S DAY

CAPITAL – **Buckeystown**, Lilypons Gardens. **www.lilypons.com**. Children's games and activities, face painting, festival foods and boat rides. (May weekend)

AAFB JOINT SERVICES OPEN HOUSE & AIR SHOW

CAPITAL – **Camp Springs**, Andrews Air Force Base. **www.andrews.af.mil/PA/JSOH.htm**. The Joint Services Open House and Air Show is the largest military open house in the United States. The Open House features vintage and state-of-the-art aircraft, demos, displays, food and refreshments, and a dazzling air show. This is the only event of its kind in the Washington metro area. FREE. (May weekend)

FREDERICK CELTIC FESTIVAL

CAPITAL – **Frederick**, Urbana Fairgrounds. Heritage demos, Scottish clan tents, Celtic music, dancing, crafts, Celtic vendors, kids activities, Highland games. **http://www.sasmm.com/celtic_festival.htm** Admission. (second Saturday in May)

ROCKVILLE SCIENCE DAY

CAPITAL – **Rockville**, Montgomery College. The event, which has free admission and parking, annually attracts thousands for an afternoon of fun with math, science, experiments and a look at the future. Entertainment, learning, rockets, astronomy, mammals, reptiles, chemistry, rocks, fossils, minerals and hands-on science. **www.rockvillescience.gov/rcsday**. FREE. (Sunday afternoon in early May)

ANNAPOLIS MARITIME HERITAGE FESTIVAL (AND VOLVO RACE)

CENTRAL – **Annapolis** City Dock. **www.oceanracechesapeake.org**. Celebrate the maritime heritage of the Chesapeake spotlighting the almost annual stop of the Volvo Ocean Race. Entertainment, blessing of fleet, display of boats, Children's Pavilion, and living history Civil War re-enactments at Avery House (waterman) in Shady Side. (first full weekend in May)

May *(cont.)*

BLUE ANGELS

CENTRAL – **Annapolis** City Dock. **www.watermarkcruises.com** The exciting Blue Angels perform over the Severn River; watch from onboard one of the boat cruise vessels. Admission. (late May Wednesday)

PREAKNESS CELEBRATION PARADE

CENTRAL – **Baltimore**, East on Pratt St. to Market Place. (877) BALTIMORE or **www.promotionandarts.com**. Marching bands, clowns, equestrian units, floats in a salute to the Preakness Stakes the following weekend. (second Saturday in May)

SUNS ON THE FARM

CENTRAL – **Brookeville**, Sharp's at Waterford Farm. **www.sharpfarm.com**. Hayride, picnic, farm animals, nature trail, family entertainment. Admission. (Sundays in May)

LITHUANIAN FESTIVAL

CENTRAL – **Catonsville** Armory, 130 Mellor Avenue. (410) 646-0261. Festival celebrating Lithuanian heritage with folk dancing, live music, food, exhibits, crafts and amber. Admission. (second weekend in May)

CIVIL WAR LIVING HISTORY DAY

CENTRAL – **Havre de Grace**, Steppingstone Museum. Living history encampment, drills, firing, artillery demonstrations, vendors, food, period music and dance. **www.steppingstonemuseum.org**. Admission. (third weekend in May)

DECOY AND WILDLIFE ART FESTIVAL

CENTRAL – **Havre de Grace**, Decoy Museum & Middle and High Schools. **www.decoymuseum.com**. 175 or so carvers, collectors and artists. Live auction, special exhibits, retriever demos and carving competitions. (first full weekend in May)

WAR OF 1812 RE-ENACTMENT – ATTACK ON HAVRE DE GRACE

CENTRAL – **Havre de Grace**, Lock House Museum, Susquehanna Museum. **www.lockhousemuseum.org/1812.htm**. Re-enactment of the British attack on Havre de Grace during the War of 1812. (first weekend in May)

GERMAN-AMERICAN FESTIVAL

CENTRAL – **Jessup**, Blob's Park. Assn. Of German-American Societies (301) 577-6488. Gemuetlichkeit for everyone. Folk dance performances, live music for dancing, vendors. Admission, children FREE. (first Sunday in May)

BLACKSMITH DAYS

CENTRAL – **Westminster**, Carroll County Farm Museum. **http://ccgov.carr.org/farm**. Blacksmiths set up forges and demonstrate "smithy" skills; hands-on opportunity, auction of blacksmith-related items. Farmhouse tours. Admission. (third weekend in May)

CIVIL WAR LIVING HISTORY RE-ENACTMENT

CENTRAL – **Westminster**, Carroll County Farm Museum. **http://ccgov.carr.org/farm**. Relive historic moments as Civil War troops re-create forgotten lifestyles. Farmhouse tours. Admission. (first weekend in May)

FLY-IN

EASTERN SHORE – **Cambridge**, Horn Point Aerodrome. (410) 228-1899. Antique aircraft fly-in, aircraft judging, meet pilots, examine planes, food-on-site, aviation vendors. (third Saturday in May)

CHESTERTOWN TEA PARTY FESTIVAL

EASTERN SHORE – **Chestertown** historic district. Re-enactment of 1774 Tea Party; crafts, Colonial parade, art show and entertainment all day. **www.chestertownteaparty.com**. (Memorial Day weekend)

May *(cont.)*

CRUISIN' OCEAN CITY

EASTERN SHORE – **Ocean City**, Inlet parking lot. (800) OC-OCEAN or **www.ococean.com**. 3,500 street rods and classic cars cruisin' the boardwalk and the city; boardwalk parades, competition, styling and profiling. Admission. (third long weekend in May)

SALUTE TO THE SERVICES

EASTERN SHORE – **Ocean City**, Citywide. Hotels, motels, restaurants and attractions offer discount to fire, EMS, police and military personnel. Admission. **www.salutetotheservices.com**. (late May thru late June)

KENT ISLAND DAY

EASTERN SHORE – **Stevensville**, Historic Cray House, Cockey Lane. (410) 604-2100. Historic Cray House, post office, railroad station; food; 18th century displays, art, crafts, children's activities, entertainment and such. (third Saturday in May)

FAIRMOUNT ACADEMY 1800'S FESTIVAL

EASTERN SHORE – **Upper Fairmount**, Fairmount Academy. **www.visitsomerset.com**. Restored school 1839-1969 with 1800s classroom and spelling bee, music, square dancing, class in session, folk art, seafood and baked goods. (Memorial Day Saturday)

LIVING HISTORY PROGRAM

SOUTHERN – Grantsville, Spruce Forest. **www.visitdeepcreek.com**. Step back in time to when George Washington traveled through Garrett County, both as a young surveyor and later as an officer in the French and Indian War. Period costumes, food and artifacts, as well as demonstrations to take you back in time. FREE. (third long weekend in May)

PINEY POINT LIGHTHOUSE WATERFRONT FESTIVAL

SOUTHERN – **Piney Point** Lighthouse Museum and Park. Enjoy a guided tour, demonstrations, exhibits, children's programs, food; lighthouse tower (is open) and historic boats. Admission. **www.stmarysmd.com/recreate/museums**. (second weekend in May)

MARITIME FOLKLIFE FESTIVAL

SOUTHERN – **Solomons**, Calvert Marine Museum. **www.cmm.com**. Visit the antique boat & marine engine show; taste traditional foods; learn crab picking, oyster shucking and fish filleting; enjoy Gospel and Old-time music; children's games and races; rides on bugeye and draketail work boats; talk with carvers, crab pot makers, watch model boat demos, test your dog in the Chesapeake Bay Retriever Trials; build a toy boat in the boat shed. Admission. (first Saturday in May)

FORT FREDERICK ANNIVERSARY CELEBRATION

WESTERN – **Big Pool**, Fort Frederick State Park. Fort Frederick celebrates its 250th plus birthday with music, reenactments, period entertainers & fireworks. **www.dnr.state.md.us/publiclands/western/ fortfrederick**. Admission. (Memorial Day weekend)

MUSEUM RAMBLE IN WASHINGTON COUNTY

WESTERN – **Hagerstown** museums around county. (301) 791-3246 or **www.marylandmemories.org**. Self-guided tour of county museums with a special event at each location. Admission. (first weekend in May)

JUNE

PUBLIC FIELD DAY

CAPITAL – **Beltsville** Agricultural Research Center. View research exhibits, guided tour hay rides, dairy tour, animal petting area, farm equipment on display. **www.ba.ars.usda.gov**. (first Saturday in June)

IMAGINATION BETHESDA

CAPITAL – **Bethesda**, Woodmont Ave and Elm Street. **www.Bethesda.org**. Children's street festival featuring performers, giveaways and hands-on activities. (first Saturday in June)

LILYPONS DAYS

CAPITAL – **Buckeystown**, Lilypons Water Gardens. **www.lilypons.com**. Arts and crafts, live entertainment, walks and children's activities. (second weekend in June)

June *(cont.)*

ROMAN DAYS

CAPITAL – **Glenn Dale**, Marietta House Museum grounds. **www.pgparks.com**. Annual encampment of Roman legionnaries and gladiators, tactical demos, fashion show, interactive activities, merchants and food. Admission. (first weekend in June)

CHARLES VILLAGE PARADE

CENTRAL – **Baltimore**, St. Paul & 23rd St. **www.charlesvillage.net**. A vibrant colorful procession, featuring creative floats, art cars, marching bands, and more, captures the heart and soul of this diverse urban village. Voted Baltimore's best parade, this funky event includes bands, antique cars, dogs on skateboards, food and craft. Various prizes will be awarded in several categories. (first weekend in June)

FLAG DAY FIREWORKS CRUISE

CENTRAL – **Baltimore**, Bay Lady & Lady Baltimore, Inner Harbor. **www.harborcruises.com**. Three hour dinner cruise with a buffet and DJ while waiting for fireworks. Admission. (Flag Day, June 14th)

FLAG DAY, NATIONAL PAUSE FOR THE PLEDGE OF ALLEGIANCE

CENTRAL – **Baltimore**, Fort McHenry National Monument. **www.flagday.org**. Annual National Pause ceremony and program, band concert, parade of state flags, entertainment, fly-over and fireworks. (Flag Day, June 14th)

HONFEST

CENTRAL – **Baltimore**, **Hampden**. **www.honfest.net**. HonFest is a unique celebration that pays homage to the neighborhoods, the language and the people of Baltimore. Over 20,000 people flock here each year at HonFest to join in the festivities. The highlight of the day is the crowning of Baltimore's Best Hon. What is a Hon? The term Hon is actually a friendly Baltimore greeting and comes from the word "honey". However, the women who become Baltimore's Best Hon are a vision of the sixties-era women with beehive hairdos, blue-eyeshadow, spandex pants and something, anything leopard print! During HonFest you too can get your own beehive in their Glamour Lounge, listen to talented local musicians, and peruse the work of local artists, while you stroll "downy Avenue". (second Saturday in June)

LATINOFEST

CENTRAL – **Baltimore**, Patterson Park. **www.latinofest.org**. A lively weekend of Hispanic art and culture, Latin music, Hispanic cuisine, costumed dancers and family activities. Admission. (last weekend in June)

BOAT FLOAT

CENTRAL–**Howard County**, near **Clydes**. **www.hocoboatfloat.com**. A challenge to design & build a person-powered, corrugated cardboard boat capable of racing a 200-yard course. (second Friday in June)

MEDITERRANEAN FESTIVAL

CENTRAL – **Hunt Valley**, St. Mary's Orthodox Church. **www.smfestival.com**. Greek & Middle Eastern food & music, pastries, dancing, children's crafts & cultural crafts. (first weekend in June)

SCOTTISH FESTIVAL

CENTRAL – **Havre de Grace**, Steppingstone Museum, Scottish clans, vendors, entertainment, sheep herding, spinning and weaving, pipe band, food and museum tours. **www.steppingstonemuseum.org**. Admission. (second Sunday in June)

SPRING MUSTER AND ANTIQUE FIRE APPARATUS

CENTRAL – **Westminster**, Carroll County Farm museum grounds. **http://ccgov.carr.org/farm**. Annual Maryland Antique Fire Apparatus Muster will feature a parade of antique fire equipment, family-oriented contests, food vendors and a flea market of fire service items. Admission. (first Saturday in June)

June *(cont.)*

SUMMER FEST AT APPLEWOOD

CENTRAL–Whiteford,ApplewoodFarm. **www.applewoodfarm.org**. Applewood express train rides, petting zoo, pony rides, horse-drawn carriage rides, music, food and storytelling. Admission. (first Sunday in June)

SPRING CARNIVAL

CENTRAL – **Woodbine**, Days End Farm Horse Rescue. Petting zoo, pony rides, games. All proceeds benefit abused, neglected horses. **www.defhr.org**. Admission. (last Saturday in June)

YOUTH FISHING DERBY

EASTERN SHORE – Cambridge, Blackwater National Wildlife Refuge. **www.blackwater.fws.gov**. Fishing event with prizes for youths 15 and under; also features turtle and frog races. (first Saturday in June)

EASTERN SHORE FISHING DERBY

EASTERN SHORE – **Salisbury** City Park. An Eastern Shore fishing tradition for kids of all ages in Salisbury's historic City Park. **www.wicomicoredandparks.org**. (first Friday in June)

STRAWBERRY FESTIVAL

EASTERN SHORE – **Sykesville** – Freedom Fairgrounds. (410) 489-5232. Crafts, flea market, games, hay wagon rides, food, baked goods, strawberries, shortcake, entertainment. (first Saturday in June)

TILGHMAN ISLAND SUMMER SEAFOOD FESTIVAL

EASTERN SHORE – **Tilghman Island** Volunteer Fire Company and adjacent Kronsberg Park. **www.tilghmanmd.com**. Local seafood, live music, crab races, crafts & fireman's parade. (fourth Saturday in June)

SOUTHERN MARYLAND SOAP BOX DERBY

SOUTHERN – **Leonardtown**, Fenwick Street (Derby Hill). (301) 863-2561. Youth racing event allowing youngsters from Southern Maryland to compete in stock/super stock cars. (second Saturday in June)

BLUE AND GRAY DAYS

SOUTHERN – **Scotland**, Fort Lincoln within Point Lookout State Park. **www.dnr.Maryland.gov**. Civil War living history demos, military and civilians of Point Lookout, no reservations required. Admission. (second weekend in June)

AFRICAN-AMERICAN FAMILY COMMUNITY DAY

SOUTHERN – St. Leonard, Jefferson Patterson Park. **www.jefpat.org**. Annual African-American Family day event features African dancing and drums, singing groups, games, face painting, crafts and food. FREE (third Saturday in June)

CHILDREN'S DAY ON THE FARM

SOUTHERN – St. Leonard, Jefferson Patterson Park. **www.jefpat.org**. Live farm animals, music, entertainment, scarecrow making, tractor parade, pony rides, wagon rides, story telling, puppet show and magician. Free admission, small fee for some activities. (first Sunday in June)

MARITIME HERITAGE FESTIVAL

SOUTHERN – **St. Mary's City** waterfront. **www.stmaryscity.org**. Big boats, little boats, work boats, play boats. Hands-on activities for children of all ages. Learn a new skill or take a cruise on the St. Mary's River. Then, cheer on your favorite contender in the model sailboat regatta. Admission. (third Saturday in June)

HERITAGE DAYS FESTIVAL

WESTERN – **Cumberland**, Washington Street historic district. **www.heritagedaysfestival.com**. 250 arts and crafts and food booths; demos, entertainment, encampments, carnival, historic tours, steam train excursions. Some admission for select activity. (second weekend in June)

RAILROAD HERITAGE DAYS

WESTERN – **Hagerstown** Roundhouse Museum. Historic railroad equipment artifacts and photos, trains for kids to run, HO and O model railroads to see. **www.roundhouse.org**. Admission. (second weekend in June)

June *(cont.)*

FLAG ON MOUNTAIN MARYLAND

WESTERN – **McHenry**, WISP Resort Hotel. A patriotic tribute to our country including music & a living American Flag. **www.visitdeepcreek.com**. (Flag Day, June 14th)

MCHENRY HIGHLAND FESTIVAL

WESTERN – **McHenry**, Garrett County Fairgrounds. Complimentary shortbread along with Celtic fun including athletic games, fiddlers, bagpipes, sheep dogs, concerts, dancing, craft and food. Admission. **www.highlandfest.info**. (first Saturday in June)

JULY

JULY 4TH CELEBRATION

CAPITAL – **Bowie**, Allen Pond Park. **www.cityofbowie.org**. One of the biggest July 4th celebrations in the country. Fireworks celebration at dark, food, live entertainment. Baysox play the annual baseball game. FREE for celebration, FEE for baseball game. (July 4th)

CIVIL WAR ENCAMPMENT

CAPITAL – **Frederick**, Rose Hill Manor Park. Civil War living history encampment; demos, skirmish, food concessions, manor tours, and children's activities. **www.rosehillmuseum.com**. Admission. (second weekend in July)

FREDERICK'S 4TH – AN INDEPENDENCE DAY CELEBRATION

CAPITAL – **Frederick**, Baker Park. **www.celebratefrederick.com**. Annual celebration with fireworks, food, four stages of entertainment, boat rides, children's activities and more. (July 4th)

4TH OF JULY CELEBRATION

CAPITAL – **Gaithersburg**, Montgomery County Fairgrounds. **www.gaithersburgmd.gov**. Independence Day celebration including music concerts, games and food. Fireworks start at dark. (July 4th)

4TH OF JULY WEEKEND

CAPITAL – **Walkersville** Southern Railroad. **www.wsrr.org**. Hot dogs and apple pie in Museum. Music on the train. Flag stickers for the kids. Admission. (Saturday before July 4th)

STAR-SPANGLED SPECIAL FIREWORKS TRAIN

CAPITAL – **Walkersville** Southern Railroad. **www.wsrr.org**. Visit the carnival in town, have dinner at the fire hall, then take an evening train ride for a view of the fireworks you will never forget. Bring a flashlight and a blanket. Admission. (Friday after July 4th)

AMERICA'S INDEPENDENCE DAY PARADE

CAPITAL-DC - Constitution Avenue. **www.july4thparade.com** Celebrate the nation's birthday in the nation's capital. Don't miss the parade, with more then 100 marching units stepping out at noon along Constitution Avenue. When that's over, popular music groups entertain from mid-afternoon until the fireworks at Washington Monument. FREE.

SMITHSONIAN FOLKLIFE FESTIVAL

CAPITAL-DC - National Mall. National, even international, celebration of contemporary living traditions. The Festival typically includes daily and evening programs of music, song, dance, celebratory performance, crafts and cooking demonstrations, storytelling, illustrations of workers' culture. The Festival encourages visitors to participate - to learn, sing, dance, eat traditional foods, and converse with people presented in the Festival program. FREE. (first two weekends, Thursday-Sunday, in July)

ALL AMERICAN FOURTH OF JULY CELEBRATION

CENTRAL – **Annapolis**, William Paca House and Garden. **www.Annapolis.org**. Period music and entertainment, Revolutionary War re-enactors, historical figures, readings of the Declaration of Independence and patriotic crafts. (July 4th)

July *(cont.)*

INDEPENDENCE DAY FIREWORKS CRUISES

CENTRAL – **Annapolis** City Dock, Watermark Cruises. 3 hours in the evening for the best seat in town for spectacular Annapolis Harbor fireworks. DJ and snacks. **www.watermarkcruises.com**. Admission. (July 4th)

JOHN PAUL JONES DAY

CENTRAL–**Annapolis**, U.S. Naval Academy. **www.navyonline.com**. Wreath laying, flag raising, historical presentations, children's activities, fifes and drums, John Paul Jones warrant signings. (second weekend in July)

ARTSCAPE

CENTRAL – **Baltimore**, Mt. Royal Avenue Corridor. The region's premier celebration of the arts; continuous music, children's activities, food, artists' market. **www.artscape.org**. (fourth full weekend in July)

BALTIMORE'S FOURTH OF JULY CELEBRATION

CENTRAL – **Baltimore**, Inner Harbor. **www.promotionandarts.com** Entertainment including a fireworks display over the Inner Harbor. Admission for 4 hour Harbor Cruise. (July 4th)

GLORIOUS FOURTH

CENTRAL – **Baltimore**, Fort McHenry National Monument. (410) 962-4290. Join the garrison of the Fort and patriotic citizens of Baltimore for fife and drum music, cannon firing, a musket salute for 18 states, period dancing and games. Twilight ceremony. (July 4th weekend)

CATONSVILLE'S JULY 4TH CELEBRATION

CENTRAL – **Catonsville**, Parade on Frederick Road. (410) 744-9655. Kids games and races, spectacular parade, Mammoth Fireworks. (July 4th)

INDEPENDENCE CELEBRATION

CENTRAL – **Havre de Grace**, Tydings Memorial Park. (410) 939-4362. Carnival, Parade, Concert & Fireworks. (first few days of July)

SUMMER FUN DAY

CENTRAL – **Havre de Grace**, Steppingstone Museum. Children's activities, ice cream eating contest, turtle races, frog jumping contest, sack races, face painting, food and the famous lawnmower races. **www.steppingstonemuseum.org**. Admission. (second Sunday in July)

FIREWORKS EXTRAVAGANZA

CENTRAL – **Middle River**, Eastern Yacht Club. **www.mtabc.org**. Annual fireworks extravaganza on Middle River. Admission. (one of first few days in July)

TOWSON AREA FOURTH OF JULY PARADE

CENTRAL – **Towson**, around courthouse. (410) 832-2190. Parade with National Guard fly-over, bands, military units, community participation, and floats. (July 4th)

CIVIL WAR ENCAMPMENT LIVING HISTORY

CENTRAL – **Union Mills** Homestead. Living history, demos, food both days, ice cream social, music, clowns, pony rides, and tours of Homestead & grist mill. **www.carr.org/carroll/tourism/un-mills.htm**. (second weekend in July)

HOWARD COUNTY POW-WOW

CENTRAL – **West Friendship**, Howard County Fairgrounds. (410) 442-1022. American Indian festival with dancers, arts and crafts, and food. Admission. (third weekend in July)

COMMON GROUND ON THE HILL

CENTRAL – **Westminster**, Carroll County Farm Museum. **www.commongroundonthehill.org**. Four stages of music, folk, Blues, old-time, bluegrass, world arts and crafts, ethnic foods, and family "world village". Admission. (second weekend in July)

July *(cont.)*

OLD-FASHIONED JULY 4TH CELEBRATION

CENTRAL – **Westminster**, Carroll County Farm Museum. Fireworks, old-fashioned family picnic, games, food, crafts and farmhouse tours. **http://ccgov.carr.org/farm**. Admission. (July 4th)

TUCKAHOE STEAM AND GAS SHOW

EASTERN SHORE – **Easton**, Tuckahoe Showgrounds. Antique steam engines, gas engines, blacksmith, museum, railroad, horse pull and auction. Children under 12 are FREE. **www.tuckahoesteam.org**. (first full weekend in July)

SALUTE TO CECIL COUNTY VETERANS CELEBRATION AND FIREWORKS

EASTERN SHORE – North East Community Park. Fireworks, music, and food. **www.northeastchamber.org**. (July 3rd)

OCEAN CITY FOURTH OF JULY JAMBOREE AND FIREWORKS JUBILEE

EASTERN SHORE – **Ocean City**, Northside Park (127th Street bayside), on beach and Boardwalk. **www.ococean.com**. Music, arts and crafts, food, family games, free concerts on beach, fireworks over the ocean. (July 4th)

ROCK HALL PARADE AND FIREWORKS

EASTERN SHORE – **Rock Hall**, The Bulkhead and Main Street. **www.kentcounty.com**. Day-long celebrations in a waterman's town. Food, music, horseshoe tournament, turtle races and a parade. Largest display on Maryland's Eastern Shore, overlooking Rock Hall Harbor. (July 3rd & July 4th)

CALVERT COUNTY FARM TOUR

SOUTHERN – County-wide, various farms. **www.calvertag.com**. One or more working farms have demos, hayrides, animals, music, food, children's activities, produce, and pony rides. (third Sunday in July)

FIREWORKS CELEBRATION

SOUTHERN – **Chesapeake Beach**, Rod Reel Restaurant. **www.chesapeakebeachresortspa.com**. Largest fireworks display on the bay; music, food and beach games. (July 3rd and 4th)

INDEPENDENCE DAY

SOUTHERN – St. Leonard, Jefferson Patterson Park. **www.jefpat.org**. Bring a picnic and enjoy the park and museum. See "12,000 years in the Chesapeake" exhibit and others on local culture, history and archaeology. In the Discovery Room, learn about American Indian and Colonial history through hands-on activities. FREE (July 4th)

TIDEWATER ARCHAEOLOGY WEEKEND

SOUTHERN – **St. Mary's**, historic area. **www.stmaryscity.org**. Help archaeologists remove pieces of the past from excavations; watch as artifacts are identified; lab tours. Admission. (last weekend in July)

CANALFEST / RAILFEST

WESTERN – **Cumberland**, CanalPlace. **www.canalplace.org**. Events and activities for visitors of all ages, this festival celebrates the transportation history of the Queen City with many modern twists. Free entertainment. (second weekend in July)

FIREWORKS AT FAIRGROUNDS PARK

WESTERN–Hagerstown, Fairgrounds Park. **www.hagerstownmd.org**. Musical entertainment and a large fireworks display. (July 4th)

DEEP CREEK LAKE FIREWORKS CELEBRATION

WESTERN – **McHenry**, Deep Creek Lake area. Food music, games and spectacular fireworks display launched off the mountain overlooking the Lake. **www.deepcreeklakeinfo.com**. (July 4th)

AUGUST

WINGS OF FREEDOM OVER FREDERICK

CAPITAL – **Frederick** Municipal Airport. The Commemorative Air Force Wings of Freedom Over Frederick Air Show – a salute to Vietnam Veterans. **www.wingsoffreedomoverfrederick.com**. Admission. (second weekend in August)

WAR OF 1812 ENCAMPMENT

CAPITAL – **Riverdale** Park, Riversdale House Museum. **www.pgparks.com**. American and British military and civilian re-enactors prepare for the Battle of Bladensburg. Admission. (second Saturday in August)

CAL RIPKEN WORLD SERIES

CENTRAL – Aberdeen, Cal, Sr.'s Yard, a youth sized version of Oriole Park at Camden Yards, located adjacent to Ripken Stadium in the heart of the Ripken Youth Baseball Academy. **www.ripkenbaseball.com**. Baseball games between 10 U.S. and 5 international teams competing for the Cal Ripken World Series championship title. Admission. (second full week in August)

BALTIMORE POW-WOW

CENTRAL – **Baltimore**, Patterson Park. **www.baic.org**. Intertribal gathering of Native American dancers, drummers, artists, crafts persons, and friends; public is cordially invited. Admission. (last weekend in August)

KUNTA KINTE CELEBRATION

CENTRAL – **Crownsville**, Anne Arundel County Fairgrounds. **www.kuntakinte.org**. African-American ethnic festival featuring exciting performances. Unusual displays of arts, crafts. Children's tent and delicious ethnic cuisine. Admission. (second weekend in August)

BACK TO THE FUTURE AT THE LOCK HOUSE

CENTRAL – **Havre de Grace**, Susquehanna Museum. Come experience the fun of living history. **www.lockhousemuseum.org**. (second weekend in August)

MARYLAND STATE FAIR

CENTRAL – **Timonium**, 2200 York Road. Livestock, crafts, produce, farm and garden exhibits, food, midway rides, Thoroughbred horse racing, and entertainment. **www.marylandstatefair.com**. Admission. (last Friday in August thru Labor Day)

OLD-FASHIONED CORN ROAST FESTIVAL

CENTRAL – **Union Mills** Homestead. Chicken platters, applesauce, rolls, sliced tomatoes, roasted corn, and tours of Homestead and grist mill; art, music and vendors, too. **http://tourism.carr.org/unionmil.htm**. Admission. (first Saturday in August)

ST. JOSEPH'S JOUSTING TOURNAMENT

EASTERN SHORE – **Cordova**, St. Joseph's Church. (410) 822-6915. Horse show and dinner. Jousting tournament and country dinner. Admission. (first Wednesday in August)

WHEAT THRESHING, STEAM AND GAS ENGINE SHOW

EASTERN SHORE – **Federalsburg**, Rte. 313, between Denton and Federalsburg. **www.threshermen.org**. See antique farm equipment in operation; flea market, steam engines, antique tractors. (first weekend in August)

BLESSING OF THE COMBINES

EASTERN SHORE – **Snow Hill**, Green Street. (410) 632-1334. Parade of combines and antique tractors, blessing, music, petting barnyard, games, food, and tractor pull. (first Saturday in August)

August *(cont.)*

CALVERT COUNTY JOUSTING TOURNAMENT

SOUTHERN – **Port Republic**, Grounds of Christ Episcopal Church. **www.christchurchcalvert.org**. Oldest tournament of Maryland's official state sport; crafts, bazaar, organ recitals and country supper. Admission. (last Saturday in August)

WWII CRADLE OF INVASION

SOUTHERN – **Solomons**, Calvert Marine Museum. Discover Solomons' historical role in WWII; displays, WWII encampments and entertainment. **www.calvertmarinemuseum.com**. (first weekend in August)

AMERICAN INDIAN HERITAGE DAY

SOUTHERN – **St. Leonard**, Jefferson Patterson Park and Museum. **www.jefpat.org**. Everyday life as it was around the Chesapeake Bay more than 500 years ago; cultural heritage through visual and performing arts and crafts (basketry, archery, stone tool making) by American Indians from the region (some hands-on participation). Discovery Room open for exploration. Admission. (second Saturday in August)

NORTH BEACH BAYFEST

SOUTHERN – **North Beach** waterfront. **www.ci.north-beach.md.us**. Craft vendors, live music, Maryland food vendors, kids entertainment and activities. (last weekend in August)

AUGUSTOBERFEST

WESTERN – **Hagerstown**, Central Parking Lot. Augustoberfest is a re-creation of the festivities found at traditional Oktoberfest celebrations – authentic German musicians, dancers, Bavarian food. A children's area features clowns, games, rides and more. **www.augustoberfest.org**. (second weekend in August)

JONATHAN HAGAR FRONTIER CRAFT DAYS

WESTERN – Hagerstown, Jonathan Hagar House. 60 craftsmen, food, Hagar House tours & Appalachian-style music. **www.hagerhouse.org**. (first weekend in August)

SEPTEMBER

OKTOBERFEST

CAPITAL–Accokeek, Hard Bargain Farm. **www.hardbargainfarm.org**. Traditional Alpine music, authentic German food and drink, homemade delicacies, hayrides. Admission. (September)

JOHN WILKES BOOTH ESCAPE ROUTE TOUR

CAPITAL – **Clinton**, Surratt House Museum. **www.surratt.org**. Narrated bus tour on the trail of President Lincoln's assassin; advance reservations required. Admission. (second and fourth Saturday in September)

GREAT FREDERICK FAIR

CAPITAL – **Frederick** Fairgrounds. **www.thegreatfrederickfair.com**. Agricultural fair, large midway, top musical entertainment. (third full weekend in September)

SHAKER FOREST FESTIVAL

CAPITAL – **Gaithersburg**, Seneca Creek State Park. Observe craftspeople dressed in Shaker-period attire, demonstrating their skills and offering their wares for sale. Shop amid a canopy of trees and mulched pathways for quality handcrafted items and artwork and enjoy performances by entertainers. At the Shaker kitchen, sample selections from delicious foods. Admission. **www.shakerforest.org**. (second and third weekend in September)

NEW MARKET DAYS

CAPITAL – **New Market**, Streets in town. **www.nmdays.com**. Celebration of long ago; civil War re-enactors, crafters, entertainment, food and ponies. (fourth weekend in September)

September *(cont.)*

MARYLAND SEAFOOD FESTIVAL

CENTRAL – **Annapolis**, Sandy Point State Park. Traditional Maryland seafood fare, crab soup cookoff, arts and crafts, music, family-oriented entertainment. Admission. **www.mdseafoodfestival.com**. (second weekend in September)

BALTIMORE BOOK FESTIVAL

CENTRAL – **Baltimore**, Mount Vernon Place. Celebration of the literary arts; local bookstores, publishers, storytellers, author signings, crafts, refreshments and entertainment. **www.promotionandarts.com** (fourth long weekend in September)

DEFENDERS' DAY- A STAR-SPANGLED BANNER WEEKEND

CENTRAL – **Baltimore**, Fort McHenry National Monument. **www.nps.gov/fomc**. Large War of 1812 re-enactment, musket firing, artillery demos, noted authors, children's programs, fireworks, ship-to-shore bombardment and military band concert. Admission. (second weekend in September)

DRAGON BOAT RACES

CENTRAL – **Baltimore** Inner Harbor. **www.returnofthedragons.com** Corporate sponsored teams compete in chessie (dragon) boat races for Catholic charities. Daylong elimination heats determine winner of the Dragon Cup. (second Saturday in September)

JOHNNY APPLESEED FESTIVAL

CENTRAL – **Baltimore** area, Weber's Cider Mill Farm – Rte. 695 exit 30B north. **www.webersfarm.com**. Hayrides, apple picking, farm animals, fresh pressed apple cider and baked fruit pies. (last full weekend in September)

STEAM DAYS AT THE B & O

CENTRAL – **Baltimore**, B & O Railroad Museum. **www.borail.org**. Celebration of American railroading including special programs, entertainment and train rides. Admission. (Labor Day weekend)

UKRAINIAN FESTIVAL

CENTRAL – **Baltimore**, Patterson Park. (410) 687-3465. Enjoy Ukrainian dance groups, ethnic food, pierogy eating contest, 40 vendors, eggs and children's area. (second weekend in September)

DUCK FAIR

CENTRAL – **Havre de Grace**, Decoy Museum grounds. 50 carvers, collectors & artists, live & silent auctions, kids activities, retrievers, carving competition. **www.decoymuseum.com**. (second weekend in September)

FALL HARVEST FESTIVAL

CENTRAL – **Havre de Grace**, Steppingstone Museum. Scarecrow making, hayrides, clowns, storytelling, pumpkin painting, apple bobbing, crafts, food, tours, country music, clogging and corn shelling. **www.steppingstonemuseum.org**. Admission. (fourth weekend in September)

CHILDREN'S DAY AT LADEW TOPIARY GARDENS

CENTRAL – Monkton, Ladew Topiary Gardens. Live entertainment, interactive performances for children of all ages, treasure hunt, face painting and balloons. **www.ladewgardens.com**. Admission. (second Sunday in September)

APPLE FESTIVAL

CENTRAL – **Sykesville**, Piney Run Park. (410) 795-6043. Crafters, demos, hayrides, live music and entertainment, face painting, scarecrow making, apple dumplings, homemade food and baked goods. Admission. (fourth Saturday in September)

HOWARD COUNTY FARM HERITAGE DAYS

CENTRAL – **West Friendship**, Clarks Eliok Farm, Sharps and Triadelphia Lake View Farm. **www.farmheritage.org**. Family fun, antique farm equipment, arts and crafts show, live music, food. (fourth weekend in September)

September *(cont.)*

STEAM SHOW DAYS

CENTRAL – **Westminster**, Carroll County Farm Museum. Antique farm machinery, antique cars, working demos, flea market, hayrides, farmhouse tours, sawmilling, & food for sale. **http://ccgov.carr.org/farm**. (second weekend in September)

FALL FESTIVAL

CENTRAL – **Woodbine**, Days End Farm Horse Rescue. **www.defhr.org**. Horses in costume. Petting zoo, pony rides, games and prizes. All proceeds benefit abused, neglected horses. Admission. (last Saturday in September)

VETERANS RECOGNITION TRIBUTE/MEMORIAL

EASTERN SHORE – **Cambridge**, Sailwinds Governor Hall. (410) 228-4692. To honor and thank all veterans, active military, law enforcement, personnel, fire fighters, and EMT's. Presentation of colors, USO show, WWII Encampment, cannon firing, 21 gun salute. (second Saturday in September)

CRAB FEAST

EASTERN SHORE – Chestertown, Wilmer Park. Extravaganza features balloon rides, fireworks & entertainment. Delicious Eastern Shore crabs. **www.chestertown.com/c-300**. (third Saturday in September)

NATIONAL HARD CRAB DERBY AND FAIR

EASTERN SHORE – **Crisfield**, Somers Cove Marina. This tiny town and its waters are responsible for supplying much of the world with crabs. Crabs representing all 50 states try to skittle to glory in the crab race; parade, crab cooking and picking contests, fireworks, games, amusement rides, boat docking, fireworks. Admission. **www.crisfieldchamber.com/events.htm**. (Labor Day weekend)

SKIPJACK RACE AND LAND FESTIVAL

EASTERN SHORE – **Deal Island** Harbor. Skipjack race. Car show, concerts, vendors, events. Home to still active commercial skipjacks. **www.webauthority.net/lions.htm** Admission. (Labor Day weekend)

MILBURN ORCHARDS

EASTERN SHORE – **Elkton**, Milburn Orchards, 1495 Appleton Road. **www.milburnorchards.com**. U-pick apples and raspberries; Barnyard Buddy demos, magic shows, entertainment, games. (weekends in September)

SUNFEST

EASTERN SHORE – **Ocean City**, boardwalk, Inlet lot. **www.ococean.com**. Ocean City's biggest festival with fine art, crafts, performers on two stages and a variety of food vendors. Fall Children's activities include pumpkin decorating and scarecrow making. The Kite Festival includes a kids workshop, kite battles and the East Coast's premier sport kite competition. Evening headline entertainers. Admission. (fourth long weekend in September)

WAR OF 1812 RE-ENACTMENT

SOUTHERN – **St. Leonard**, Jefferson Patterson Park and Museum. **www.jefpat.org**. Re-enactment at the site of the Battle of St. Leonard Creek; British and American encampments, musket and cannon demonstrations, 19th century crafters and vendors. Tours of Lab offered. Admission. (last Saturday in September)

WOODLAND INDIAN DISCOVERY DAY

SOUTHERN – **St. Mary's City** , historic area. **www.stmaryscity.org**. Explore American Indian culture & skills through demos & hands-on activities. Try a traditional dance, shoot a bow and arrow, learn to start a fire without a match. Storytelling. Admission. (second Saturday in September)

APPLE BUTTER BOIL

WESTERN – **Oakland**, Harrington Manor/Swallow Falls State Park. **www.dnr.state.md.us**. Enjoy arts, crafts, and music while stirring the apple butter and feasting on a corn roast. Admission to State Park. (Labor Day weekend)

September *(cont.)*

SHARPSBURG HERITAGE DAY

WESTERN – **Sharpsburg**, downtown. Commemorating Battle of Antietam, period music, children's activities, crafts and local food. **www.sharpsburghistoricalsociety.org**. Colonial Kids Camp at the Agricultural Education Center where kids will get hands-on experience in colonial skills and trades, while learning from one of the many historical interpreters. (third Saturday in September)

SEPTEMBER / OCTOBER

THE MAZE AT CRUMLAND FARMS

CAPITAL – **Frederick**, Crumland Farms. **www.crumland.com**. 6 acres of twisty-turny joy in the middle of a real working cornfield, truly an a-Maze-ing way to get lost in the fun. Admission. (late September thru October)

WINTERBROOK FARMS MOONLIGHT MAZE

CAPITAL – **Thurmont**, Winterbrook Farms (Route 550). Pumpkin cannon shoot, largest corn mazes in the state with seven miles of trails. **www.mazeplay.com**. Admission. (Friday-Sunday from late September thru October)

MARYLAND RENAISSANCE FESTIVAL

CENTRAL – **Annapolis**, Crownsville Road. **www.rennfest.com**. 16th century English festival with 10 stages, 5,000 seat jousting arena, zoo performers, 140 food and craft shops. Admission. (weekends in September and October)

NORTH RUN FARM

CENTRAL – **Baltimore** area, North Run Farm, 1703 Greenspring Valley Road, just west of Villa Julie College. **www.northrunfarm.com**. Hayride to pick your own pumpkin patch, GPS designed corn maze, farm animal zoo, barnyard fun. Admission. (long weekends late September thru early November)

BRADS PRODUCE

CENTRAL – **Churchville**, Brad's Produce, 550 Asbury Road. **www.bradsproduce.com**. This farm is a full-time farming operation raising fresh produce, flowers and grain. In the fall, they open the Corn Maze Adventure. Each year with a different theme. Each maze is designed to share history, too. Hayrides to the Pumpkin patch on weekends. Admission. (Labor Day thru end of October)

PUMPKIN PATCH

EASTERN SHORE – **Elkton**, Milburn Orchards. Unlimited access to hayrides, bail trail, corn maze, boo barn, Johnny's chicken coop, tractor tunnel, gigantic sand dig, entertainment shows and Milky Sway. **www.milburnorchards.com**. Admission (month-long in October)

CRAZY CORN MAZE

SOUTHERN – **Mechanicsville**, Forrest Hall Farm and Orchard. **www.forresthallfarm.com**. More than two miles of trails through a five-acre maze. Ticket includes hayride, visit with farm animals, maze and a pumpkin. Admission. (open to general public on weekends, by appointment on weekdays in September/October)

COVE RUN FARMS CORN MAZE

WESTERN – **Accident**, Cove-Run Farms (I-68 exit 14A, 3.5 mile south to right on Cove Run). **www.coverunfarms.com**. Ten-acre educational corn maze, play area, pedal tractor track, barn tours of working dairy farm – milk or feed cows, snacks for purchase. Admission. (mostly Friday – Sunday afternoons/evenings, other weekdays by appointment in September/October)

TWIGGTOWN HARVEST FESTIVAL

WESTERN – **Twiggtown**, J and B Farms. **www.jandbfarms.com**. Bring your family out for a day of fun and activity on the farm. Purchase a pumpkin and enjoy painting it or take a hay ride or grab some farm fresh food. There will also be antique tractors, clowns, crafts, a corn maze, a straw maze and mums. Admission. (weekends late September and October)

OCTOBER

TASTE OF BETHESDA

CAPITAL – **Bethesda**, Fairmont, Norfolk, St. Elmo, Cordell and Del Ray avenues. **www.bethesda.org**. Features 50 restaurants, four entertainment stages and a children's area for young visitors. (first Saturday in October)

INTERNATIONAL FESTIVAL

CAPITAL – **Bowie**, Allen Pond Park. **www.cityofbowie.org**. Celebrate cultures and countries from around the world through performing arts, visual arts, & exotic cuisines. (first Saturday in October)

BRUNSWICK RAILROAD DAYS

CAPITAL – **Brunswick**, East and West Potomac Streets, Railroad Square, Fire Hall. **www.brunswickmd.gov**. Craft, car, motorcycle, and train show, carnival, pony and MARC train rides, live entertainment. (first weekend in October)

FAMILY FESTIVAL AT THE FARM

CAPITAL – **Buckeystown**, Lilypons Gardens. **www.lilypons.com**. Garden tours, birding walks, face painting, nature crafts, festival foods. (third weekend in October)

FALL OPEN HOUSE

CAPITAL – **Colesville**, National Capital Trolley Museum. **www.dctrolley.org**. Go behind the scenes in the museum's trolley restoration and storage barn. (third Sunday in October)

FARM MUSEUM FALL FESTIVAL

CAPITAL – **Frederick**, Rose Hill Manor Park. Family festival; demos and activities relating to the agricultural heritage of the area. **www.rosehillmuseum.com**. Admission. (first weekend in October)

IN THE STREET

CAPITAL – **Frederick**, Market Street in downtown. **www.inthestreet.info**. Eight city blocks filled with music, food and children's activities. (first Saturday in October)

OKTOBERFEST

CAPITAL – Frederick Fairgrounds. **www.frederickoktoberfest.com**. German oompah bands, dancers, food, crafters, children's area, polka, contests. Admission. (first weekend in October)

SUMMERS FARM FALL FOR ALL FESTIVAL

CAPITAL – **Frederick**, Summers Farm. **www.summersfarm.com**. Pumpkin patch, hayrides, giant slides, five-acre corn maze, hayloft jumping, farm animals, pony rides and concession. Admission. (weekends in October)

OKTOBERFEST

CAPITAL – **Gaithersburg**, Kentlands Village Green. Horse-drawn hayrides, scarecrow making and demos, food booths and sampling of authentic German fare. **www.gaithersburgmd.gov**. (second Sunday in October)

SUGARLOAF CRAFTS FESTIVAL

CAPITAL – Gaithersburg, Montgomery County Fairgrounds. **www.sugarloafcrafts.com**. This exciting show features 450 fine artists and crafters, delicious food, craft demos, and children's entertainment. Admission. (second long weekend in October)

BUTLER'S ORCHARD PUMPKIN FESTIVAL

CAPITAL–Germantown, Butler's Orchard. **www.butlerorchard.com**. Pumpkins, hayrides, pony rides, hayloft jumping, food, crafts, animals, entertainment, straw maze and caramel apples. Admission. (weekends in October)

MEDIEVAL FAIRE

CAPITAL – Glenn Dale, Marietta House Museum. **www.pgparks.com**. Living history camps (11th-15th century); battle reenactments, music, crafts, period merchants, entertainment, food. Admission. (October)

PATUXENT WILDLIFE FESTIVAL

CAPITAL – **Laurel**, National Wildlife Visitor Center. Discover wildlife through behind-the-scenes tours, tram tours, live animals, research exhibits and kids crafts. **http://patuxent.fws.gov**. FREE. (second Saturday in October)

October *(cont.)*

KINDERFEST

CAPITAL – **Upper Marlboro**, Watkins Regional Park. Fall festival that celebrates Prince George's county children and families. Enjoy entertainment, workshops and exhibits, moon bounces, carnival games, pumpkin patch, farm and nature activities. **www.pgparks.com**. (first Sunday in October)

CAPITAL CHALLENGE HORSE SHOW/ WASHINGTON INTERNATIONAL

CAPITAL – **Upper Marlboro**, Show Place Arena/Prince George's Equestrian Center. **www.showplacearena.com**. See Olympians and Olympic hopefuls in one of the largest hunter/jumper equestrian competitions in the U.S. FREE. (October)

MARITIME REPUBLIC OF EASTPORT'S ANNUAL TUG OF WAR

CENTRAL – **Annapolis**, Second Street, next to Chart House. **www.themre.org**. The longest tug of war over a body of water in the world. The tug of war between the maritime Republic of Eastport and Downtown Annapolis features 1700 foot rope, more than 450 tuggers, and more than 1,000 spectators. Proceeds benefit charity. (last Saturday in October)

PUMPKIN WALK

CENTRAL – **Annapolis**, Hammond Harwood House. Old-fashioned fall fun especially for children. Festivities include story telling, apple bobbing, a parade and more. **www.hammondharwoodhouse.org**. Admission. (third Friday in October)

UNITED STATES SAILBOAT SHOW

CENTRAL – **Annapolis** City Dock & Harbor. **www.usboat.com**. Nation's oldest & largest in-water sailboat show, new sailboats, sailing accessories, equipment & services. Admission. (first full weekend in October)

UNITED STATES POWERBOAT SHOW

CENTRAL – **Annapolis** City Dock and Harbor. **www.usboat.com**. Nation's oldest and largest in-water powerboat show; new boats, accessories and services. Admission. (second weekend in October)

CZECH AND SLOVAK FESTIVAL

CENTRAL – **Baltimore (Parkville)**. **www.czslha.org**. Ethnic costumes, food, bands, & dancing. Sokol gymnastics, vendors, exhibits, instrumental & vocal music. Admission. (third Sunday in October)

FALL APPLE FESTIVAL

CENTRAL – **Baltimore**, North Street in Shot Tower Park. (410) 837-5424. Apple festival features foods, arts, crafts, live music, pie-eating contests, children's and adult games. (second Thursday in October)

FESTIFALL

CENTRAL – **Baltimore**, Clyburn Arboretum. Family harvest festival for all. **www.cylburnassociation.org**. Parking fee. (second Saturday in October)

LIVING AMERICAN FLAG PROGRAM

CENTRAL – **Baltimore**, Fort McHenry National Monument. **www.flagday.org**. 3,500 plus 3rd, 4th and 5th graders from public, private and home schools in Maryland recreate the first "Human Flag" (Living American Flag). (morning of October 6)

RUSSIAN FESTIVAL

CENTRAL – **Baltimore**, Holy Trinity Russian Orthodox Church. **www.russianfestival.latest-info.com**. Celebration of Russian culture & food, homemade breads, samovar, live Balalaika Orchestra, chorus, dancers, imports. Admission. (third full weekend in October)

LOHR'S ORCHARDS

CENTRAL – **Churchville**, Lohr's Orchard, Snake Lane. (410) 836-2783. Free wagon rides out to pick apples and pumpkins, fresh apple cider. (weekends in October)

October *(cont.)*

INTERNATIONAL FALL FESTIVAL

CENTRAL – **Columbia**, Oakland Mills Village Center. **www.columbiavillages.org/oaklandmills**. Moon bounce, crafts, drum circle, Chinese Dragon dance, entertainment, foreign car show, food and health screenings. (second Saturday in October)

SCOTTISH HIGHLAND GAMES

CENTRAL – **Crownsville**, Anne Arundel Fairgrounds. Massed pipebands, Scottish athletics, Highland dancing, fiddling, sheepdogs, Highland cattle, Clydesdales, Scottish entertainment, food and vendors. **www.annearun.com/aasfi**. Admission. (second Saturday in October)

DARLINGTON APPLE FESTIVAL

CENTRAL – **Darlington**, Shuresville Road. Take a step back in time. Apples, pumpkins, mums, crafts, entertainment, art, country market & refreshments. **www.darlingtonapplefest.org**. (first Saturday in October)

PUMPKIN WEEKENDS

CENTRAL – **Ellicott City**, Clark's Elioak Farm. Each weekend provides a little different theme – Storytime at the Farm, Pumpkin Growing Contest, Pumpkin Patch, Teddy Bear Farm visit, homemade cider, face-painting, hayrides, Scarecrow making, & Pumpkin Chucking. **www.clarklandfarm.com**. Admission. (month-long in October)

SWANFEST

CENTRAL – **Havre de Grace**, Swan Harbor Farm. (410) 939-6767. Spend a day on the farm with crafters, hayrides, pumpkins, entertainment, children's activities and food. Admission. (third Sunday in October)

FALL HARVEST FESTIVAL

CENTRAL – **Millersville**, Kinder Farm Park. Hayrides, children's games, music, scarecrow making, pumpkin painting, blacksmith demo, farm animals, ponies, food & more. **www.kinderfarmpark.org**. (second Saturday in October)

FALL FESTIVAL

CENTRAL – **Mount Airy**, Historic Main Street. (301) 829-2112. 150 juried artisans and crafters, entertainment, food, contests, children's section, scarecrow making and pumpkin painting. (first weekend in October)

WEST RIVER HERITAGE DAY AND OYSTER FESTIVAL

CENTRAL – **Shadyside**, Captain Salem Avery House Museum. **www.averyhouse.org**. Great food including raw oysters, oyster fritters, fried oysters, oyster stew, crab cakes, fresh fish, cream of crab soup, picnic food, desserts and refreshments. Musical entertainment and children's activities. Admission (age 13+). (third Sunday in October)

SUGARLOAF CRAFTS FESTIVAL

CENTRAL – **Timonium**, Maryland State Fairgrounds. A show featuring 350 fine artists and craft designers, delicious food, craft demos and children's entertainment. **www.sugarloafcrafts.com**. Admission. (first weekend in October)

FALL HARVEST AT BAUGHER'S

CENTRAL – **Westminster**, 3 miles west of town on Rte. 140. **www.baughers.com**. Pick your own pumpkins, hayrides, pony rides, scarecrow making, face painting, petting zoo, food, farm market, ice cream and play area. Admission. (weekends in October)

FALL HARVEST DAYS

CENTRAL – **Westminster**, Carroll County Farm Museum. Scarecrow making, wagon rides, apple butter making, country food, crafts, entertainment, puppet theater, games, farmhouse tours. **http://ccgov.carr.org/farm**. Admission. (first weekend in October)

APPLEWOOD FARM

CENTRAL – **Whiteford**. **www.applewoodfarm.org**. Petting zoo, hayrides, pony rides, pick-your-own pumpkins, decorated barn, train gardens, children's maze. Admission. (weekends in October)

October *(cont.)*

WILDLIFE REFUGE OPEN HOUSE

EASTERN SHORE – **Cambridge**, Blackwater National Wildlife Refuge Visitor Center. **www.blackwater.fws.gov**. Event highlighting wildlife and refuge management programs, featuring demos, tours, wildlife exhibits and children's programs. (second Saturday in October)

FLY IN

EASTERN SHORE – **Ocean City** Municipal Airport. 800-OC-OCEAN or **www.ococean.com**. Annual Fly-In offers fun for the whole family. Display aircraft include restored vintage planes along with aircraft from the MD National Guard, United States Air Force, United States Coast Guard, United States Marine Corps & MD State Police. Educational presentations, demonstrations, food & music. (first weekend in October)

OKTOBERFEST

EASTERN SHORE – **Ocean City**, Convention Center, 40th St. & Bay. **www.oceanpromotions.info**. Three full days of continuous entertainment including Jolly Joe & the Bavarians, the Polka Jets & the Alpen Rose Dancers. Eat, drink & be merry with schnitzels, wursts & arts and crafts. Admission. (first weekend in October)

1812 HERITAGE FESTIVAL

EASTERN SHORE – **Princess Anne**, Grounds of Teackle Mansion and Bending Water Park. **www.teackle.mansion.museum**. 1812 military encampment, interactive weapons drills, singing and period music, children's activities. (third weekend in October)

CHESAPEAKE WILDFOWL EXPO

EASTERN SHORE – **Salisbury**, Ward Museum of Wildfowl Art. **www.wardmuseum.org**. Shootin' stool competition, old decoy contest, auction, search/rescue dog demos, pig roast, water fowling, cooking demonstrations. (second long weekend in October)

CHESAPEAKE CELTIC FESTIVAL

EASTERN SHORE – **Snow Hill**, Furnace Town Living Heritage Museum. **www.celticfest.net**. Bagpipe bands, sheep herding, Celtic music & dance on three outdoor stages, medieval encampment, ethnic foods, marketplace & more. Admission. (first weekend in October)

MID-ATLANTIC SMALL CRAFT FESTIVAL

EASTERN SHORE – **St. Michaels**, Chesapeake Bay Maritime Museum. **www.cbmm.org**. Amateur and professional boat builders and enthusiasts bring their kayaks, canoes, and skiffs to show and race. Museum open too. Admission. (first Saturday in October)

TILGHMAN ISLAND DAY FESTIVAL

EASTERN SHORE – **Tilghman Island**. **www.tilghmanmd.com**. Local seafood, live music, watermen contests, artisans, championship docking, oyster shucking, crab picking contests and an auction. Admission. (third Saturday in October)

SOUTHERN MARYLAND FARM LIFE FESTIVAL

SOUTHERN – **Charlotte Hall**, Green Manor Farm. 60,000 square feet of indoor farm life exhibits, live demos, antique tractors, pop engine show and Christmas in April. Proceeds help fund the annual rebuilding/repairs of needy homes. **www.christmasinaprilsmc.org**. Admission. (second weekend in October)

BLESSING OF THE FLEET

SOUTHERN – **Colton's Point**, St. Clement's Island/Potomac River Museum. **www.blessingofthefleet.net**. Seafood demos, rides for kids, parades and food. Admission. (first weekend in October)

OYSTER FESTIVAL

SOUTHERN – **Leonardtown**, St. Mary's County Fairgrounds. **www.usoysterfest.com**. National shucking contest and oyster cook-off, lots of other seafood, exhibits, arts and crafts and live entertainment. Admission. (third weekend in October)

October *(cont.)*

PATUXENT RIVER APPRECIATION DAYS FESTIVAL

SOUTHERN – **Solomons**, Calvert Marine Museum grounds. Celebrating Maryland's largest intrastate river; boat rides, lighthouse, children's activities, live music, parade and arts & crafts show. **www.calvertmarinemuseum.com**. (first weekend in October)

GRAND MILITIA MUSTER

SOUTHERN – **St. Mary's City**, Largest gathering of 17th century reenactment units in the nation. "Competitions! Color! Pageantry!" Visit with militia families at one of the largest gatherings of 17th-century re-enactors in the U.S. Hearth cooking, mock battle, drills, and sutlers. **www.stmaryscity.org**. Admission. (third Saturday in October)

HARVEST HOEDOWN

WESTERN – **Hagerstown**, Fairgrounds Park. A wonderful autumn event for children featuring hay rides, barrel rides and pumpkin painting. **www.hagerstownmd.org**. (first Saturday in October)

AUTUMN GLORY FESTIVAL

WESTERN – **Oakland**, County-wide. **www.deepcreeklake.info.com** Fall foliage festival. Two parades, official Maryland state banjo and fiddle championships, crafts, Oktoberfest, square dancing, bagpipes, bluegrass, storytellers festival, and a fly-in. 40 events in all. Admission for some. (five days mid-October)

NOVEMBER

TRAIN SPOTTING DAY

CAPITAL – **Bowie Station** Museum. (301) 809-3088. Amtrak presses some amazing and unusual stock into service to accommodate the holiday weekend travelers. Enjoy a fun free afternoon of counting the unusual & old, rare equipment working the line. FREE. (November)

VETERAN'S DAY PARADE

CAPITAL – **Brunswick**, East & West Potomac Streets. One of the oldest Veterans Day parades in Maryland. Over four states, large variety of units. **www.brunswickmd.gov**. (first Sunday in November)

MADRIGAL FEASTE AND REVELS

CAPITAL – **Frederick**, All Saints Episcopal Church. Come discover the two men born in 1564, one month apart, and how they help create joy and mirth. Hearty fare from the Queen's kitchen. Admission. **www.frederickchorale.org**. (third weekend in November)

SUGARLOAF CRAFTS FESTIVAL

CAPITAL – **Gaithersburg**, Montgomery County Fairgrounds. **www.sugarloafcrafts.com**. Show features 500 fine artists and craft designers, delicious food, craft demos and children's entertainment. Admission. (third long weekend in November)

COLONIAL DOG SHOW

CENTRAL – **Annapolis**, Hammond Harwood House. Features breeds of dogs popular and available in the 18th century. Special tour of house and parade of dogs. **www.hammondharwoodhouse.org**. Admission. (first Saturday in November)

FESTIVAL OF TREES

CENTRAL – **Annapolis (Timonium)**, Maryland State Fairgrounds. **www.festivaloftrees.kennedykrieger.org**. Ring in the holiday season with crafts, ginger bread gardens and much more at this benefit of the children of Kennedy Krieger Institute. Admission. (Thanksgiving weekend in November)

THANKSGIVING PARADE

CENTRAL – **Baltimore**, East on Pratt Street to Market Place. **www.promotionandarts.com**. Santa Claus, floats, marching bands and equestrian units usher in the holiday season. (third Saturday in November)

November *(cont.)*

HISTORIC SAVAGE MILL HOLIDAY OPEN HOUSE

CENTRAL – **Savage**, throughout the mill. **www.savagemill.com**. Annual display of holiday trees; home décor and fashion, live music. (third weekend in November)

DOWNRIGGING WEEKEND SULTANA

EASTERN SHORE – **Chestertown** Town Dock. Sultana's Downrigging weekend with a tall ships parade of sail; cruises on the Chester River; tours of tall ships. **www.schoonersultana.com**. Admission. (first full weekend in November)

FESTIVAL OF TREES

EASTERN SHORE – **Easton**, Tidewater Inn and throughout Easton. **www.talbothospice.org**. Fabulous decorated Christmas trees and decorations, gifts, home tours and many other events. Admission. (last full weekend in November)

FALL FAMILY FESTIVAL

EASTERN SHORE – **Ridgely**, Adkins Arboretum. Catch the fall spirit with hayrides, guided walks through the woods, children's seasonal crafts & activities. **www.adkinsarboretum.org**. Admission. (second Saturday in November)

OYSTERFEST

EASTERN SHORE – **St. Michaels,** Chesapeake Bay Maritime Museum. Shucking, tonging, nippering, children's activities, live music, boat rides and purchase raw, steamed and fried oysters. Admission. (first Saturday in November)

VETERAN'S DAY PARADE

SOUTHERN – **Leonardtown**, Washington Street. Marching bands, military units, bagpipers, antique cars; Native American dancers, horses, scouts, Memorial ceremony and placing of wreaths. **www.leonardtown.somd.com**. (second Saturday in November)

HEARTH AND HOME IN EARLY MARYLAND

SOUTHERN – **St. Mary's City**, historic. **www.stmaryscity.org**. Discover the ways Maryland's first citizens prepared for winter before supermarkets and department stores. Hands-on activities. Admission. (thanksgiving weekend in November)

FALL PEAK COLOR EXCURSION

WESTERN – **Hagerstown** Railroad Museum. **www.roundhouse.org**. Join a trip through the Valley of the Bald Eagles. Travel from Brunswick, MD and Martinsburg, WV to Romney, WV. Because of the topography of the area, the colors come later in the season – this is the time of peak color and views of eagles. Admission. (first Saturday in November)

NOVEMBER / DECEMBER

WINTER LIGHTS

CAPITAL – **Gaithersburg**, Seneca Creek State Park. 3 1/2 mile drive through a winter wonderland light display; 350 displays, 60 of them animated. Large capacity vehicles welcome. Admission. **www.gaithersburgmd.gov**. (Thanksgiving thru end of December)

GINGERBREAD HOUSE CONTEST AND SHOW

CAPITAL – **Upper Marlboro**, Darnall's Chance. **www.pgparks.com**. Children of all ages marvel at the creativity and talent of local bakers. Visitors can choose the best houses on display - presented to both favorite adult and child entries. Small Fee. (Thanksgiving thru mid-December)

WINTER FESTIVAL OF LIGHTS

CAPITAL – **Upper Marlboro**, Watkins Regional Park. **www.pgparks.com**. Light up the holidays with this scenic show. Enjoy a festive, animated drive along a 2 1/2 mile course of more than one million twinkling lights, animated displays and arrangements. Admission. (nightly late November thru New Years Day)

November / December *(cont.)*

SANTA TRAINS

CAPITAL – **Walkersville** Southern Railroad. **www.wsrr.org**. Ride the train with Santa. Admission. (Thanksgiving weekend and first two weekends of December)

HOLIDAY FESTIVAL OF TRAINS AT THE B&O RAILROAD MUSEUM

CENTRAL – Baltimore and Ohio Railroad Museum. **www.borail.org**. The kick-off of the B&O's winter holiday celebration featuring model train gardens. Admission. (Thanksgiving through December)

SYMPHONY OF LIGHTS

CENTRAL – **Columbia**, Howard County General Hospital Symphony Woods. **www.hcgh.org**. Annual holiday drive-through light display to benefit maternal child services. Admission per car. (mid-November through first full week of January)

CAROUSEL WINTER WONDERLAND

EASTERN SHORE – **Ocean City**, Carousel Resort Hotel, 118th St. **www.carouselhotel.com**. Dazzling holiday decorations, indoor ice skating rink open to the public. Admission to the ice skating rink includes skates. (mid-November to late December)

WINTERLAND OF LIGHTS

EASTERN SHORE – **Ocean City**, Townwide, Inlet Lot; Northside Park. **www.ococean.com**. Dazzling lights on cold winter nights put everyone in a holiday mood. Tour the tunnel of lights and the Inlet where you'll find the beach filled with lights boasting a nautical theme. Travel the avenues of Ocean City to see the old-fashioned lighted wreaths, then on to Northside Park to see hundreds of animated lighted displays. Browse the gift shop, have a photo taken with Santa and enjoy hot chocolate in the heated, decorated tent while you wait to board the Winterfest Express to tour the lights. Small Fee to ride Tram (age 12+). (evenings mid-November to New Years Day)

VICTORIAN CHRISTMAS CELEBRATION

WESTERN – **Cumberland**, Gordon-Roberts House. Victorian Christmas celebration; the Christmas Garden. Christmas tea served with tours. **www.historyhouse.allconet.org**. Admission. (Tuesday-Saturday Thanksgiving thru end of December)

OLD-FASHIONED COWBOY CHRISTMAS

WESTERN – **Hagerstown, www.antietamrecreation.com**. Antietam Recreation. Start off with a hayride through the Wild West Town (look for outlaws, animals and a nativity scene). Grab your partner for some good old-fashioned barn dancing to build your appetite for dinner. Enjoy the generous meal of BBQ beef, baked potato, baked beans, applesauce, biscuits and gingerbread. Then, sit back and relax as they perform the exciting Wild West Christmas Show – bull-whip tricks, romance, comedy, and stunts with a touching Christmas message. Admission. (most Thursdays, Fridays and Saturdays from mid-November thru December)

DECEMBER

CHRISTMAS PARADES

CENTRAL – **Annapolis** City Harbor, **www.eastportyc.org**. (second Saturday in December)

EASTERN SHORE – **Cecil County** - North East, Main Street & Perryville Holly Tree Park (off Jackson Station Rd). Bands, floats, Santa's house. Annual lighting of the B&O Railroad's Travelers Christmas Tree – the Holly Tree with local performers and food vendors. (first Saturday in December)

EASTERN SHORE – **Easton**, Town Center. Olde Tyme Holiday Parade. **www.eastonmd.org**. Victorian-themed parade includes horses and carriages, floats, costumed characters; 2 tree-lighting ceremonies. (first Saturday in December)

EASTERN SHORE - **Ocean City** Christmas Parade, 100th St to 115th St. **www.ococean.com**. Professionally judged parade with bands, floats, marching units & more. (first weekend in December)

December - Christmas Parades *(cont.)*

EASTERN SHORE – **Oxford** waterfront. Parade of Lights (Talbot Twinkles). **www.tourtalbot.org**. Lighted boat parade led by Santa. (first Saturday in December)

WINTER'S EVE CELEBRATION

CAPITAL – **Accokeek**, National Colonial Farm, Piscataway Park. **www.accokeek.org**. The farm will celebrate the beginning of the winter season with a cup of colonial cranberry tea, cookies, popcorn, and carols by the fire. Features special musical entertainment and a gift shop. FREE. (December)

BETHESDA'S WINTER WONDERLAND

CAPITAL – **Bethesda**, various locations. **www.bethesda.org**. Winter wonderland features carolers, arts and crafts, storytelling, holiday treats and Santa Claus. (second weekend in December)

FAMILY HOLIDAY FUN

CAPITAL – **Bowie**, Fire House 9th Street, Belair Mansion and other downtown locations. **www.cityofbowie.org**. Enjoy holiday music, dance and children's arts and crafts stations. Mr. And Mrs. Claus, too. (first Sunday in December)

VICTORIAN YULETIDE BY CANDLELIGHT

CAPITAL – **Clinton**, Surratt House Museum. **www.surratt.org**. Holiday tours, period greens, antique dolls and toys, 19th century cards and ornaments, refreshments. Admission. (weekend in December)

HOLLY TROLLEYFEST

CAPITAL – **Colesville**, National Capital Trolley Museum, Northwest Branch Park. **www.dctrolley.org**. Ride with Santa aboard a trolley and see toy trains in operation. Admission. (first three weekends in December)

HOLIDAY TRAINS AND PLANE

CAPITAL – **College Park** Aviation Museum. The museum is all decked out in the Yuletide spirit complete with an encore exhibit. Miniature trains, villages, tunnels and depots bring history to life. Santa fly-in the first weekend. **www.collegeparkaviationmuseum.com.** Admission. (Saturdays in December)

BETHLEHEM MARKETPLACE

CAPITAL – **Frederick**, Evangelical Lutheran Church, 31 E Church Street. (301) 663-6361. Walk-thru dramatization of Bethlehem at the time of Jesus' birth; culminates with a live nativity. Admission. (second weekend in December)

CANDLELIGHT HOUSE TOUR

CAPITAL – **Frederick**, downtown historic district. Self-guided tour of private homes elaborately adorned with holiday décor in historic Frederick. **www.celebratefrederick.com.** Admission. (first weekend in December)

HOLIDAY MAGIC

CAPITAL – **Frederick**, Rose Hill Manor Park. Holiday programming for children and their families; hands-on activities, snacks, magic shows. **www.rosehillmuseum.com.** Admission. (first Saturday in December)

MUSEUMS BY CANDLELIGHT

CAPITAL – **Frederick**, various museums. Interpretive tours, seasonal music, decorations, hearth demos, children's activities, holiday traditions of the past. **www.fredericktourism.org.** (second Saturday in December)

HOLIDAY CANDLELIGHT TOURS

CAPITAL – **Glenn Dale**, Marietta House Museum. **www.pgparks.com.** Enjoy Federal, Civil War and Victorian era decorations. Program includes reenactor escorts, live music, storyteller, light refreshments. Admission. (December)

December *(cont.)*

HOLIDAY CANDLELIGHT TOURS

CAPITAL – **Laurel**, Montpelier Mansion. **www.pgparks.com**. Refreshments, live holiday music by area performers, tours of the mansion decorated with green and lit by candlelight. (second long weekend in December)

WINTER EVENINGS

CAPITAL – **Riverdale** Park, Riverdale House Museum. **www.pgparks.com**. Step back in time to see the candlelit house, with re-enactors, games and refreshments. Admission. (last Thursday and Friday in December)

HANSEL & GRETEL TEA PARTY

CAPITAL – Upper Marlboro, Darnall's Chance. **www.pgparks.com**. Visit Darnall's Chance when it is decorated like a gingerbread house, listen to the story of Hansel and Gretel and enjoy tea and dessert. Reservations and Fee apply. (third Saturday in December)

NUTCRACKER PERFORMANCES

No holiday season is complete without Tchaikovsky's The Nutcracker. Enjoy breathtaking scenery, extravagant costumes, and dance that thrills adults and children alike. Admission.

> **CAPITAL-DC -** American Ballet Theatre: The Nutcracker, Kennedy Center. 202-467-4600, **kennedy-center.org**.

> **CAPITAL-DC -**Washington Ballet: The Nutcracker, Warner Theatre, Georgetown. 1299 Pennsylvania Ave. NW. (202) 397-7328, **washingtonballet.org**. The Nutcracker bears a striking resemblance to George Washington and the Rat King looks a bit like King George III

HOLIDAY HOMECOMING

CAPITAL-DC - Warm up your holiday season with spectacular art exhibitions and lively performances in the nation's capital. Lighting of the National Christmas Tree (White House Ellipse), Discovery

Theatre children's performances (Discovery of Light), house tours, Creche Nativity display and Christmas Pageant at National Cathedral. **www.washington.org/holidayhomecoming/**. Some events require fee. (December)

CANDLELIGHT STROLL

CENTRAL – **Annapolis**, City Dock. **www.watermarkcruises.com**. A Christmas candlelight walk through historic Annapolis; reservations required. Admission. (weekends in December)

GREENS SHOW AND SALE

CENTRAL – **Annapolis**, Hammond Harwood House. This event features the sale of fresh holiday decorations from the 18th century. **www.hammondharwoodhouse.org**. Tour the house dressed in holiday splendor. Admission. (second weekend in December)

HOLIDAY OPEN HOUSE

CENTRAL – **Annapolis**, William Paca House and Garden. **www.Annapolis.org**. Period home enhances candlelight and daylight tours of the William Paca House in all of its holiday grandeur. Admission. (almost daily in December)

LIGHTS ON THE BAY

CENTRAL – **Annapolis**, Sandy Point State Park. (410) 481-3161. Annual drive through holiday lights show sponsored by the Anne Arundel Medical Center (benefits hospital). Admission. (month-long in December)

STATE HOUSE BY CANDLELIGHT

CENTRAL – **Annapolis**, Maryland State House. (410) 974-3400. Decorated for the holiday season; a variety of musical entertainment. State House guided tours. (first weekend in December)

BREAKFAST WITH SANTA

CENTRAL – **Baltimore**, Bay Lady and Lady Baltimore Harbor Cruises. **www.harborcruises.com**. Two hour cruise with breakfast buffet, Santa, DJ and holiday sing-along. Admission. (weekends in December leading to Christmas)

December *(cont.)*

MONUMENTAL OCCASION

CENTRAL – **Baltimore**, Mount Vernon Place. Annual lighting of the Washington Monument by the mayor and First Family of Baltimore. **www.promotionandarts.com**. Live entertainment, refreshments, colorful fireworks finale. (first Thursday in December)

CHRISTMAS OPEN HOUSE

CENTRAL – **Catonsville** Historical Society, 1824 Frederick Road. **www.catonsvillehistory.org**. Annual holiday house tour, rooms decorated by local community groups, firehouse, train garden, refreshments served. (first weekend in December)

CANDLELIGHT TOUR

CENTRAL – **Havre de Grace**, historic city streets. Tour of homes, museums, and B&Bs in historic HdG. **www.lockhousemuseum.org**. Admission. (second Sunday in December)

HOLIDAY OPEN HOUSE @ STEPPINGSTONE

CENTRAL – **Havre de Grace**, Steppingstone Museum and Park. **www.steppingstonemuseum.com**. Farmhouse decorated for the holidays, cookies, cider & more. FREE. (first weekend in December)

CHRISTMAS AT AN ENGLISH COUNTRY HOUSE

CENTRAL – **Monkton**, Ladew Topiary Gardens. Festively decorated manor house; fresh greens, unique holiday decorations for sale. **www.ladewgardens.com**. Admission. (second weekend in December)

FESTIVE CHRISTMAS LUNCH

EASTERN SHORE – **Elkton**, Historical Sinking Springs Herb Farm. **www.cecilcounty.com/sinkingsprings**. 130-acre historic farm near Chesapeake City has guided house tours with Colonial decorations, lunch buffet with reservations. Admission. (first Saturday in December)

LIVE NATIVITY

EASTERN SHORE – **North East**, Hart's Amphitheater and Tailwinds Farm. (410) 658-8187. Saturday at Hart's and Sunday evening at Tailwinds, read the Christmas story as the stable is full of live music and animals. Donations Accepted. (third weekend in December)

CANDLELIGHT TOUR

EASTERN SHORE – **Port Deposit**, Historic homes and buildings. (410) 378-4480. Late 1700s and early 1800s homes and buildings are seasonally decorated and opened for this event; Civil War activities planned. Admission. (first Saturday in December)

CANDLELIGHT TOUR

EASTERN SHORE – **Quantico**, Main Street. (410) 546-1557. A traditional candlelight walking tour of historic homes and churches. Admission. (second weekend in December)

GRAND ILLUMINATION AND CANDLELIGHT CAROLING WALK

EASTERN SHORE – **Ridgely**, Adkins Arboretum. The Arboretum's holiday decorations are illuminated, carolers lead visitors along lighted paths through the forest and Santa pays a visit. Admission. **www.adkinsarboretum.org**. (first Saturday in December)

VICTORIAN CHRISTMAS CELEBRATION

EASTERN SHORE – **Snow Hill**, Julia A. Purnell Museum, 208 W. Market St. **www.purnellmuseum.com**. Attend an old-fashioned holiday party with Victorian music, decorations & refreshments. Admission. (first Saturday in December)

19TH CENTURY CHRISTMAS

EASTERN SHORE – **Snow Hill**, Furnacetown. Open house with the village trimmed for Christmas. Animals, crafts and shopping. **www.furnacetown.com**. Admission. (first two Saturdays in December)

December *(cont.)*

HOLIDAY TOUR

EASTERN SHORE – **Westminster**, Carroll County Farm Museum. **http://ccgov.carr.org/farm**. Holiday theme tours, Santa, wagon rides on weekends, food. Museum. Admission. (first two long weekends in December)

CANDLELIGHT TOURS OF THE MANSION AT SOTTERLEY

SOUTHERN – **Hollywood**, Sotterley Plantation. **www.sotterley.org**. Special tours by candlelight; historical drama; live seasonal music, food and drink available; reservations required. Admission. (first weekend in December)

MARYLAND STATE POLICE SHIVER IN THE RIVER

SOUTHERN – **Newburg**, behind Gilligan's Pier Seafood. **www.somd.org**. Join hundreds of dunkers as they brave the river; benefits Special Olympics of Maryland. (first Saturday in December)

CHRISTMAS ON THE BEACH

SOUTHERN – **North Beach** boardwalk. **www.ci.north-beach.md.us**. Tree decorating and lighting, caroling, Yule log, refreshments; meet Santa. (first Saturday in December)

GARDEN IN LIGHTS

SOUTHERN – **Solomons**, Annmarie Garden. Delightful holiday light show full of imaginative creations and "Holiday I Spy" game for kids. **www.annmariegarden.org**. Admission. (nightly from second Friday thru New Years Day, except Christmas Eve)

VICTORIAN CHRISTMAS

SOUTHERN – **Waldorf**, Dr. Samuel A. Mudd House Museum. **www.somd.lib.md.us/museums/mudd.htm**. Refreshments, Civil War exhibits, music entertainment, Mr. & Mrs. Claus, and walk-through tours. Admission. (first weekend in December)

NORTH POLE & SANTA'S EXPRESS TRAINS

WESTERN – **Cumberland**, Canal Place depot. **www.wmsr.com**. The North Pole Express departs Cumberland at 6:00pm (Santa's Express departs at 11:30am), and the round trip lasts approximately 3 1/2 hours. Jolly Santa meets the train at the Depot in Frostburg, where riders will be served cookies and hot chocolate or candy canes. Admission. (Thursday, Friday and Saturdays in December, up to weekend before Christmas)

CHRISTMAS IN THE VILLAGE

WESTERN – **Grantsville**, Spruce Forest Artisan Village. **www.spruceforest.org**. Visit artisan studios as you stroll through candle-lit villages. Storytelling, complimentary refreshments, concerts. Admission. (first weekend in December)

FESTIVAL OF TREES

WESTERN – **Hagerstown**, Robinwood Medical Center. Benefit for special care nursing at Washington County Hospital, decorated trees, holiday gift shop, entertainment & special event activities. Admission. **www.festivaloftreesinhagerstown.org.** (first long weekend in December)

TRAINS OF CHRISTMAS

WESTERN – **Hagerstown** Roundhouse Museum. 300 S. Buthans Blvd (US 11). (301) 739-4665 or **www.roundhouse.org**. The visions, sounds, & snows of Christmas past & present on an "O" Gauge railroad. Admission. (every Friday-Sunday, except Dec. 24th, in December)

MOUNTAIN REFLECTIONS

WESTERN – **Rocky Gap** State Park. **www.mtreflections.com**. A community celebration in lights, held nightly during the Christmas holiday season. Over 30 large and many animated light displays are part of the scenic drive or walk through the park. Fees collected benefit the Western Potomac Chapter of the American Red Cross. Admission. (nightly in December)

NEW YEARS EVE CELEBRATIONS
FIRST NIGHT

A New Year's Eve celebration of family and the arts with no alcohol allowed. The downtown areas are transformed into a theater-without-walls, and non-stop stage entertainment is shown in various venues. Early programs for children, midnight waterfront fireworks finale. Admission.

CENTRAL – **Annapolis. www.firstnightannapolis.org**.
EASTERN SHORE – Easton Town Center. **www.easternshore.com/firstnighttalbot**.

DUCK DROP

CENTRAL – **Havre de Grace** Middle School, Lewis Lane. (410) 939-2100. Duck drops at Midnight followed by a fireworks spectacular. FREE.

1812 Heritage Festival, 210
18th Century Market Fair, 178
19th Century Christmas, 223
4th Of July Celebration, 188
AAFB Joint Services Open House &
  Air Show, 179
Adkins Arboretum, 108
Adventure Park USA, 13
African-American Family Community
  Day, 187
African-American Heritage Walking
  Tour, 172
Airmen Memorial Museum, 19
Albert Einstein Planetarium, 34
Allegheny Highlands Trail Of
  Maryland, 145
All American Fourth Of July
  Celebration, 189
America's Independence Day
  Parade, 189
American Chestnut Land Trust, 130
American Deli And Nutter's Ice
  Cream, 168
American Indian Heritage Day, 196
American Visionary Art Museum, 61
Annapolis Ice Cream Company, 87
Annapolis Maritime Heritage Festival
  (And Volvo Race), 179
Annapolis Maritime Museum, 45
Annapolis Symphony Orchestra, 40
Annmarie Garden, 132
Antietam Battlefield, 165
Antietam Recreation & Wild West
  Shows, 154
Applewood Farm, 209
Apple Butter Boil, 201
Apple Festival, 199
Artscape, 190
Assateague Adventure, 102
Assateague Island National Seashore &
  State Park, 92

Audubon Naturalist Society, Woodend
  Sanctuary, 5
Augustoberfest, 196
Autumn Glory Festival, 212
Babe Ruth Birthplace, 61
Backbone Mountain, 163
Back To The Future At The Lock
  House, 195
Baltimore's Fourth Of July
  Celebration, 190
Baltimore Area Sports, 49
Baltimore Book Festival, 198
Baltimore Civil War Museum, 51
Baltimore Maritime Museum, 70
Baltimore Museum Of Art, 59
Baltimore Museum Of Industry, 62
Baltimore Orioles, 49
Baltimore Pow-Wow, 194
Baltimore Public Works Museum, 53
Baltimore Ravens, 49
Baltimore Streetcar Museum, 57
Baltimore Symphony Orchestra, 50
Baltimore Waterfront Festival, 175
Banneker-Douglass Museum, 41
Barbara Fritchie House, 11
Battle Creek Cypress Swamp
  Sanctuary, 131
Bayside Inn, 121
Beltsville Agricultural Research
  Center, 3
Bethesda's Winter Wonderland, 218
Bethlehem Marketplace, 219
Big Bus Company Of Baltimore, 65
Big Run State Park, 153
Blacksmith Days, 181
Blackwater National Wildlife
  Refuge, 92
Black Panther Shipwreck Preserve, 129
Blessing Of The Combines, 195
Blessing Of The Fleet, 211
Blue And Gray Days, 187
Blue Angels, 180

Boat Float, 185
Bowie Baysox, 3
Bowie Heritage Day, 178
Brads Produce, 203
Breakfast With Santa, 221
Breezy Point Beach, 124
Broadford Lake Recreation Area, 164
Brooks Barrel Company, 93
Brunswick Railroad Days, 204
Brunswick Railroad Museum / C&O
   Canal Visitors Center, 4
Buddy's Crabs & Ribs, 87
Bunny Trains, 175
Bureau Of Engraving & Printing
   Tour, 28
Butler's Orchard Pumpkin Festival, 205
B & O Railroad Museum, 59
C&O Canal Paw Paw Tunnel, 158
Calvert Cliffs State Park, 127
Calvert County Farm Tour, 192
Calvert County Jousting
   Tournament, 196
Calvert Marine Museum, 132
Cal Ripken World Series, 194
Cambridge Lady Cruises, 94
Canalfest / Railfest, 193
Canal Place Heritage Area, 144
Candlelight House Tour, 219
Candlelight Stroll, 221
Candlelight Tour, 222, 223
Candlelight Tours Of The Mansion At
   Sotterley, 224
Capital Challenge Horse Show /
   Washington International, 206
Capitol Building, United States, 32
Carousel Winter Wonderland, 216
Carrol's Creek Café, 87
Casselman River Bridge State
   Park, 153
Catoctin Furnace, 20
Catonsville's July 4th Celebration, 190

Celebrate Maryland Archaeology
   Month, 177
Celtic Festival & Highland
   Gathering, 177
Charles Carroll House, 42
Charles Village Parade, 184
Chase Lloyd House, 42
Cherry Blossom Festival, 175
Chesapeake Bay Environmental
   Center, 101
Chesapeake Bay Maritime
   Museum, 118
Chesapeake Beach Railway
   Museum, 124
Chesapeake Beach Waterpark, 124
Chesapeake Biological Lab Visitors
   Center, 134
Chesapeake Celtic Festival, 211
Chesapeake Children's Museum, 46
Chesapeake Farms, 96
Chesapeake Fishing Adventures, 114
Chesapeake Sailing Cruises &
   Tours, 119
Chesapeake Wildfowl Expo, 210
Chessies, 65
Chestertown Tea Party Festival, 181
Chick & Ruth's Delly, 85
Children's Day, 179
Children's Day At Ladew Topiary
   Gardens, 199
Children's Day On The Farm, 187
Choptank Riverboat Company, 101
Christmas At An English Country
   House, 222
Christmas In The Village, 225
Christmas On The Beach, 224
Christmas Open House, 222
Christmas Parades, 217
Civil War Encampment, 188
Civil War Encampment Living
   History, 191
Civil War Living History Day, 180

Civil War Living History
  Re-enactment, 181
Clara Barton National Historic
  Site, 14
Clipper City Tall Ship, 69
College Park Aviation Museum &
  Airport, 6
Colonial Dog Show, 213
Comfort Inn, 121
Common Ground On The Hill, 191
Concord Point Lighthouse, 76
Conowingo Hydroelectric Plant, 97
Cotoctin Wildlife Preserve And
  Zoo, 19
Cove Point Lighthouse, 132
Cove Run Farms Corn Maze, 203
Crab Feast, 200
Cranesville Subartic Swamp, 160
Crazy Corn Maze, 203
Crisfield Walking & Trolley Tours, 97
Cruisin' Ocean City, 182
Crystal Grottoes Caverns, 142
Cumberland Full Scale C & 0 Canal
  Boat Replica, 145
Cumberland Theatre, 146
Cunningham Falls State Park, 20
Czech And Slovak Festival, 207
C & D Canal Museum, 95
C & O Canal National Historical Park,
  18
C & O Canal National Historical Park
  Visitor Center, 145
C & O Canal Visitor Center, 158
Dans Mountain State Park, 160
Darlington Apple Festival, 208
Day Basket Factory, 83
DC Ducks, 37
Decoy And Wildlife Art Festival, 180
Deep Creek Lake Fireworks
  Celebration, 193
Deep Creek Lake State Park &
  Discovery Center, 151

Defenders' Day- A Star-spangled
  Banner Weekend, 198
Delmarva Shorebirds Baseball, 111
Discovery Station, 155
Discover Annapolis Trolley Tour, 46
Downrigging Weekend Sultana, 214
Dr. Samuel Mudd Home, 138
Dragon Boat Races, 198
Drum Point Lighthouse, 134
Duck Drop, 226
Duck Fair, 199
Eagle Festival, 173
Eastern Neck National Wildlife Refuge,
  109
Eastern Shore Fishing Derby, 186
Easter Brunch Cruise, 176
Easter Egg Hunt, 178
Easter Kids Fair, 176
Easter Sunrise Service, 177
Ed Kane's Water Taxi, 65
Elk Neck State Park And Forest, 102
Ellicott City B&O Railroad Station
  Museum, 73
Enchanted Forest & Clarkland Farm, 72
Evans Seafood, 139
Fairmount Academy 1800's Festival,
  182
Fall Apple Festival, 207
Fall Family Festival, 214
Fall Festival, 200, 209
Fall Harvest At Baugher's, 209
Fall Harvest Days, 209
Fall Harvest Festival, 199
Fall Open House, 204
Fall Peak Color Excursion, 215
Family Festival At The Farm, 204
Family Holiday Fun, 218
Farm Museum Fall Festival, 204
Farm Museum Family Festival, 174
Fells Point Maritime Museum, 51
Festifall, 207
Festival Of Trees, 213, 214

Festive Christmas Lunch, 222
Fireside Deli, 169
Fireworks At Fairgrounds Park, 193
Fireworks Celebration, 193
Fireworks Extravaganza, 191
Fire Museum Of Maryland, 82
First Night, 226
Flag Day, National Pause For The
    Pledge Of Allegiance, 184
Flag Day Fireworks Cruise, 184
Flag House & Star Spangled Banner
    Museum, 54
Flag On Mountain Maryland, 188
Flag Ponds Nature Park, 128
Fly-In, 181, 210
Fort Foote, 8
Fort Frederick, 142
Fort Frederick Anniversary Celebration,
    183
Fort McHenry National Monument &
    Historic Shrine, 63
Fort Washington Park, 8
Franklin D. Roosevelt Memorial, 25
Frederick's 4th – An Independence Day
    Celebration, 188
Frederick Celtic Festival, 179
Frederick Douglass - Isaac Myers
    Maritime Park, 55
Frederick Keys Baseball, 10
Frontier Town Western Park, 107
Frostburg State University Planetarium,
    152
Furnace Town Living Heritage
    Museum, 116
Gambrill State Park, 20
Garden In Lights, 224
Gathland State Park & Townsend
    Museum, 144
George Washington's Headquarters,
    146
Geppi's Entertainment Museum, 50
German-American Festival, 181

Gingerbread House Contest And Show,
    215
Glorious Fourth, 190
Gordon-Roberts House, 146
Grand Militia Muster, 212
Great Frederick Fair, 197
Greenbrier State Park, 143
Greens Show And Sale, 221
Greenwell State Park, 126
Green Ridge State Forest, 152
Gunpowder Falls State Park / Jerusalem
    Mill, 81
Hagar House, 157
Hagerstown City Park, 157
Hagerstown Speedway, 155
Hagerstown Suns Baseball, 156
Hampton Inn, 139
Hampton Inn & Suites, 22
Hampton National Historic Site, 85
Hansel & Gretel Tea Party, 220
Harborplace, 64
Harvest Hoedown, 212
Havre De Grace Decoy Museum, 76
Havre De Grace Maritime Museum, 78
Hayride In Bunnyland, 174
Hearth And Home In Early Maryland,
    215
Heritage Days Festival, 187
Herrington Harbour Inn, 86
Herrington Manor State Park, 161
Hessian Barracks, 12
Hirshhorn Gallery, 35
Historical Electronics Museum, 81
Historic Londontown, 71
Historic Savage Mill Holiday Open
    House, 214
Historic St. Marys City, 136
Historyquest, 41
Holiday Candlelight Tours, 219, 220
Holiday Festival Of Trains At The B&O
    Railroad Museum, 216
Holiday Homecoming, 220

Holiday Magic, 219
Holiday Open House, 221
Holiday Open House @ Steppingstone, 222
Holiday Tour, 224
Holiday Trains And Plane, 219
Holly Trolleyfest, 218
Honfest, 184
Howard County Farm Heritage Days, 199
Howard County Pow-Wow, 191
Husky Power Dogsledding, 147
Hyatt Regency Baltimore, 88
Hyatt Regency Chesapeake Bay, 120
Imagination Bethesda, 183
Independence Celebration, 191
Independence Day, 193
Independence Day Fireworks Cruises, 190
International Fall Festival, 208
International Festival, 204
International Spy Museum, 24
In The Street, 204
Island Grille, The, 121
J.C. Lore & Sons Oyster House, 135
Janes Island State Park, 98
Jefferson Memorial, 26
Jefferson Patterson Park And Museum Opening Celebration, 177
Jerusalem Mill, 81
Johnny Appleseed Festival, 198
John Paul Jones Day, 190
John Wilkes Booth Escape Route Tour, 174, 197
Jolly Roger Amusement Parks, 103
Jonathan Hagar Frontier Craft Days, 197
July 4th Celebration, 188
Kent Island Day, 182
Kinderfest, 206
Kunta Kinte, 42
Kunta Kinte Celebration, 194

Lacrosse Museum And National Hall Of Fame, 57
Ladew Topiary Gardens, 82
Lady Baltimore Or Bay Lady Harbor Cruises, 65
Lakeside Creamery, 169
Latinofest, 185
Laurrapin Grille, 89
Library Of Congress, 33
Lighthouse & Civil War Museum, 131
Lilypons Days, 183
Lincoln Memorial, 27
Linda's Café, 139
Lithuanian Festival, 180
Live Nativity, 223
Living American Flag Program, 207
Living History Program, 182
Lohr's Orchards, 207
Lonaconing Iron Furnace And Park, 160
MacGregors Restaurant, 89
Madrigal Feaste And Revels, 213
Maple Sugarin' Festival, 173
Maple Syrup Festival, 173
Marching Through Time, 174
Maritime Folklife Festival, 183
Maritime Heritage Festival, 187
Maritime Republic Of Eastport's Annual Tug Of War, 206
Martin Luther King Jr. Birthday Celebration Parade, 172
Maryland Aviation Museum, Glenn L. Martin, 59
Maryland Day, 173, 174
Maryland Historical Society Museums, 50
Maryland International Kite Exposition, 176
Maryland Renaissance Festival, 202
Maryland Science Center, 70
Maryland State Fair, 195
Maryland State House, 42

Maryland State Police Shiver In The River, 224
Maryland Symphony Orchestra (MSO), 156
Maryland Zoo In Baltimore, 58
Maze At Crumland Farms, 202
McHenry Highland Festival, 188
Medieval Faire, 205
Medieval Times Dinner & Tournament, 48
Mediterranean Festival, 185
Memorial Day Parade, 178
Merkle Wildlife Sanctuary & Visitors Center, 20
Mid-Atlantic Small Craft Festival, 211
Milburn Orchards, 201
Monocacy National Battlefield, 10
Monumental Occasion, 222
Mountain Reflections, 225
Mt. Zion One-room School Museum, 116
Museums By Candlelight, 219
Museum Ramble In Washington County, 183
NASA Goddard Space Flight Center, 15
Nation's St. Patrick's Day Parade, 173
National Air & Space Museum, 35
National Aquarium, 30
National Aquarium In Baltimore, 66
National Archives, 33
National Capital Trolley Museum, 6
National Colonial Farm In Piscataway Park, 2
National Cryptologic Museum, 75
National Gallery Of Art, 34
National Great Blacks In Wax Museum, 58
National Hard Crab Derby And Fair, 200
National Mall, 27
National Museum/American History, 36

National Museum Of Civil War Medicine, 12
National Museum Of Dentistry, 51
National Museum Of Natural History, 36
National Museum Of The American Indian, 36
National Postal Museum, 36
National Wildlife Visitor Center, 16
National Zoo, 24
Newseum, 34
New Germany & Big Run State Parks, 153
New Market Days, 197
New Years Eve Celebrations, 226
North Beach Bayfest, 196
North Point State Park, 81
North Pole & Santa's Express Trains, 225
North Run Farm, 202
Oakland Heritage Square, 161
Ocean City Boardwalk, 103
Ocean City Boat Tours, 104
Ocean City Fourth Of July Jamboree And Fireworks Jubilee, 192
Ocean City Life-saving Station Museum, 106
OC Jamboree, 108
Oktoberfest, 197, 205, 210
Old-fashioned Corn Roast Festival, 195
Old-fashioned Cowboy Christmas, 217
Old-fashioned July 4th Celebration, 192
On The Mall, 35
Oxon Hill Farm At Oxon Cove Park, 17
Oysterfest, 214
Oyster Festival, 211
Patapsco Valley State Park, 74
Patuxent River Appreciation Days Festival, 212
Patuxent River Naval Air Museum, 127
Patuxent Wildlife Festival, 205
Peggy Stewart House, 42

Pemberton Hall Plantation, 111
Phillips Seafood, 64
Pickering Creek Audubon Center, 101
Piney Point Lighthouse Museum, 129
Piney Point Lighthouse Waterfront
    Festival, 182
Pirate's Cove Restaurant, 86
Pirate Adventures On The Chesapeake,
    47
Piscataway Indian Museum & Trading
    Post, 137
Plaza Hotel, 168
Pleasant Valley Dream Rides, 162
Plumpton Park Zoo, 109
Pocomoke River State Park & Forest,
    117
Point Lookout State Park, 131
Polar Bear Plunge, Maryland State
    Police, 172
Port Discovery, The Children's
    Museum, 56
Potomac-Garrett State Forest/ Backbone
    Mountain, 163
Preakness Celebration Parade, 180
Princess Royale Resort Hotel, 122
Public Field Day, 183
Pumpkin Patch, 203
Pumpkin Walk, 206
Pumpkin Weekends, 208
Purnell Museum, 117
Radisson Hotel Largo, 22
Railroad Heritage Days, 187
Reginald F. Lewis Museum Of
    Maryland African American History
    & Culture, 56
Richardson Maritime Museum &
    Boatworks, 95
Ride The Ducks, 67
Ripken Stadium / Ironbirds, 40
Ripley's Believe It Or Not!, 105
Rocks State Park, 80
Rockville Science Day, 179

Rock Creek Park And Nature Center,
    25
Rock Hall Museum, 110
Rock Hall Parade And Fireworks, 192
Rock Run Grist Mill, 80
Roger Brooke Taney House, 8
Roman Days, 184
Rose Hill Manor Park/ Children's &
    Farm Museum, 9
Russian Festival, 207
Sackler Gallery, 37
Salisbury Pewter Outlet, 112
Salisbury Zoo, 112
Salute To Cecil County Veterans
    Celebration And Fireworks, 192
Salute To The Services, 182
Sandy Point State Park, 43
Savage River State Forest, 153
Schmankerl-stube Bavarian Restaurant,
    167
Schooner Sultana, 96
Schooner Woodwind, 43
Scottish Festival, 185
Scottish Highland Games, 208
Seneca Creek State Park, 13
Shaker Forest Festival, 197
Sharpsburg Heritage Day, 202
Shops At Canal Place, 146
Sideling Hill Exhibit Center & Wildlife
    Management Area, 159
Simon Pearce Glassblowing, 164
Six Flags America, 16
Skipjack Martha Lewis, 78
Skipjack Nathan Of Dorchester, 95
Skipjack Race And Land Festival, 200
Smallwood State Park, 128
Smiley's Funzone Pizzeria, 149
Smithsonian Environmental Research
    Center, 72
Smithsonian Folklife Festival, 189
Smithsonian Institution, 35
Smith Island, 114

Smith Island Cruises & Smith Island, 100
Soldier's Delight Natural Environmental Area, 84
Sotterley Plantation, 126
Southern Maryland Farm Life Festival, 211
Southern Maryland Soap Box Derby, 186
South Mountain State Battlefield, 143
Sports Legends @ Camden Yards, 52
Spring Carnival, 186
Spring Celebration, 176
Spring Muster And Antique Fire Apparatus, 185
Spring Open House, 178
Spruce Forest Artisan Village, 154
St. Clements Island Museum, 125
St. Clements Island State Park, 125
St. Joseph's Jousting Tournament, 195
St. Mary's River State Park, 126
St. Patrick's Day Parade And Festival, 173
Star-spangled Special Fireworks Train, 189
State House By Candlelight, 221
Steam Days At The B & O, 198
Steam Show Days, 200
Steppingstone Museum, 80
Strawberry Festival, 186
Sturgis One Room School Heritage House, 108
Sugarloaf Crafts Festival, 174, 176, 205, 209, 213
Suggested Lodging And Dining, 22, 85, 120, 139, 167
Summers Farm Fall For All Festival, 205
Summer Fest At Applewood, 186
Summer Fun Day, 191
Sunfest, 201
Suns On The Farm, 180

Surratt House Museum, 5
Susquehanna Museum Of Havre De Grace Lock House, 79
Susquehanna State Park / Rocks State Park, 80
Swallow Falls State Park, 163
Swanfest, 208
Symphony Of Lights, 216
Taste Of Bethesda, 204
Tawes, J. Millard, Historical Museum, 99
Thanksgiving Parade, 213
Thirsty Crab, The, 168
Thomas Stone National Historic Site, 130
Thrasher Carriage Museum, 152
Tidewater Archaeology Weekend, 193
Tilghman Island Day Festival, 211
Toby's Dinner Theatre, 64
Tourmobile, 37
Townsend Museum, 144
Towson Area Fourth Of July Parade, 191
Trader's Coffee House, 168
Trains Of Christmas, 225
Trains Of Christmas, The, 172
Train Room, The, 156
Train Spotting Day, 212
Tuckahoe State Park, 108
Tuckahoe Steam And Gas Show, 192
Twiggtown Harvest Festival, 203
U.S. Naval Academy, 44
U.S Army Ordnance Museum, 40
Ukrainian Festival, 199
United States Holocaust Memorial Museum, 28
United States Powerboat Show, 207
United States Sailboat Show, 206
USS Constellation, 68
Vandiver Inn, 88
Veteran's Day Parade, 213, 214
Veterans Day Parade, 213

Veterans Recognition Tribute/memorial, 200
Victorian Christmas, 224
Victorian Christmas Celebration, 217, 223
Victorian Yuletide By Candlelight, 218
Walkersville Southern Railroad, 21
Walters Art Museum, 53
Ward Museum Of Wildfowl Art, 113
War Of 1812 Encampment, 194
War Of 1812 Re-enactment, 201
War Of 1812 Re-enactment – Attack On Havre De Grace, 181
Washington County Rural Heritage Museum, 166
Washington Monument, 29
Washington Monument State Park, 144
Washington Redskins Football, 16
Waterman's Museum, 110
Watermark Cruises & Walking Tours, 47
Watkins Regional Park, 21
Way Off Broadway Dinner Theater & Children's Theater, 9
Western Maryland Rail Trail, 160
Western Maryland Scenic Railroad, 147
West River Heritage Day And Oyster Festival, 209
Wheat Threshing, Steam And Gas Engine Show, 195
Wheels Of Yesterday, 105
White's Ferry, 7
Whitehouse Easter, 175
White House, 31
Wildlife Refuge Open House, 210
William Paca House, 42
Wilson Country Store/ One Room Schoolhouse, 157
Wings Of Freedom Over Frederick, 194
Winter's Eve Celebration, 218
Winterbrook Farms Moonlight Maze, 202

Winterland Of Lights, 216
Winterlights: A Celebration Of Chesapeake Bay Lighthouses, 172
Winter Evenings, 220
Winter Festival Of Lights, 215
Winter Lights, 215
Wisp Resort At Deep Creek Lake, 149
Woodland Indian Discovery Day, 201
World Carnival, 177
World Trade Center "Top Of The World", 68
WWII Cradle Of Invasion, 196
Wye Grist Mill And Museum, 120
Wye Island Natural Resources Management Area, 109
Yogi Bear's Jellystone Park, 167
Youth Fishing Derby, 186

Activity Index

PROUDLY

MADE IN THE USA

AMUSEMENTS

CAPITAL - Frederick (New Market) *Adventure Park USA*, 13

CAPITAL – Largo, *Six Flags America*, 16

CAPITAL - Upper Marlboro, *Watkins Regional Park*, 21

CENTRAL - Baltimore, Inner Harbor, *Harborplace*, 64

EASTERN SHORE - Ocean City, *Jolly Roger Amusement Parks*, 103

EASTERN SHORE - Ocean City, *Ocean City Boardwalk*, 103

EASTERN SHORE - Ocean City, *Ripley's Believe It Or Not!*, 105

EASTERN SHORE - Ocean City, West, *Frontier Town Western Park*, 107

SOUTHERN - Chesapeake Beach, *Chesapeake Beach Waterpark*, 124

WESTERN - Deep Creek Lake, (McHenry), *Smiley's Funzone Pizzeria*, 149

ANIMALS & FARMS

CAPITAL – Thurmont, *Cotoctin Wildlife Preserve And Zoo*, 19

CENTRAL – Baltimore, *Maryland Zoo In Baltimore*, 58

CENTRAL - Baltimore, Inner Harbor, *National Aquarium In Baltimore*, 66

CENTRAL - Ellicott City, *Enchanted Forest & Clarkland Farm*, 72

CAPITAL – DC – *National Zoo*, 24

EASTERN SHORE – Chestertown, *Chesapeake Farms*, 96

EASTERN SHORE - Rising Sun, *Plumpton Park Zoo*, 109

EASTERN SHORE – Salisbury, *Salisbury Zoo*, 112

WESTERN – Hagerstown, *Antietam Recreation & Wild West Shows*, 154

HISTORY

CAPITAL – Accokeek, *Nat'l Colonial Farm In Piscataway Park*, 2

CAPITAL – Brunswick, *Brunswick Railroad Museum / C&O Canal Visitors Center*, 4

CAPITAL – Clinton, *Surratt House*, 5

CAPITAL – Colesville, *National Capital Trolley Museum*, 6

CAPITAL - College Park, *College Park Aviation Museum & Airport*, 6

CAPITAL - Fort Washington, *Fort Washington Park*, 8

CAPITAL – Frederick, *Roger Brooke Taney House*, 8

CAPITAL – Frederick, *Rose Hill Manor Park/Children's & Farm Museum*, 9

CAPITAL – Frederick, *Monocacy National Battlefield*, 10

CAPITAL – Frederick, *Barbara Fritchie House*, 11

CAPITAL – Frederick, *Hessian Barracks*, 12

CAPITAL – Frederick, *Nat'l Museum Of Civil War Medicine*, 12

CAPITAL - Glen Echo, *Clara Barton National Historic Site*, 14

CAPITAL - Oxon Hill, *Oxon Hill Farm At Oxon Cove Park*, 17

CAPITAL – Potomac, *C & O Canal National Historical Park*, 18

CAPITAL – Suitland, *Airmen Mem'l*, 19

CAPITAL – DC – *Franklin D. Roosevelt Memorial*, 25

CAPITAL – DC – *Jefferson Mem'l*, 26

CAPITAL – DC – *Lincoln Memorial*, 27

CAPITAL – DC – *National Mall*, 27

CAPITAL – DC – *United States Holocaust Memorial Museum*, 28

CAPITAL – DC – *Washington Monument*, 29

CAPITAL – DC – *Capital Building, United States*, 32

CAPITAL – DC – *National Archives*, 33

CAPITAL – DC – *Library/ Congress*, 33

HISTORY *(cont.)*

CAPITAL – DC – *Smithsonian Institution*, 35

CENTRAL – Aberdeen, *U.S. Army Ordnance Museum*, 40

CENTRAL – Annapolis, *Maryland State House*, 42

CENTRAL – Annapolis, *Annapolis Maritime Museum*, 45

CENTRAL – Baltimore, *Maryland Historical Society Museums*, 50

CENTRAL – Baltimore, *National Museum Of Dentistry*, 51

CENTRAL – Baltimore, *Flag House & Star Spangled Banner Museum*, 54

CENTRAL – Baltimore, *Frederick Douglass - Isaac Myers Maritime Park*, 55

CENTRAL – Baltimore, *Reginald F. Lewis Museum Of Maryland African American History & Culture*, 56

CENTRAL – Baltimore, *Baltimore Streetcar Museum*, 57

CENTRAL – Baltimore, *National Great Blacks In Wax Museum*, 58

CENTRAL – Baltimore, *Maryland Aviation Museum, Glenn L. Martin*, 59

CENTRAL – Baltimore, *B & O Railroad Museum*, 59

CENTRAL – Baltimore, *Baltimore Museum Of Industry*, 62

CENTRAL – Baltimore, *Fort McHenry National Monument & Historic Shrine*, 63

CENTRAL - Baltimore, Inner Harbor, *USS Constellation*, 68

CENTRAL - Baltimore, Inner Harbor *"World Trade Center, - Top Of The World"*, 68

CENTRAL - Baltimore, Inner Harbor, *Baltimore Maritime Museum*, 70

CENTRAL – Edgewater, *Historic Londontown*, 71

CENTRAL - Ellicott City, *Ellicott City B&O Railroad Station Museum*, 73

CENTRAL - Fort George G. Meade, *National Cryptologic Museum*, 75

CENTRAL - Havre de Grace, *Concord Point Lighthouse*, 76

CENTRAL - Havre de Grace, *Havre de Grace Maritime Museum*, 78

CENTRAL - Havre de Grace, *Susquehanna Museum Of Havre de Grace Lock House*, 79

CENTRAL – Linthicum, *Historical Electronics Museum*, 81

CENTRAL – Lutherville, *Fire Museum Of Maryland*, 82

CENTRAL – Towson, *Hampton National Historic Site*, 85

EASTERN SHORE – Cambridge, *Richardson Maritime Museum*, 95

EASTERN SHORE - Chesapeake City, *C & D Canal Museum*, 95

EASTERN SHORE – Crisfield, *Tawes, J. Millard, Historical Museum*, 99

EASTERN SHORE - Ocean City, *Ocean City Life - Saving Station Museum*, 106

EASTERN SHORE – Pocomoke, *Sturgis One Room School Heritage House*, 108

EASTERN SHORE - Rock Hall, *Rock Hall Museum*, 110

EASTERN SHORE - Rock Hall, *Waterman's Museum*, 110

EASTERN SHORE – Salisbury, *Pemberton Hall Plantation*, 111

EASTERN SHORE - Snow Hill, *Furnace Town Living Heritage Museum*, 116

EASTERN SHORE - Snow Hill, *Mt. Zion One-Room School*, 116

EASTERN SHORE - Snow Hill, *Purnell Museum*, 117

EASTERN SHORE - St. Michaels, *Chesapeake Bay Maritime Museum*, 118

HISTORY (cont.)

EASTERN SHORE - Wye Mills, *Wye Grist Mill & Museum*, 120

SOUTHERN - Chesapeake Beach, *Chesapeake Beach Railway Museum*, 124

SOUTHERN - Colton's Point, *St. Clements Island Museum*, 125

SOUTHERN – Hollywood, *Sotterley Plantation*, 126

SOUTHERN - Piney Point, *Piney Point Lighthouse Museum & The Black Panther Shipwreck Preserve*, 129

SOUTHERN - Port Tabacco, *Thomas Stone National Historic Site*, 130

SOUTHERN - St. Marys City, *Historic St. Marys City*, 136

SOUTHERN – Waldorf, *Piscataway Indian Museum & Trading Post*, 137

SOUTHERN - Waldorf (Beantown), *Dr. Samuel Mudd Home*, 138

WESTERN - Big Pool, *Ft. Frederick*, 142

WESTERN – Burkittsville, *Gathland State Park & Townsend Museum*, 144

WESTERN – Cumberland, *Canal Place Heritage Area*, 144

WESTERN – Cumberland, *Gordon-Roberts House*, 146

WESTERN – Hagerstown, *Hagar House & Hagerstown City Park*, 157

WESTERN - Hagerstown (Clear Spring), *Wilson Country Store/ One Room Schoolhouse*, 157

WESTERN – Hancock, *C & O Canal Visitor Center*, 158

WESTERN – Oakland, *Oakland Heritage Square*, 161

WESTERN – Sharpsburg, *Antietam Battlefield*, 165

WESTERN – Sharpsburg, *Washington County Rural Heritage Museum*, 166

MUSEUMS

CAPITAL – DC – *International Spy Museum*, 24

CAPITAL – DC – *Newseum*, 34

CENTRAL – Annapolis, *Chesapeake Children's Museum*, 46

CENTRAL – Baltimore, *Geppi's Entertainment Museum*, 50

CENTRAL – Baltimore, *Baltimore Public Works Museum*, 53

CENTRAL – Baltimore, *Port Discovery, Children's Museum*, 56

CENTRAL - Havre de Grace, *Havre de Grace Decoy Museum*, 76

EASTERN SHORE - Ocean City, *Wheels Of Yesterday*, 105

EASTERN SHORE – Salisbury, *Ward Museum Of Wildfowl Art*, 113

SOUTHERN - Lexington Park, *Patuxent River Naval Air*, 127

WESTERN – Frostburg, *Thrasher Carriage Museum*, 152

WESTERN – Hagerstown, *Discovery Station*, 155

WESTERN – Hagerstown, *The Train Room*, 156

OUTDOOR EXPLORING

CAPITAL - Chevy Chase, *Audubon Naturalist Society, Woodend Sanctuary*, 5

CAPITAL – Gaithersburg, *Seneca Creek State Park*, 13

CAPITAL – Thurmont, *Cunningham Falls State Park / Catoctin Furnace/Gambrill State Park*, 20

CAPITAL – DC – *Rock Creek Park & Nature Center*, 25

CENTRAL – Annapolis, *Sandy Point State Park*, 43

CENTRAL - Ellicott City, *Patapsco Valley State Park*, 74

CENTRAL - Havre de Grace, (Jerrettsville), *Susquehanna State Park / Rocks State Park*, 80

OUTDOOR EXPLORING (cont.)

CENTRAL – Kingsville, *Gunpowder Falls State Park/Jerusalem Mill*, 81

CENTRAL - Owings Mills, *Soldier's Delight Environmental Area*, 84

EASTERN SHORE – Berlin, *Assateague Island National Seashore & State Park*, 92

EASTERN SHORE – Cambridge, *Blackwater National Wildlife Refuge*, 92

EASTERN SHORE – Crisfield, *Janes Island State Park*, 98

EASTERN SHORE – Easton, *Pickering Creek Audubon Center*, 101

EASTERN SHORE – Grasonville, *Chesapeake Bay Environmental Center*, 101

EASTERN SHORE - North East, *Elk Neck State Park And Forest*, 102

EASTERN SHORE - Queen Anne, *Tuckahoe State Park*, 108

EASTERN SHORE – Queenstown, *Wye Island Natural Resources Management Area*, 109

EASTERN SHORE - Rock Hall, *Eastern Neck National Wildlife Refuge*, 109

EASTERN SHORE - Snow Hill, *Pocomoke River State Park & Forest*, 117

SOUTHERN - Chesapeake Beach, *Breezy Point Beach*, 124

SOUTHERN – Hollywood, *Greenwell State Park*, 126

SOUTHERN – Leonardtown, *St. Mary's River State Park*, 126

SOUTHERN – Lusby, *Calvert Cliffs State Park*, 127

SOUTHERN – Lusby, *Flag Ponds Nature Park*, 128

SOUTHERN – Marbury, *Smallwood State Park*, 128

SOUTHERN - Port Republic, *American Chestnut Land Trust*, 130

SOUTHERN – Scotland, *Point Lookout State Park*, 131

WESTERN – Boonsboro, *Greenbrier State Park*, 143

WESTERN – Boonsboro, *South Mountain State Battlefield*, 143

WESTERN – Boonsboro, *Washington Monument State Park*, 144

WESTERN - Deep Creek Lake, (McHenry), *Wisp Resort At Deep Creek Lake*, 149

WESTERN – Flintstone, *Green Ridge State Forest*, 152

WESTERN – Grantsville, *Savage River State Forest / New Germany & Big Run State Parks*, 153

WESTERN – Hancock, *Western Maryland Rail Trail*, 160

WESTERN – Lonaconing, *Dans Mountain State Park*, 160

WESTERN – Oakland, *Cranesville Subartic Swamp*, 160

WESTERN – Oakland, *Herrington Manor State Park*, 161

WESTERN – Oakland, *Potomac-Garrett State Forest / Backbone Mountain*, 163

WESTERN – Oakland, *Swallow Falls State Park*, 163

WESTERN - Oakland (Mountain Lake Park), *Broadford Lake Recreation Area*, 164

SCIENCE

CAPITAL - Beltsville (Powder), *Beltsville Agricultural Research Center*, 3

CAPITAL – Greenbelt, *NASA Goddard Space Flight Center*, 15

CAPITAL – Laurel, *National Wildlife Visitor Center*, 16

CAPITAL - Upper Marlboro, *Merkle Wildlife Sanctuary & Visitors Center*, 20

CAPITAL – DC – *National Aquarium*, 30

SCIENCE (cont.)

CAPITAL – DC – *Albert Einstein Planetarium*, 34

CENTRAL - Baltimore, Inner Harbor, *Maryland Science Center*, 70

CENTRAL – Edgewater, *Smithsonian Environmental Research Center*, 72

SOUTHERN - Prince Frederick, *Battle Creek Cypress Swamp Sanctuary*, 131

SOUTHERN – Solomons, *Calvert Marine Museum*, 132

SOUTHERN - Solomons Island, *Chesapeake Biological Lab Visitors Center*, 134

WESTERN – Boonsboro, *Crystal Grottoes Caverns*, 142

WESTERN - Deep Creek Lake (Swanton), *Deep Creek Lake State Park & Discovery Center*, 151

WESTERN – Frostburg, *Frostburg State University Planetarium*, 152

WESTERN – Hancock, *Sideling Hill Exhibit Center & Wildlife Management Area*, 159

SPORTS

CAPITAL – Bowie, *Bowie Baysox,* 3

CAPITAL – Frederick, *Frederick Keys Baseball*, 10

CAPITAL – Landover, *Washington Redskins Football*, 16

CENTRAL – Aberdeen, *Ripken Stadium / Ironbirds*, 40

CENTRAL – Baltimore, *Baltimore Area Sports*, 49

CENTRAL – Baltimore, *Sports Legends @ Camden Yards*, 52

CENTRAL – Baltimore, *LaCrosse Museum And National Hall Of Fame*, 57

CENTRAL – Baltimore, *Babe Ruth Birthplace*, 61

EASTERN SHORE – Salisbury, *Delmarva Shorebirds Baseball*, 111

SPORTS (cont.)

WESTERN – Hagerstown, *Hagerstown Speedway*, 155

WESTERN – Hagerstown, *Hagerstown Suns Baseball*, 156

THE ARTS

CAPITAL – Frederick, *Way Off Broadway Dinner Theater & Children's Theater*, 9

CAPITAL – DC – *National Gallery of Art*, 34

CENTRAL – Annapolis, *Annapolis Symphony Orchestra*, 40

CENTRAL - Annapolis (Hanover), *Medieval Times Dinner & Tournament*, 48

CENTRAL – Baltimore, *Baltimore Symphony Orchestra*, 50

CENTRAL – Baltimore, *Walters Art Museum*, 53

CENTRAL – Baltimore, *Baltimore Museum Of Art*, 59

CENTRAL – Baltimore, *American Visionary Art Museum*, 61

CENTRAL - Baltimore & Columbia, *Toby's Dinner Theatre*, 64

CENTRAL – Monkton, *Ladew Topiary Gardens*, 82

EASTERN SHORE - Ocean City, West, *OC Jamboree*, 108

SOUTHERN – Solomons, *Annmarie Garden*, 132

WESTERN – Cumberland, *Cumberland Theatre*, 146

WESTERN – Grantsville, *Spruce Forest Artisan Village*, 154

WESTERN – Hagerstown, *Maryland Symphony Orchestra (MSO)*, 156

TOURS

CAPITAL – Dickerson, *White's Ferry*, 7

CAPITAL – Walkersville, *Walkersville Southern Railroad*, 21

TOURS *(cont.)*

CAPITAL – DC – *Bureau of Engraving & Printing Tour*, 28
CAPITAL – DC – *White House*, 31
CAPITAL – DC – *Tourmobile*, 37
CAPITAL – DC – *DC Ducks*, 37
CENTRAL – Annapolis, *History Quest*, 41
CENTRAL – Annapolis, *Schooner Woodwind*, 43
CENTRAL – Annapolis, *U.S. Naval Academy*, 44
CENTRAL – Annapolis, *Discover Annapolis Trolley Tour*, 46
CENTRAL – Annapolis, *Pirate Adventures On The Chesapeake*, 47
CENTRAL – Annapolis, *Watermark Cruises & Walking Tours*, 47
CENTRAL - Baltimore, Inner Harbor, *Big Bus Company Of Baltimore*, 65
CENTRAL - Baltimore, Inner Harbor, *Lady Baltimore or Bay Lady Harbor Cruises*, 65
CENTRAL - Baltimore, Inner Harbor, *Ride The Ducks*, 67
CENTRAL - Baltimore, Inner Harbor, *Clipper City Tall Ship*, 69
CENTRAL - Havre de Grace, *Skipjack Martha Lewis*, 78
CENTRAL - North East, *Day Basket Factory*, 83
EASTERN SHORE – Cambridge, *Brooks Barrel Company*, 93
EASTERN SHORE – Cambridge, *Cambridge Lady Cruises*, 94
EASTERN SHORE – Cambridge, *Skipjack Nathan Of Dorchester*, 95
EASTERN SHORE – Chestertown, *Schooner Sultana*, 96
EASTERN SHORE – Conowingo, *Conowingo Hydroelectric Plant*, 97
EASTERN SHORE – Crisfield, *Crisfield Walking & Trolley Tours*, 97
EASTERN SHORE – Crisfield, *Smith Island Cruises & Smith Island*, 100
EASTERN SHORE – Hurlock, *Choptank Riverboat Company*, 101
EASTERN SHORE - Ocean City, *Assateague Adventure*, 102
EASTERN SHORE - Ocean City, *Ocean City Boat Tours*, 104
EASTERN SHORE – Salisbury, *Salisbury Pewter Outlet*, 112
EASTERN SHORE - Smith Island, (Tylerton), *Chesapeake Fishing Adventures*, 114
EASTERN SHORE - Tilghman Island, *Chesapeake Sailing Cruises & Tours*, 119
SOUTHERN – Solomon's Island, *J.C. Lore & Sons Oyster House*, 135
WESTERN – Cumberland, *Western Maryland Scenic Railroad*, 147
WESTERN - Deep Creek Lake, (Accident), *Husky Power Dogsledding*, 147
WESTERN – Oakland, *Pleasant Valley Dream Rides*, 162
WESTERN - Oakland (Mountain Lake Park), *Simon Pearce Glassblowing*, 164

Travel Journal & Notes:

Travel Journal & Notes:

Travel Journal & Notes:

Travel Journal & Notes:

Need more great ways to keep the kids busy?

www.KidsLoveTravel.com

Best-selling "Kids Love" Travel Guides now available for:

Florida, Georgia, Illinois, Indiana, Kentucky, Maryland, Michigan, North Carolina, Ohio Pennsylvania, Tennessee, and Virginia.

State Coloring Books:

Kids can color and learn new facts. Lots and fun and educational too. Includes State Characters, Places, Facts and Fun. Color your way around the state! All ages will enjoy these books. Various states.

State Big Activity Books:

Kids will learn about State History, Geography, People, Places, Nature, Animals, Holidays, Legend, Lore and much, much more by completing these enriching activities. Includes dot-to-dots, mazes, coloring, matching, word searches, riddles, crossword puzzles, word jumbles, writing, and many other creative activities. Each book is state specific fun! Reproducible. Grades 1-5. Correlates with State Academic Standards. Various states.

State Pocket Guides:

This handy easy-to-use guide is divided into 7 color coded sections (State Facts, Geography, History, People, Places, Nature, and more). Riddles, recipes, and surprising facts make this guide a delight. Various states.

Invisible Ink Book Sets:

(Includes special marker). Hours of "clean" fun for all. The special marker is clear so it doesn't make a mess. The invisible ink pen reveals invisibly printed pictures or answers to quizzes and games. What are you interested in? Sports ... Trivia ... History ... The Bible ... Fascinating Facts ... or just plain fun ...

(Just a sample of the many titles available below)

Kids Love Travel Memories!

Now that you've created memories with your family, it's time to keepsake them by scrapbooking in this unique, family-friendly way!

"Travel Mystery Books"

Kids Our kids love these books! A great way to engage the kids and learn about places they may visit. An EXCITING new series of mystery books for kids ages 7 to 14 featuring REAL KIDS in REAL PLACES! This series plunks real children in a current-day adventure mystery set in famous settings across America. Historical facts add powerful educational value! Students read about famous places like the Whitehouse, Biltmore House, Mighty Mississippi, the first flight of Orville and Wilbur Wright, Historic times of the Underground Railroad, Blackbeard the Pirate, New York City, and more.

Travel Games:

Travel Bingo, Magnetic Paper Dolls Travel Tins, Games in a CD case, etc.

www.KidsLoveTravel.com